Grow Up America!

Learning *to* Live *the* Happy, Responsible Life

By Michael J. Hurd, Ph.D.

Living Resources Press
Washington, DC

Acknowledgments

To my readers around the world.

To Jon Howard, for his outstanding and
dedicated work on the design of the book.

Most of all to Bob Yesbek, for his unwavering
commitment in every step of the process.

ISBN 0-9674218-0-2

Living Resources Press
Washington, DC

Introduction

America.... It's Time To Grow Up.

It's time to Grow Up and stop suing one another over spilled coffee, pinched fingers and other mishaps that result from the lack of common sense.

It's time to Grow Up and stop suing manufacturers for not labeling a cup of coffee "hot," a knife "sharp," or a gun "deadly."

It's time to Grow Up and quit allowing exasperated teachers and fawning psychiatrists to rename our kids' lack of focus and discipline as fictitious diseases.

It's time to Grow Up and end our whining about hurt feelings or others' "lack of sensitivity" about what we are or what we choose to be.

It's time to Grow Up and stop electing officials who promise to be our nannies—and then lie, cheat, and laugh in our faces.

It's time to Grow Up and end our submissive dependence on the government's less-than-mediocre "management" of our health care and our social security, simply because we cannot muster up the self-control to put away the credit cards and save a little money.

It's time to Grow Up and stop squandering our wealth and our young peoples' lives every time some impotent dictator in some backward nation decides to rattle his pitiful chains.

It's time to Grow Up and teach our schoolkids about the real world of commerce, profit and self-interest—and the comforts and joys that result—rather than the "good-little-citizen" nonsense that foists legions of illiterate, resentful graduates on a world that, by definition, cannot be nearly as "politically correct" as the feel-good psychologists, intellectuals, educators and media would have us think.

It's time to Grow Up and stop the sanction of media-hungry politicians who jump at the chance to condemn our greatest entrepreneurs so they can ooze sensitivity and concern for second-rate competitors who couldn't make it any other way.

It's time to Grow Up and become more judgmental—acting on the facts rather than our feelings—in our personal lives, our choice of leaders and mates. We would be rewarded with less mental dysfunction, fewer meddling politicians, and fewer divorces.

We have become a Nation trained to accept "service" from the questionably qualified. In the name of "goodness" and religion, we guiltily sacrifice to—who else: the self-appointed collectors of those sacrifices.

It's time we became responsible for our own money, our dignity and our happiness.

America... It's time to Grow Up!

Table of Contents

Table of Contents

Chapter 1

Coping

STRESS-BUSTING

Have you ever suffered from any of the following symptoms?

Poor concentration. Forgetting to do important tasks. A pervasive sense of helplessness or hopelessness. Nervous behaviors (shaking leg, biting nails). High blood pressure. Blowing up or snapping at loved ones and co-workers. Accelerated heart rate.

If so, you may be suffering from stress.

Stress is the psychological and/or physiological experience of being overwhelmed, under pressure, or unable to cope. Stress manifests itself in a number of ways. Additional symptoms include dry mouth, nausea, choking sensations, disrupted breathing, intrusive irrational thoughts, and reduced work performance.

Regardless of the specific symptoms, stress usually involves an evaluation or belief that you are incapable of handling the tasks you (or others) expect of yourself. Sometimes, such a belief is entirely rational and easily proved by the facts of the situation. For example, if you have four deadlines to meet at work in one day, you have to meet with your child's teacher about school performance problems, and your car breaks down on the highway, you clearly have too much to do in a very short period of time. In other situations, the belief might be an exaggeration or distortion of the facts. For instance, you feel you *must* work seventeen hours a day, seven days a week, in order to be efficient, when perhaps you could ultimately be more productive if you allowed for recreational breaks and set more realistic expectations for yourself.

In either case, stress management skills are essential to coping with daily life—especially if you have set high standards for yourself. Stress management is important for two reasons: first, to accomplish your desired goals, and second, to *enjoy* the process of achieving your goals. People who successfully manage stress both perform better and have more fun in the process.

What are the essential principles of stress management?

Make promises carefully, not indiscriminately. At work, take on new tasks only when you are confident that you are managing the old ones reasonably well. Allow yourself time to think before making important decisions. If you are pressured to make a decision quickly, then ask the person who pressures you for a specific time period (one hour, one week, one month) to think it over. When the time period ends, follow up as promised.

Don't act blindly under pressure. When feeling pressured, ask yourself if the pressure is really coming from outside forces or from within yourself; many feelings of pressure arise from internal, unrealistic expectations people subconsciously impose on themselves. (Example: I must be able to do anything anyone asks of me at all times, no exceptions). Sometimes others are expecting the impossible of themselves, and consequently they will expect the same of you. Remember that this is their problem, not yours. Trying to do the impossible ultimately makes you look foolish, even dishonest. Do your best, and do it well.

Prioritize. Judge and rank the importance of various contacts in both your professional and personal life, and act accordingly. Return the most important phone calls first. Set lunch dates with the clients or associates who do the most for you. Remember that every second of your life is an investment of time. Invest your time wisely, as if it were money. If you have many different social or business options to either accept or reject, ask yourself to rank the options in order of importance. You do not owe your time to anybody, and you should not give your time to anybody unless you expect something for yourself (financially, emotionally, etc.) in return.

Think benevolently and avoid the adversarial mentality. Give people the benefit of the doubt unless their actions prove they do not deserve it. Remember that dishonesty and other undesirable traits ultimately reveal themselves as long as you are alert and willing to make judgments. Just as it is naive to think everybody is honest and nobody will do harm to you, so too is it naive to assume that everyone is out to get you and cannot be trusted. If you assume that rational, benevolent relationships with others are impossible, then this assumption will turn into a self-fulfilling, and self-defeating, prophecy. Adversarial, chronically suspicious individuals, while believing they are protecting themselves from pain, also "protect" themselves from valuable, rewarding relationships because they alienate those who really do deserve the benefit of the doubt.

Adopt a day-to-day policy of optimistic realism. When feeling negative, train yourself to see positive facts and not only the negative. Try to turn negative events into positives. If you lose a major client in your business, ask yourself, "What does this free me up to do instead?" If a personal relationship ends or breaks up, ask yourself the same question. When you are swamped with work, remind yourself that business is good and that this is a nice problem to have. When things are slower, remind yourself that you have earned a break, and use the opportunity to find new clients, attend a conference, and enjoy lunch with friends or associates. Try to realize that your mind needs optimistic realism as desperately as your body needs food and nourishment. Negative thinking leads to self-destructive action, which in turn reinforces the negative thinking. Optimistic realism represents the only psychological antidote to this vicious cycle.

Be a fact-oriented egoist, not a conventional egoist. Healthy egoists want to know the facts, and only the facts. They enjoy being right *not* because of how it makes them look to others, but because they enjoy being in touch with reality. Conventional egoists, of which there are far too many in the world, are in fact pseudo-egoists. They want to be right not because they enjoy knowledge and competence; they want to be right so that others will like them, respect them, or perhaps even fear them.

If someone you respect criticizes or questions you, do not become defensive or hostile; consider the criticism or question and judge for yourself if it is valid or not. It is OK to be wrong, so long as you are intellectually honest and willing to correct an error when you see evidence of one. Nothing creates more stress than the false, irrational belief that you must never be seen making an error. Human beings, while capable of great things when they use their minds intelligently and rationally, are also capable of error. Accept this fact and deal with it.

Take care of the body as well as the mind. The mind and the body exist simultaneously and interactively. Just as a healthy body is of little value if you are paralyzed by anxiety and low self-worth, so too is a sound and intelligent mind of little value if your body does not work properly. Eat sensibly. Exercise regularly. Keep your home and office environment clean and organized. Practice good hygiene. Pay attention to the details, such as dressing properly in cold weather and washing your hands after contact with someone who has a cold. Poor or mediocre physical health is a major contributor to stress.

Process your feelings, and introspect, regularly. When you encounter a dilemma or issue, discuss it with a close friend, a professional counselor, or yourself (e.g., in the form of a diary or journal). Ignoring, repressing, or evading a personal issue will not make it go away. On the contrary: the people most ruled by their emotions are the rationalists who pride themselves on never looking inward at their feelings.

Strive to be rational, but recognize that being rational includes accepting the fact that you have feelings. You need to process these feelings so they do not overwhelm you or lead you to inappropriate, self-destructive behaviors. Schedule regular emotional/mental "tune-ups" either with yourself or, if more practical, with a professional or loved one who is willing and able to listen.

Work productively, not compulsively. Productive work means focusing on the task you are doing while you are doing it. Concentrate on what you are doing, and strive to do it well (even enjoyably) rather than focusing or dwelling on what your next task will be. Many people under stress take on one activity and, instead of focusing on the task itself, think to themselves, "How am I going to get the next task done? And the next one? I've got so much to do, how will I ever finish?" The anxiety and stress levels build and build. Such thoughts do nothing to make the workload any lighter; in fact, they make things worse because they distract you from successfully, competently and enjoyably finishing your current task.

Instead of thinking about everything you have to do in one hour, one day, or one week, try to focus exclusively on what you are doing now. Organize yourself and plan ahead, but limit the amount of time you spend on planning. Planning and looking ahead are crucial; but they are of little use if they distract you from competence and enjoyment in the here-and-now.

Set limits and boundaries on others. When you are busy, you cannot always say "yes" to others, even to others who are of value to you. Remember that it is OK to say "no" to an invitation or a request to do a favor. You are not obliged to sacrifice for anyone, even loved ones; and they are not obliged to sacrifice for you. Remember, too, that non-sacrificial compromise is often an option. For example: " I really want to get together with you. This weekend is not good for me. How about a week from Sunday?"

Stand back from your personal and business relationships, from time to time, and objectively analyze them. Ask yourself such questions as: "Am I getting back what I'm putting into this relationship? Is it a good investment of my time, energy, money, etc.?" If not, then perhaps you should minimize or even end the business or personal relationship in question.

Create an environment in all your relationships where it is OK for you to ask for what you want, and it is OK for the other individual to do the same. (Double standards are unfair, and do not work). Such an environment encourages honest, authentic relationships rather than relationships based upon false niceties, self-sacrifice, and dishonesty. In the short run you may lose some people by setting such honest standards, but over the long run you will enjoy relationships of only the highest quality.

Practice rational communication. It is in your own self-interest to communicate with those of value to you (personally or professionally) in a reasonable way. In a discussion, listen to what the other has to say rather than rehearsing your response; listen critically, but still listen. Avoid interrupting. If interrupting is unavoidable, then ask, "Can I say something, please?" rather than plunging in with your statement.

Recognize that many disagreements are simply not going to be resolved, no matter how well you argue. You can request discontinuing the discussions at any time if you find you are getting nowhere. The possibility exists that the other person will give your points serious thought later on, even if it does not seem likely at the time.

If a point is not clear to you, then ask the other party to clarify it; nobody can read minds. Never be embarrassed to ask if you do not recognize the name of a person or concept someone else identifies; if you don't know it, you don't know it, and it is fraudulent to pretend that you do. If tensions build to where you are too emotional to go on, then ask the other person if you may continue the discussion at a specified time (and keep your promise to continue it; don't merely put them off).

Avoid defensiveness, and opt instead for calm explanation. Defensiveness implies to the other party that you have no valid point, or that your point is insufficiently thought out. Explanation, on the other hand, shows you have given careful thought to your case and that it at least merits respect and attention.

Accept the absolutism of reality. What is, *is*. Merely wishing something to be different cannot make it so. Use your intellect to distinguish between what is certainly outside of your control (e.g., the weather, death, others' choices) from what is potentially under your control (e.g., good school/work performance, achievement of a goal with persistence and practice). Focus on that which is under, or at least potentially under, your control.

Remember that reality does not have a will and consciousness of its own. Reality is not a person. Reality is not a conscious entity. Contrary to what you were taught, no invisible hand governs the universe. Planes crash because pilots make errors, and because of faulty engine parts. Car accidents happen because of inadequate roads, faulty cars, or poor judgment by drivers. Coincidences happen because coincidences happen. People get diseases because of bacteria, viruses, and other causes not yet discovered, but potentially discoverable. Things happen for a reason—but for logical reasons, not mystical reasons.

Existence exists, and only existence exists: not "fate," nor other mystical fantasies. Neither empirical evidence, nor logical argumentation derived from it, even hints at the existence of mystical forces. We live in a rational universe where not everything is known (at least, not yet), but everything is, at least potentially, knowable.

All that happens, however mysterious it may sometimes seem, nevertheless follows certain logical laws. The laws of gravity operated long before scientists discovered and named them. The earth revolved around the sun in the Middle Ages, even while people were put to death for believing so. Scientists do not yet fully understand what is needed to cure cancer or AIDS; but thankfully they are using logic and reason to discover cures, rather than waiting for "fate" to do its work.

Rational people understand, intellectually, that existence does not have a will or a consciousness, but nevertheless experience conflicting premises on the emotional level. Example: "Why me? Why did my train have to be delayed? Why is everything going wrong for me today?" (Do you ever, by the way, ask such questions when everything goes *well* on a given day?) The implication of such a feeling is that some unseen force is acting against you, trying to make your life miserable and to block you in your goals. Now *that's* a stressful way to think. Although your own life should be your most important value, it is still irrational to assume (even subconsciously) that the universe revolves around you, and even more irrational to think that some force is deciding when some people suffer while others prosper. If you really want to conquer stress, consider this the root premise upon which all the other methods of stress management depend: existence, and *only* existence, exists.

TWELVE WAYS TO REDUCE STRESS

1. Take breaks when possible — even a 10 minute walk can help.

2. Take deep breaths throughout the day to help maintain relaxation and calm.

3. Exercise regularly, based upon your physician's recommendations.

4. Set realistic expectations for each day, allowing time for unexpected events.

5. Don't make promises or commitments you cannot keep.

6. Treat those whom you love well; respecting those you value is a form of self-respect.

7. Prioritize; do most important things first, and do not allow yourself to feel guilty for judging some people and activities as more important than others.

8. Strive for excellence and competence, not infallibility.

9. Allow yourself extra time before going to appointments or work.

10. Don't let issues or resentments build; handle them while it is still easy to do so rationally.

11. Recognize that how you think about a situation determines your emotions about it; strive for realistic optimism.

12. Don't try to always be proving yourself, or showing others you're right; your view of yourself and your understanding of reality are what count the most.

LEARN TO LOVE YOUR WORK

Q: I suffer from stress in my job. Though I really like the work, I often experience fatigue, resentment, and a hard time motivating myself. How can this be?

A: Sometimes the way a person looks at his work affects the level of stress he experiences. Consider an example. A man works very hard for many years to establish a successful business. After years of effort, he finally achieves both the income level and the types of clients he desires.

At times, however, the man notices emotions of frustration and irritation over how busy he is. He even feels resentful of his clients. Sometimes he wishes that his demanding clients would "go away." He might snap at them, or act less than professional towards them. In the process, he violates his own high business standards and harms his self-interest. He understands the irrationality of his behaviors, yet finds himself continuing to engage in them.

In effect, this man forgets that he's doing the work he loves and *chose* to do. He set an ambitious goal and is now achieving it. This is cause for rejoicing—not misery! By not allowing himself to feel pride, happiness, and a sense of self-worth, he defaults to stress—rather than joy—at doing the work he loves.

Why does he not allow himself to feel pride, self-worth, and happiness in his work? Numerous explanations are possible. Perhaps he's losing perspective, or not seeing the full context. Productive, detail-oriented people often fall into this trap. Maybe he finds it hard to recognize his overall progress, because he values excellence and wants every detail of his work to be perfect. If he does anything in a less than perfect way, he quickly becomes demoralized.

While there is nothing wrong with pursuing excellence, the man ought to respect reality as well. He should strive to be excellent at the possible—not at the impossible. Excellence is not the same as infallibility. He can treat his errors as opportunities for learning rather than disasters.

Guilt is another factor. Perhaps this man was taught (like so many of us) to believe that pride is a sin or a vice. Intellectually, he might recognize that pride is healthy, appropriate, and moral. Nevertheless, he does not always feel this way on the emotional level. A part of his mind slams shut at the first feeling of pride. His subconscious mind erroneously tells him, "Don't be a braggart! Pride is a deadly sin. Don't let yourself feel it for even a moment!"

He might also worry that if he allows himself to feel pride, he will slip into mediocrity and inefficiency. Again, he must try to remember that excellence and infallibility are not one and the same.

The man's emotion that pride is somehow improper represents "stale thinking" from his past. He needs to vigorously "talk back" to the stale thinking. He must repeatedly show his subconscious mind the errors in the mistaken emotions each time he experiences them (or at least as often as possible). He must teach and re-teach himself that pride and accomplishment are virtues, not vices. Introspection and self-reflection, including psychological counseling if necessary, can help him accomplish this task.

If you identify with any of this man's problems, then try the following exercise as an experiment. At the end of each day, spend a few minutes writing down everything that you did well. You might write, "I finished all the paperwork on my desk." Or, "I handled my difficult client with calm, poise, and professionalism." The possibilities are limitless. The important thing is to thoroughly identify the facts of your accomplishments—what you did well—each day.

The exercise, if done consistently, will give you a sense of perspective, of seeing the full factual context. Perspective and objectivity are tremendous antidotes to stress. Stress causes people to lose touch with the positive facts of reality. They see the objectively negative facts but not the objectively positive ones. Staying in touch with reality includes recognizing positive facts, particularly about your own performance.

From time to time, allow yourself to stand back and look at your recent accomplishments. Doing so will not compromise your commitment to excellence. It's OK to tell yourself, "These are the things I did well today," so long as you also ask yourself, "How, if at all, can I do even better tomorrow?" Contrary to what you might believe, the pursuit of excellence does not mean a refusal to ever compliment yourself.

Imagine, for example, that you hire an employee. Suppose you only tell the employee what he does poorly, while you never tell him what he does well (even though much of what he does *is*, in fact, very good). What kind of loyalty and hard work can you expect to inspire in him?

The same principle applies to your relationship with yourself. If you always criticize yourself, but never identify your good points, your motivation will suffer and your stress level will increase. Without positive feedback, you won't work well for yourself. The result: heightened stress.

In summary, remember the "three P's" for reducing stress: pride, perspective, and positive thinking.   ✆

Chapter 2

Getting a Grip
on Reality

WHO DECIDES WHAT'S TRUE—YOU, OR OTHERS?

Many people have accepted the erroneous view that facts and truth reside in the opinions of others, rather than in objective reality. This mistaken premise represents the underlying cause of many emotional problems.

Consider one example. A man differs from his colleagues about a work-related issue. He bases this viewpoint on careful observation of facts and draws what he honestly believes to be the only logical conclusion. When he voices his viewpoint at an office meeting, many of his colleagues dismiss it. Some even belittle it. The man immediately feels, "I must be wrong. Boy, am I stupid."

Think about another example. A high school student experiments with marijuana and cocaine. She believes drug use is a mistake, but she does it anyway. Why? Because she feels that "Everyone else is doing it, so there must be something to it." This is the extent of her thinking on the subject.

Consider still another example. A college student wants to join a fraternity. The fraternity subjects him to traumatic initiation rites. Although he is otherwise an intelligent, accomplished person, he endures physical pain and public humiliation so that he can be accepted into the fraternity. His girlfriend, who usually admires him for his integrity and intelligence, is horrified. "Why are you doing this to yourself?" she asks him. When faced with this question, his immediate feeling is: "Because I'm not worthwhile unless I belong to this group. My other accomplishments mean nothing."

In each of the three examples, the error contained within the person's emotional reaction is the same: the notion that truth resides somewhere other than in objective reality.

The man in the office believes truth resides in the opinions and minds of his colleagues, rather than in the facts of objective reality which his own mind can ascertain. The high school student believes the validity of drug abuse lies in the subjective "truth" of her friends' opinions and values, rather than in an objective reality based upon facts and logical consequences.

Finally, the college student believes the truth of his self-worth lies not in his objective accomplishments and his integrity, but in whether or not the fraternity accepts or rejects him.

All three individuals depend on others—rather than on their own reasoning minds—for the definition of truth. To each of them, truth is what somebody else *says* it is.

How People Seek to Evade Objective Reality and Truth

Not everybody looks to members of a group for the definition of truth. Some look to a mystical entity, such as God, or to some God-like authority here on earth. Members of cults, for example, sacrifice their independent judgment to whatever an admired authority figure tells them to think. Cult members who kill themselves for the sake of the group leader's proclamation that a better world awaits them (in the

Beyond, or perhaps on a spaceship behind a comet), have long since concluded that truth resides somewhere other than in objective reality.

In order to develop genuine self-esteem, and to avoid such mistakes, every individual must first resolve this most fundamental of questions for himself: Where does truth come from?

If truth resides somewhere other than in objective reality, then something other than common sense, rational judgment, and reason must be the means of assessing truth. Independent judgment of facts and conclusions drawn from those facts mean little when compared to the unreasoned edict of an authority figure. "He thinks it, so it must be so," or "They do it, so it must be right," best summarizes the underlying mentality of people who ignore objective reality in this way.

Sadly, this anti-objectivity provides the emotional climate necessary for the development of many psychological syndromes including anxiety, depression, drug addiction, obsessive-compulsive personality, and schizophrenia. Why? Because without confidence in your ability to rationally and independently think and draw conclusions, the consistent experience of mental stability is impossible. If you do not know how to think, then you can never feel good about yourself.

The Psychological Consequences of Evading Objective Truth and Reason

If a person fails to see that he possesses the capacity for reason and objective, independent judgment, he will not develop the self-esteem "mind muscle" required to ward off psychological disorder. Reason and objectivity are to the psyche what the disease-fighting immune system is to the body. Without recognizing—and repeatedly using—one's capacity for reason, a person will develop the mental equivalent of a physical disease.

A large number of psychological disorders arise from the false, irrational belief that the suffering individual must be liked by everybody or else he is not worthwhile. Usually, he consciously understands that this expectation is ridiculous and defies common sense. What he generally does *not* recognize, however, is that his underlying premises about where truth resides make his feeling that everyone must like him both logical and inevitable. If he holds the view, "Who am I to reason and judge?" then he cannot help but feel, "I must rely on others to tell me whether I'm correct, or worthwhile, or good." If he does not trust his own judgment, then he will naturally depend upon others to tell him when he is right or wrong, good or bad.

Certain emotions can make it even more difficult for a person to recognize, and internalize, that his mind is capable of discerning objective truth. Two examples of such intrusive yet common emotions are fear and resentment.

Many people feel afraid to make independent judgments, for a variety of reasons. They might fear making a mistake. Or they might fear being *seen* making a mistake. They are so afraid of making a mistake that they become paralyzed. Or they are so concerned about the risk of being "judgmental" or "mean" or offending someone that they give up on rational judgment altogether.

Still others resent the idea of having to make judgments. They would rather act solely on feelings, because identifying feelings requires less work than making conscious, reasoned evaluations and critical, objective judgments. "Life is stressful enough," they often feel. "Someone else should judge for me." So they turn over their intellectual and psychological independence to an authority figure, or to the group—the "group" being defined as anything from an assortment of friends or relatives to a collection of colleagues to an influential newspaper.

In extreme cases, the failure to resolve questions about the nature of reality can contribute to psychosis. Psychosis refers to a total, complete break with reality: the layman's notion of "crazy." The cult member who believes suicide will place him on a spaceship behind a comet is obviously psychotic. So too are people who believe that their thoughts are being broadcast on the radio waves, that a television newscaster is addressing them personally, or any other delusional belief for which no evidence exists and for which the believer sees no need for evidence.

Far more common psychological consequences of ignoring the need for objectivity and reason include anxiety and depressive syndromes, as well as drug and alcohol abuse. These self-esteem problems arise from a prevailing conviction within a person that he is not in command of his existence, that he is mentally unable to grasp and cope with external reality. This lack of a sense of control and mastery over one's life and mind stems from the mental habit of looking towards others to define truth, rather than towards oneself. Like a child lost in the woods, an emotionally troubled or drug abusing adult feels existentially abandoned in a hostile world because he has lost—or perhaps never learned about—his capacity for independent reason and objectivity.

Preventative Measures

To prevent such mental problems, you need to learn (at the earliest age possible) to consistently ask these two questions when faced with various life experiences:

1. What are the *facts* of this situation?
2. What *conclusion* is the logical one to draw from these facts?

Answering these questions can take minutes, days, or years, depending upon the complexity and importance of the specific issue.

If you desire mental health, then strive to be fact-oriented. Do not, however, focus solely on facts. Be willing to draw abstract conclusions from the facts you observe. Do not be afraid to make judgments and draw conclusions. You need not expect your reasoning to always be error-free; you should only demand of yourself that your reasoning be thorough and honest. Simply recognize that reason is the only viable, human method of making judgments about reality.

Regarding disagreements with others, it is best to avoid the temptation to become defensive. Defensiveness usually implies that you have something of which to be ashamed. Yet if you made an honest effort to consider all of the relevant facts and draw the most reasonable, sensible conclusion, then there is no reason to feel ashamed. Perhaps you made an honest, innocent mistake. Simply learn from the mistake, and move forward.

At the same time, it is wise to avoid rushing to the conclusion that the person who disagrees with you is right and you are wrong. If you have some basis for trusting this person, then ask him his reasons for disagreeing. Then calmly consider, for yourself, the merit or lack of merit in his points. Ask yourself if his conclusions make logical sense given the available facts. Write down all the relevant facts; look at them and judge whether your conclusion or his conclusion more logically follows from the facts. Stand by your own viewpoint *until* or *unless* a new fact is raised or a new argument is given which compels you, in all honesty, to change your conclusion.

People might use manipulative tactics to prey upon your insecurities. Emotionally manipulative people will be skillful at intimidating you into thinking you are wrong, even in the absence of factual/logical evidence to *prove* you are wrong. They will substitute various psychological "tricks" in place of logical proof. These tricks are designed to scare and intimidate you rather than genuinely convince you. Consider the following examples.

Guilt. "Who are you to think you know everything?" "You're too big for your britches!" Notice that these statements are not arguments. People who say such things do not point out your factual or logical errors. Instead, they simply try to distract you from their own low self-esteem and ignorance by implying that there is no such thing as objective truth, that nobody ever really knows anything. If they can convince you that objective truth is an illusion, then they can also intimidate you into intellectually and psychologically "wallowing" with them in their ignorance and low self-esteem.

Appeal to authority. "You're mistaken. Attention deficit disorder is a medical disease. A doctor told me it's a disease." "Government control of education is correct because this is just how it has always been." "Everyone likes this new movie. It has to be good." None of these statements appeal to rational persuasion. They simply presume that something is true because an alleged authority claims it to be so. The authority may consist of an individual, a group of individuals, or the mere existence of time-honored tradition. None of these views express why a position is supposedly correct; they only prove that certain other people believe it to be correct.

Mockery. Sarcasm, sneering, laughter, intimidation—all of these are designed to distract you from the arguments and facts at hand. They represent attempts to substitute emotions for rational persuasion.

Appeal to faith. "Trust me. Don't fight me. I know." "Follow me. I will show you the way." "Don't worry if you see no concrete results; just trust." Such statements imply that facts and reason are unnecessary, and that an individual need not ascertain the truth using his own mind. Instead, he must rely on faith in the absence of facts and logic. Such ideas are not exclusive to religion; the atheistic Communists compelled millions of people to place blind faith in their leaders. Similarly, many psychotherapists urge their clients to trust that, somehow, years of unfocused dependence on a counselor will adequately substitute for the need to think independently and responsibly.

Shouting, interrupting. Such behaviors follow from the principle that "might makes right;" that the one with the loudest voice wins. Many college campus activists, particularly in the 1960's, used this technique to "persuade" college administrators to change their policies. Teenagers will often try this approach with their parents. People who resort to such measures generally have little confidence in their viewpoints; otherwise they would attempt to use reason rather than shouting, interrupting, or rioting.

Labeling. "That's simplistic." "That's extreme." Notice that people who make such accusations generally do not attempt to point out logical or factual errors. Rather, they conclude that because your statement makes sense and is coherent, it is "simplistic," and necessarily wrong. They conclude that because you are consistent, you are "extreme" and therefore irrational. People with little confidence in their ability to reason are threatened by the coherent, the certain, and the consistent whenever they encounter it. They sense that only a confident mind can stand by its reasoned conclusions, and the presence of such a mind makes them feel insecure and resentful. So they resort to labeling.

The common factor in each of these defensive psychological tactics is, once again, the false view that truth resides somewhere other than in external reality. The extent to which you have accepted this false view is the extent to which you will be subject to intimidation by others. The more you improve the capacity to use your own mind to draw conclusions based upon facts you know, the less influence irrational psychological tactics will have on you. The more knowledge you acquire and the more skillful you become at critical, objective thinking, the more self-esteem and mental health you will enjoy.

The best way to combat these defensive tactics—without becoming defensive yourself—involves the use of two simple requests of the intimidator:

1. "Please tell me the facts which support your view."
2. "Tell me how you reached your conclusions given these facts."

An intellectually honest person will answer these questions in a straightforward, thorough, and patient manner. His goal, after all, is to honestly persuade you. If he is not intellectually honest, he will persist in trying to intimidate you and appeal to your emotions rather than to your reason.

Why the Complexity of Today's World is Not an Excuse for Abandoning Reason

In today's technically sophisticated world, many people conclude that since they cannot possibly validate all information independently and first-hand, then they might as well give up altogether on the ideas of objectivity and independent judgment. In other words: "Since I don't have the knowledge of a physician, a surgeon, a farmer, a car mechanic, a computer programmer, and everything else required for life in the modern world, then the idea of independence and objectivity is an illusion." Since you cannot be omniscient and God-like, your mind is impotent to know reality.

This view is an over-reaction, as well as a distortion of the actual facts. It is true that you have to, in a sense, "hand over" your first-hand judgment when relying upon a surgeon, a stock broker, or any other expert with specialized knowledge. But you still can—and, indeed, must—use your first-hand judgment to assess the expert's character, his reputation, his track record, and whether or not his recommendations make any logical sense. In our complex, division-of-labor society, delegating to others the task of learning specialized knowledge is both logical and necessary. To delegate, however, is not the same as to surrender independent thought altogether. Quite the contrary; in a complex, specialized society, a continuous focus on reality with the use of independent, rational judgment, is more essential than ever. We all must make day-to-day choices about whose expertise to solicit and whose to ignore.

Why Conventional "Egoists" Do Not Really Adhere to Objective Reality

Just as reality does not reside within the minds of others, neither does it reside in your own mind. In order to achieve intelligence and self-esteem, you have to accept the responsibility of disciplining your mind, with the aid of reason, to ascertain what in fact exists "out there" in objective reality. Many pseudo-advocates of objective reality are too lazy or insecure to use reason. Instead, they operate on the unacknowledged premise that "It's true because it's in my mind." They fail or refuse to consider that you cannot assume something is true simply because you think it, especially when new knowledge contradicting your current conclusion becomes available.

A classic example of this error involves racial prejudice. An ignorant white person who does not live near many black people, for example, may have the idea that all black people are, by their very natures, stupid and unsophisticated. One day he meets a black individual who is highly educated and well spoken. If the ignorant person is intellectually honest, and a true proponent of objective reality, then he feels the intellectual obligation to reconcile the new factual data (the existence of a sophisticated black person) with his previous belief ("All blacks are stupid."). In other words, he will have to abandon his mistaken prejudice. The same principle will apply to the correction of other prejudices, including: "women cannot be rational;" "all homosexuals hate people of the opposite sex;" "immigrants are fundamentally different from other human beings;" and so forth.

People who claim to favor objective reality but in actuality are too lazy to use reason are typically labeled as "egoists." They are, in a sense, "subjective egoists," which represents a contradiction in terms since the "ego" actually refers to one's ability to grasp *objective* reality. Nevertheless, these subjective, phony "egoists" drive their professional colleagues and loved ones crazy by operating on the principle, "It's my way or the highway." They are psychological autocrats who insist they are right *not* because the facts support their viewpoints, but merely because they say and feel that they are right.

Instead of experiencing the calm and self-confidence which inevitably results from habitually drawing conclusions from facts and reason, the psychological autocrat is angry, controlling, defensive, and even hostile. People exposed to these psychological autocrats, especially in childhood, sometimes draw the mistaken conclusion that such problems are the inevitable result of being egoistic. In actual fact, the precise opposite is true. People who recognize objective reality and seek to honestly identify and adhere to it—*rational* egoists—will, for the most part, be calm, confident, sensitive people. This is because their basic philosophic premise—that reason is the means to objective knowledge—gives them a legitimate sense of control over their own lives and existence.

The Intellectual Roots & The Cultural Consequences of Today's Growing Irrationalism

Under the influence of contemporary philosophy, psychology, and educational theory, growing numbers of people are giving up on reason and replacing it with various forms of subjective emotion-worship. This is why we read about growing numbers of cult movements and mass suicides. This is why we see more violence in public schools and in the larger society than ever before. This is why divorces happen more frequently and parents do not always honor their responsibilities. This is also why integrity is on the decline in both the political and business arenas. As man abandons reason, he is more prone to be ruled either by his own emotions or the emotional whim of others—simply because there is nothing else left for him.

Consider the problem of troubled adolescents. Once they become teenagers, children outgrow the tendency to blindly accept adult authority. They can now act as their own authorities through the use of abstract, objective cognition. However, instead of replacing unthinking allegiance to adults with independent reason and critical thinking, teens all too often turn to a group of peers to do their thinking for them. "Should I skip class today?" a teenager might ask himself. "Well, I don't know. . . probably not . . . but the others are doing it, so it can't be that bad."

Notice how, in this example, the teenager does not independently and objectively weigh the long- and short-term consequences of his choice to skip school. He simply acts according to what he assumes everyone else thinks, as if "everyone else" were somehow the definition of reality. He delivers himself to the unreasoned whims of his peers.

Adults, who face daily responsibility for survival, have no choice but to develop some degree of reliance on reason and independent judgment, even if they resent or fear the requirement to do so. However, remnants of mistaken premises from childhood and adolescence often influence some of their feelings and actions as adults. For instance, many young couples will have children simply because it is the "thing to do." Instead of carefully reasoning about why and when to have a child, they simply observe the fact that everyone in their age group is already having children and conclude that they, therefore, must do the same. I have learned as a therapist that many couples, remarkably enough, never even discuss this very important decision rationally and explicitly ahead of time.

People succumb to drug and alcohol abuse more easily today because they do not use reason to solve personal problems and, not having learned any other means of coping, consequently feel the need for some kind of escape from reality.[1] Marriages often break up unnecessarily because couples rely upon unchallenged emotion rather than reason for resolving disputes. My therapy practice is full of examples to support this claim.

Psychological syndromes are common today because many people feel over-whelmed and powerless. They are taught, by too many teachers and psychologists, to doubt reason and objective reality, and to place more trust in emotions. All too often, "How do you *feel?*" represents the emphasis in classrooms and therapy offices rather than, "What do you think?" and, "What should you do?"

As reason declines and emotionalism grows in influence throughout our culture, we will see more and more people making choices based on the erroneous premises described throughout this chapter.

For most of the twentieth century, American schools have been under the influence of the idea that "social adjustment," rather than intellectual mastery, constitutes the essential purpose of education.[2] Consequently, the purpose of modern education has been to produce "good" little citizens and "good" little members of society rather than intellectually confident, independent young men and women. Under irrational ideo-logical influences, schools increasingly emphasize emotional well-being and social accommodation over the use of reason, critical thinking, and independent judgment. Schools "dumb down" text books and test scores so that kids' feelings will not be hurt. Teaching reverence for the environment and the federal government is more common than teaching reverence for the human intellect. Instilling "self-esteem," and helping kids "feel good about themselves" is seen as more important than the virtues of achievement and rationality which make genuine self-esteem possible.

The impact of these mistaken educational philosophies is spreading. This is why Americans end up with Presidents like George Bush and Bill Clinton, who were edu-cated at the finest schools yet stand for almost nothing and desperately want to please everybody. They offer quite a contrast to principled men of integrity like Thomas Jefferson, James Madison, and George Washington. If people-pleasers and poll-obsessors like George Bush and Bill Clinton had been the "leaders" of the eighteenth century, you can be sure there would be no Bill of Rights or constitutional govern-ment in existence today.

Ironically, contemporary educational philosophy rests on the same premise as the mental state of a depressed or otherwise neurotic individual. The neurotic premise is that reality resides in the opinions and the whims of others, rather than in an objec-tive reality which can be grasped by an individual mind, through the use of reason and sensory observation.

Without the correct educational philosophy to guide today's school programs, too many kids grow up to be insecure and superficially arrogant, rather than genuinely calm, happy, and intelligent. Instead of knowing how to read, write, and think, they mainly know how to "fit in." They become experts at blindly accepting the opinions of others, sacrificing their individuality to teachers, politicians, media personalities, preachers, therapists, drug addiction and crime.

Reason and the Recognition of
Objective Reality: Life's Essential Resources

The only alternative to today's irrational influences is a reality-based premise: that truth resides in the facts of objective reality, and that a logical, thinking mind is capable of ascertaining that truth.

The truth is not the truth simply because an authority says so.

Nor is the truth the truth because "everybody" feels it is.

Nor is the truth the truth simply because *you* feel it is; you need clear proof of your accuracy.

The truth is what it is—independent of what anyone may think. You can access objective reality through the use of your own mind, and through the use of logic and reason—provided you are willing to focus and discipline yourself. The principles of logic and reason are universal, and all members of the human race are capable of utilizing them. There is no such thing as "black" logic, "Asian" logic, "female" logic, and so forth. The methodology of reason applies to all human minds, because all humans live in the same, objective reality and are of the same fundamental nature.

Reason, logic, critical consideration of facts, and independent judgment all constitute the basic tools, or resources, of life. If you want to be happy and successful, then you must make use of these living resources every single day.

WHAT TO DO WHEN REALITY "STINKS"

Do you wish your husband or wife or boss would change?

Are you often angry, or frustrated, with life?

Do you sometimes feel that reality stinks, and there's nothing you can ever do about it?

If it often seems like an unseen force is governing your life (whether or not you believe in unseen forces), you may need to look at how you are pursuing happiness.

Human happiness is the consequence of rational ideas. In order to be happy, serene, and mentally healthy, you must be willing to apply reality-oriented principles to everyday living.

Today, too many people look for short-cuts to happiness: drug and alcohol abuse, compulsive spending, casual sex, religious zealotry or visits to a therapist who tells you whatever you want to hear, whether it is true or not.

None of these attempts to fake happiness will ever work. None will ever serve as a substitute for accepting reality, choosing to think, and becoming independent.

"Accept reality?" you might ask. "But what if reality stinks?"

The answer: reality is all you have; but reality does not have to stay exactly as it is. You can use your creative, thinking mind not only to develop a more positive attitude, but to also set goals to change the objective reality in which you live.

You can pursue an interesting career, for example. Or you can fight for an intellectual or political/social cause in which you believe. Or you can resolve to do an excellent job raising your children. In short, you can pursue values through continuous goal-setting and achievement. *There is no magical, mystical route to happiness.*

"Reality stinks" is usually nothing more than an excuse for a deeper, more passionately held belief which, if it became conscious, would say, "I don't want to think or reason. I don't want to plan goals and work on them. I'd just rather do drugs or be mediocre or live for today only."

If you want to live for today only, then do so. But don't complain when it inevitably leads to a sense of muddled, hollow despair.

Acceptance of Reality

Acceptance of reality is the core of good mental health. To accept reality does not mean to passively give up and assume that you cannot change anything. It simply means that you should spend your precious energies on the changeable rather than the unchangeable.

For example, it makes no sense to spend any emotional or mental energy on the fact that it is raining when you wish it were sunny. It makes no sense to try to change others who do not want to be changed. It *does* make sense to improve yourself by making your new business profitable; or finishing your college or graduate degree; or painting your kitchen, listening to good music, or watching an uplifting movie or play. The combination of long-range goals and short-term, pleasurable activities is crucial to preventing depression and other psychological problems.

How can anti-reality thinking cause depression? Depressed people focus on all the things they cannot change: the fact that we will die, and the fact that life can be difficult and full of obstacles and at times even tragedy. Rational, optimistic, nondepressed people, on the other hand, focus primarily on the many possibilities for changing the external environment, from rearranging the living room furniture to finding a cure for cancer and everything in between.

In today's cynical age, it is fashionable to sneer at rationality and optimism. Psychologists too often dismiss these qualities as neurotic "denial." Politicians and moralists condemn them as harsh and cruel. Yet without the existence of rational, optimistic people—the ones who take action and show initiative—the world as we know it would come to a complete halt. Without the material prosperity and general benevolence made possible by rationality and optimism, our lives would be of a lower quality than the poorest of third-world countries.

How would planes fly, grocery shelves be filled, and life-enhancing technologies such as the Internet or television or the automobile develop if everyone adopted the attitude of gloom-and-doom increasingly in evidence today? Rational, optimistic people are well aware that obstacles and tragedy exist; sometimes, they even experience them. But they minimize them, and place them in perspective, because they recognize that ultimately life's joys, pleasures and achievements are what really matter.

How controlling others leads to unhappiness. What is, is. In order to be happy you need to separate, in your mind, the things you *can* control from the things you cannot. You can control your own actions and choices, but you cannot control or take responsibility for the actions of others. You can reason with others, provided they are open to persuasion and are motivated to listen to you; but you cannot force them to think or bend to your intellectual will. Attempts to make them do so will invariably backfire.

Consider your spouse, or romantic partner. You cannot change him. You can ask him to do certain things which you believe represent a reasonable compromise, but you cannot ask him to compromise his basic self, or soul, or personality. You cannot command or wish your quiet, passive husband into becoming a domineering, assertive man. You can, however, ask that he make the decision about where you will take your next vacation, or where you will eat dinner tonight, so that you do not have to make all of his decisions for him. If he is quiet and withdrawn, you can ask him to work on being more open with you about his thoughts and feelings. But you cannot change his basic personality.

The same principle applies to children. As a parent, you are obliged to provide your child with food, clothing, shelter, nurturing, and education. You are also obliged to impose on him logical consequences for his actions, in the form of incentives and punishments, so he can learn to take full responsibility for himself.

You possess neither the right nor the ability to control your child's mind. Kids, even very young kids, make their own choices. You can punish your child and teach him your values; but he remains free to think what he wants, and to act the way he wants when you are not looking. You can tell him not to break his toys or touch the hot stove; but he might choose to do so anyway. He is still an autonomous individual.

The futility of wallowing in anger. Dwelling on injustices and wallowing in anger represents another failure to accept reality. Objective injustices certainly do exist. It makes sense to allow yourself to feel anger when confronted with evidence of such an injustice. If you do not let yourself feel the anger, it will fester and contribute to the development of psychological problems, such as depression.

When allowed to mushroom without the guidance of reason, however, anger is probably the least productive of all human emotions. You need to keep normal and healthy anger from turning into a liability. Even while still feeling the anger, you can tell yourself: "When my anger subsides, the reality of the situation will still be the same. What should I do about the situation? Or is there anything I can do? Or do I just need to work on letting go of the anger and moving on?"

Learn to think about your anger, and not merely feel it. Dwelling on anger and frustration can break your spirit and motivation like nothing else. Either you should work on accepting the fact you cannot change something; or, if you can change or influence an injustice, then place your energies into decisively doing so.

If you are angry, for example, at how your parents mistreated you as a child, then you might consider telling them what you think. You can also refuse to pretend that everything was OK in the past when you know it was not: no more "make believe." If necessary, you can reduce or even cut off contact with family members who remain in a state of unhealthy denial. Many options are possible. To spend any additional time on the anger, however, will only intensify the injustice and victimize yourself further. Ruminating on anger keeps you from moving forward in the present, where you do have choices and control.

How to cope with reality when feeling a loss of control. Consider some other examples of people who find it hard to cope with harsh reality.

Bill. Bill's brother was recently murdered. A crucial first step in Bill's coping is, of course, accepting the reality of his feelings. His feelings of anger, sadness, and shock are self-evidently rational; at first, he simply needs to feel them.

As time progresses, Bill needs to take concrete action to cope with his feelings so he does not wallow in despair and anger forever. A first step is to decide how to honor the memory of his brother. Initially, this takes the form of a memorial service or a funeral. Later on, he might decide to become an activist for victims of violent crimes. This option will give him a sense that he still has some control over factors relating to his brother's death—specifically, influencing the system of justice—even though Bill cannot bring his brother back to life. Still another option might be to carry out his brother's wishes about his estate. Or, perhaps Bill could complete some task, goal, or project his brother had started.

Martha. Martha is married to a chronically uncooperative husband. If she is reality-oriented, she will not focus on trying to "make" him be reasonable. Only *he* can make himself reasonable, with great effort and motivation on his own part. If he refuses, for example, to shop for furniture with her (for no real reason), then she needs to go without him. She reminds him that he has a choice: he can have a say in the selection of the furniture, or he will have to live with what she picks out on her own. Chances are he will begin to cooperate once he sees she is serious.

If Martha starts to feel angry and helpless, she should remind herself that she cannot change her husband, that she can only control her *own* choices and actions. As Aristotle said, "A is A." In this case, "A" refers to her husband's repeated choices to act unreasonably. Martha must accept that her husband's choice to be unreasonable is real and unalterable on her part. She cannot *force* his mind to initiate rational thought. Instead, she needs to make sure that her own choices are sensible and to move forward in life—without him, if necessary.

Andrea. Andrea is in love with Tony, who feels much warmth and admiration for her in return. However, Tony also loves and is involved with a different woman. Andrea feels angry, resentful, and powerless, especially when she sees the happy couple together or thinks about them together. She begins to feel like a victim, and that romance will never be possible for her. She dwells on what she cannot change—i.e., Tony's choice to stay involved with the other woman.

Andrea needs to end this victim thinking and remind herself she has a choice: she can continue wallowing over the unchangeable, or she can put her thoughts into other matters, such as career, hobbies, friendships, and meeting new men. If she chooses to be rational, she will accept the facts of reality, and will resist the temptation to let Tony have his cake and eat it too by spending time with him. She will work on letting him go, and moving on to better things.

Using Reason and Objectivity

Reason refers to a continuous process of identifying facts and drawing logical conclusions, with your own mind, about these facts. Happy, rational people accept that reason is fallible. Mistakes are possible, but you will make far fewer mistakes with reason than simply going on whim, "intuition," or what you think others want you to do.

To reject reason and objectivity amounts to accepting the view: "Who am I to judge?" As a consequence of accepting this mistaken view, you will feel morally guilty or hopelessly ineffective whenever you do try to make a judgment or decision. Judgments and decisions are crucial to your survival and your happiness. Without conscious judgment, you leave the course of your life to others or to mere chance.

Consider the application of reason to an important life decision. Joe engages in the following talk with himself: "Do I marry Emily or not? What are the facts here? She's attractive. We have a good sex life. We share the same basic values. She is honest, straightforward, and career-oriented—qualities I want in a partner. Like me, she wants to have one or two kids, but not for at least five years. We like the same kinds of things, but are different enough to keep it interesting. For instance, I never considered skiing but now I like it because she taught me how to do it. Sometimes we fight, but we recover quickly.

"On the negative side, I wish she were closer to my age—she's three years older, but that's not really a problem. I also wish she were a little more outgoing and intellectual. But these negatives are minor when compared to the positives. I need to consider that it's hard to find a compatible partner and we have both invested several years in this relationship already. She's trying to improve, and she's making progress. I think I should definitely marry her."

Notice how Joe considered the full context of facts and reached his conclusion accordingly. Contrary to popular opinion, decisions about romantic love need reason and objectivity no less than other areas of life. Joe could bypass reason and decide to marry Emily simply because he feels in love with her, at least for the moment. Yet without the use of reason, Joe gambles his future on the hope that his unexamined emotions happen to be correct.

Even more, Joe needs to know the reasons for his decision in order to develop genuine conviction. Imagine that two years into their marriage, Joe and Emily have a terrible fight. Emily leaves home for a couple of days to stay with a friend. Joe begins to wonder if Emily has changed, or if he made the right decision in marrying her.

If Joe cannot recall the many reasons why he married Emily, because he never examined them in the first place, then it will be harder for him to cope with the marital crisis. He will wail, "I don't have the loving feeling anymore! It's gone! The marriage must be over." If he operates on reason, however, he will think, "I remember the reasons why I married her. I don't think that I misjudged her. We can probably get through this crisis; or, at least it's worth a major effort."

Knowing *why* you made a decision gives you more emotional conviction and perspective, especially when something happens to call that decision into question.

It is easier, for example, to be faithful to your spouse and to have a happier, stronger relationship if you know the basic reasons why you love the person. Knowing the reasons for remaining faithful make it much easier to actually stay faithful when you may be tempted, at some point, to have an extramarital affair.

A life consistently lived by reason gives you strength and perspective for the harder times. It does not leave you at the mercy of whims, feelings, or the opinions of others. Reason is your only true "higher power."

Consider another example. A young woman tries to decide whether to drop out of her doctoral dissertation program. Her feelings of wanting to drop out are stronger than her feelings of wanting to stay. If feelings alone are to be her decision criteria, then she should obviously drop out. However, when she stops to look at the facts and to use reason she reaches a different conclusion.

"Writing a dissertation is hard," she says to herself (or a friend, or a counselor). "Several of my dissertation committee members are less than supportive. My friend Betsy recently dropped out and she strongly urges me to do the same. Recently, I have started to doubt my ability to complete the project. I am also not convinced the doctoral degree will be of much use to me if I eventually choose a business career rather than an academic one.

"At the same time," she continues, "I really believe I should complete something once I start it. If I quit now, how can I be sure I won't quit again when the going gets rough in the future? The dissertation will be of some value even if I choose a business career over an academic one. Potential employers will know that I am hard working and intelligent by virtue of the fact that I was able to complete a doctoral degree. Plus, I enjoy the subject I am studying.

"Despite my self-doubts, there is no reason to assume I am incapable of completing the dissertation. How could I survive all these years of education, including moving this far through the dissertation process, if I were fundamentally incapable of finishing it? It just does not make sense. There is no mystery here. The same general principles—perseverance, focus, careful use of time—that helped me get this far will help me through to the end.

"So, in summary, here are my reasons for dropping out: (1) My friend Betsy suggests I do so; (2) I might not pursue an academic career; and (3) I am having feelings of self-doubt.

"Here are my reasons for finishing the degree: (1) It will be of use even in a business career; (2) Staying with a project once I start it will be a major, long-range self-esteem boost; (3) No intrinsic reason exists to prove that I cannot finish it once I start it; and, (4) I enjoy the subject."

Her purely emotional conclusion? Drop out. Her rational, reasoned-out determination? Stay.

The use of this example should not imply that it is always wrong to drop out of a dissertation program. Nor is it always wrong to change one's mind. Nor are emotions always mistaken. Sometimes a process of reason will actually prove the emotions correct.

The point to understand is the method by which you should make such an important life decision. Is the method going to be reason, using facts and logic? Or is the method going to consist of pure emotion, or of relying uncritically on others' opinions, without the sort of introspective process described above?

People who consistently make decisions using reason feel much more in control of their lives than people who rely primarily on emotions or the opinions of others. I know—because people who rely mostly on emotions end up in my office, overwhelmed by psychological symptoms. Using emotions, without facts and reason, for making decisions is like choosing which house to buy or what college to attend by rolling dice or flipping a coin. The roll of the dice or the flip of the coin may, by accident, lead you to the correct decision—but only by accident. You will not know why it was the correct decision and, consequently, you will not feel competent to make similarly good decisions in the future. You will have no choice but to attribute your success to luck or vague, undefinable "instincts."

People with psychological problems such as depression almost always feel that they are not in control of their lives. Do you want to feel in charge of your life and prevent mental problems such as depression? Then you need to habitually and consistently use the proper method of assessing reality and making choices.

Living By the Rule of Self-Interest

Accepting reality and using reason involves effort. If you accept this responsibility, it only seems to make sense that you let yourself enjoy the benefits as well. This means living your life according to your own self-interest.

Responsible people can and should live by their own interest. Indeed, they have earned the right to do so by accepting absolute responsibility for themselves. This means that they guiltlessly choose their own careers and their own styles of life.

Healthy people are not altruistic self-sacrificers. They do not feel compelled to spend their weekends in soup kitchens; to flee a wealthy country to live among the poverty-stricken so they can feel superior; or to give away time and money to "friends" and relatives who act as if they have a right to them.

Genuinely reality-oriented individuals do not consider themselves to be their brothers' keepers. They are their own keepers—and, instead of sharing, they *trade*. They trade value for value: dollars, in the economic marketplace, and personal virtues and compatibilities, in the arenas of friendship and romance. They live by the trader principle, rather than by the principle of self-sacrifice. When they give, they expect something in return. They recognize that others can and should also expect something in return (material *or* psychological). They want all their relationships—professional and personal—to be entirely uncoerced and voluntary.

Healthy, happy people are long-range hedonists. They live life to the fullest, respecting the equal right of everyone else to seek out the same. They acquire as much wealth and physical comfort as they can and want, without committing fraud or initiating physical force against anyone else. They seek to act in their own objective self-interests, rather than merely groping for what feels good at the moment.

Mindless hedonism and rational self-interest are not the same. If a mindless hedonist sees a woman he wants to sleep with, then he sleeps with her—forgetting the longer-range consequences to himself or those he values, such as his wife. If a rational egoist sees a woman he wants to sleep with, he stops and considers the consequences; he recognizes that while it might feel good at the time, the alternatives of hurting his wife, whom he loves more, or else having to lie to her, are simply not acceptable. He chooses to refrain from the sexual affair not because he is selfless—but because he is too selfish to hurt himself and those whom he values.

Most of us have been taught to "lump" together the mindless hedonist and the rationally self-interested person. Consequently, we tend to think our only choice consists of being a selfless saint or a mindless sinner. Such a "lumping" represents both an outrageous injustice and a profound inaccuracy. It makes no sense whatsoever to label a mindless hedonist—a crack addict, a fraudulent businessman, a cheater—as "selfish." To be selfish means to act in one's self-interest—and people who live by their whims, rather than by objectivity and reason, are certainly not acting in their own objective interests.

For centuries, the "lumping" of mindlessness and rational self-interest has led to tragic human dilemmas. People either try to become self-sacrificers—refusing to live for themselves, even in the rational sense—or, when they cannot take it any longer, they just do whatever they feel like, ignoring the consequences. Psychologically, they become caught in the false alternative of either being selfless and "good," on the one side, or mindlessly "selfish" and "bad," on the other. It is a ludicrous, utterly unrealistic choice. As a consequence many individuals vacillate back and forth between the two—working at a soup kitchen on Sunday, for example, and then cheating one's business partner on Tuesday, and then on Friday delivering a speech to high school graduating seniors on the alleged virtues of selflessness, sacrifice, and community service.

More than a decade of experience as a psychotherapist has shown me that a very large percentage of psychological conflicts are the result of the clash, in an individual's subconscious mind, between these two false alternatives. The psychological symptoms people experience—depression, anxiety, obsession, attention-deficits, and so forth—represent a "crying out" on the part of a subconscious mind pleading for a resolution. "Resolve me!" or "Fix me!" your subconscious mind is shouting to you, when you are emotionally troubled. The question remains: what exactly are you supposed to resolve?

The solution consists of accepting the rule of self-interest. Not self-interest in the mindless, hedonistic sense; but rather, self-interest grounded in the principles of accepting reality and living by reason. If you choose to think rationally, you will start to see that no inherent conflict exists between being a good person and a happy, efficacious person. If you define "good" as being reality- and reason-oriented, then happiness will flow logically.

You will begin to accept absolute responsibility for things over which you do have control—setting goals, going to school, making a living, taking vacations, raising children, pursuing interesting careers. You will also begin to let go of responsibility for things over which you will never have control—others' minds, others' choices, the fact you cannot have something for nothing, and the fact that both survival and happiness require conscious, willful action.

Conclusion

Living a happy and meaningful life requires three basic tools: (1) a commitment to accepting reality and not trying to change the unchangeable; (2) a commitment to reason, as opposed to either blind emotionalism or mindless adherence to others' opinions; and, (3) a refusal to live for anyone else except yourself and those you personally value such as spouse, friends, and children.

If you follow these principles consistently, day after day, the emotional rewards of serenity, benevolence, and happiness will become the norm rather than the exception. You will become much more able to handle everyday stress and even occasional tragedy.

Such broad abstractions are easier to preach than to practice. Try to apply them one-issue-at-a-time. Recognize that internalizing healthy ideas and behaviors takes time. See for yourself how well they work. Give them a chance. Progress usually comes in small, gradual steps—and so will the happiness resulting from such progress.

Keep working at it. Your life is worth it.   Ⓣ

1. Jack Trimpey, *The Small Book: A Revolutionary Alternative for Overcoming Alcohol and Drug Dependence* (New York: Dell, 1989, 1992).
2. See Charles J. Sykes, *Dumbing Down Our Kids* (New York: St. Martin's Press, 1995); Thomas Sowell, *Inside American Education* (New York: The Free Press, 1993); and, Ayn Rand, "The Comprachicos," in *The New Left: The Anti-Industrial Revolution* (Signet, 1970).

Chapter 3

Emotions

EMOTIONS—WHAT ARE THEY AND WHY SHOULD I CARE?

All human beings have emotions and feelings. Emotions and feelings are simply automatic thoughts. The thoughts may be rational, irrational, or some combination of the two. Pursuing mental health requires paying attention to these thoughts rather than repressing or evading them. If you repress or evade the feelings, they will gradually come to control you and your actions. If you refuse to pay attention to the resentment you feel towards your boss, for example, you run the risk of snapping at or even blowing up at him, thereby endangering your job. If you repress or evade the anxiety you feel about your fiancé, you run the risk of experiencing a panic attack the morning of the wedding. In order to manage or "control" your feelings, you first have to be aware of them.

What is the alternative to evasion and repression of emotions? The popular approach today is to "get in touch" with emotions, to feel them, to demand that others listen to them, and to even follow them blindly. In short: emotional self-indulgence. Clearly, such an approach is no better than evasion or repression; in some respects, it is even worse. If you simply tell your boss that you feel angry at him, without knowing why or whether the basis for the anger warrants a confrontation, you endanger your job unnecessarily. If you tell your fiancé that you're not sure you love him before carefully weighing the reasons for this doubt, you might needlessly hurt him or even break off a relationship that could have, in fact, worked out.

Both emotional repression *and* emotional self-indulgence represent a basic misunderstanding about what causes emotions and the role of reason in handling emotions. Ironically, these two opposing "extremes" actually reinforce one another. As psychologist Nathaniel Branden wrote in *The Objectivist* (August 1966), "It is an interesting paradox that repression and emotional self-indulgence are often merely two sides of the same coin. The man who is afraid of his emotions and represses them, sentences himself to be pushed by subconscious motivation—which means, to be ruled by feelings whose existence he dares not identify. And the 'hedonist,' the man who follows his emotions blindly, has the best reason to be afraid of them—and, at least to some extent, is driven to repress out of self-preservation."

The goal of developing a healthy psychology requires a willingness to accept that your emotions exist and do have an influence on you, while at the same time recognizing that you do not have to act blindly on those emotions. Being a rational person, contrary to the conventional idea of "rational," does not mean emotional repression. Nor, of course, does it mean blindly acting on your emotions and demanding that others accept them without proof.

Being rational means facing your emotions and acting on them, indeed enjoying them, only when you know for a fact they are consistent with objective reality. If you experience anger towards your boss, then sit down with someone (or by yourself) and determine to what extent, if any, there is a valid basis for your emotion of anger. The emotional experience of anger generally suggests a belief that some injustice has occurred. For example, maybe you have reason to believe that your boss lied to you, or that he passed you up for a promotion which the facts show you have earned. Or, upon introspecting, you might discover that you see no evidence of injustice, other than the fact that your boss' personality or style gets on your nerves.

The facts of the situation, discoverable only after introspection and thought, will provide you with clues regarding the appropriate action to take. If an objective injustice has taken place, then a discussion with your boss about your concerns is most likely appropriate. If no objective injustice has occurred, and you are experiencing anger for no clear or valid reason, then it is better to focus your attention on what is really bothering you (e.g., perhaps needing a new job or new career) rather than displacing your anger onto your boss.

Keeping a journal of your emotions, feelings and thoughts can make a big difference to your mental health. A journal represents the mental equivalent of working out; if done properly and consistently, it helps build "emotional muscle."

What does keeping a journal do? A journal is your tool of introspection. A journal serves as a confidante-counselor-friend, one that you can confide in any time of day or night. First you write in your journal all of your thoughts and feelings on a particular subject. During this initial phase of the journal entry, do not censor, inhibit or judge your feelings in any way. Simply *feel* them, to your heart's content, and write them all down. Then, immediately afterwards or, if you prefer, after a small break, begin to rationally analyze them. Ask yourself such questions as, "What facts, if any, support the truth of these feelings? What facts, if any, refute the truth of these feelings? Upon what more basic premises are my feelings based? What other possible explanations, if any, need to be ruled out before I accept this conclusion? What percentage (0, 20, 50, 90, 100%) of my feelings conform to objective facts I know for certain are true?"

Many journal formats are possible. Some people prefer a highly structured journal with routine questions to pry the necessary information out of them. Others prefer a blank notebook, and manage to work on the incongruity between emotions and reason in their own way. The specific technique is optional. The fact that human beings, in order to maintain mental health, need to introspect about their emotions with the use of logic and reason is *not* optional. Either you rationally introspect, or you succumb to the two-headed disaster of emotional repression/emotional indulgence. The choice is yours.

Introspection does mean work. It does require you to, first, confront your emotions, which is not always an easy task. It requires, second, that you be willing to rationally analyze your emotions, which is not always easy either. Try to fight the idea that mental health should not have to be work, and that psychotherapy is a passive, medical process where you sit back and let the sessions "cure" you. In truth, psychotherapy is closer to working out than sitting back. Just as you work to trim physical fat and build physical muscle in the gym or on the treadmill, so too must you work to trim emotional fat and build emotional muscle in the therapy office and during your introspective exercises and journal keeping. The pace and the magnitude of the cure is ultimately in your hands.

The more you face your emotions head on, and take responsibility for rationally analyzing them, the sooner you will see progress. How do you measure progress, in psychotherapy or with emotional problems in general? When your thoughts and your emotions start to come into harmony, you know you are getting better. When your feelings begin to catch up with—and correspond to—what you know is reality, then you know you are getting healthier.

As an illustration, consider a common—and quite painful—example. Imagine you are attracted to a romantic partner whom you know is unhealthy for you. This romantic partner treats you badly, and you know, in your head, that it can lead to nowhere but disaster. Or maybe he does not treat you badly; maybe he's a good person, but you simply know that you are incompatible for a variety of reasons. Either way, you have to keep your mind in focus and continuously remind your emotions that he is not the man you initially thought (or hoped) he was. If you act in accordance with what your head tells you, despite the onslaught of contradictory emotions, then your emotions will, in time, catch up to your head. The more consistently you work at it, the sooner you will achieve this harmony.

The same general principle applies to all kinds of psychological problems: depression, anxiety, panic disorder, attention-deficit syndrome, personality disorder, substance abuse, addictive behavior, obsessive-compulsive behavior, anger control, low self-esteem and less severe forms of psychosis. The exact techniques and the degree of difficulty, however, varies widely from individual to individual and from problem to problem. Cognitive-behavioral therapy, when practiced properly, can help you bring your emotions and your rational intelligence into harmony. *You* do the work; your therapist actively guides, coaches, and teaches you as necessary. Cognitive-behavioral therapy, of which journal keeping is one component, teaches the only rational alternative to emotional repression and emotional self-indulgence. There is no miracle cure. Instead, there is something much more powerful involved: taking charge of your own mind, and your own life.

The results will be exhilarating and lasting.

DEFINITIONS OF COMMON EMOTIONS

Emotions refer to broad categories of feelings and self-statements which are an expression of your ongoing value judgments, ideas, and observations. Emotions represent such value judgments and ideas in automatized, immediate form.

Anger, for example, qualifies as an emotion. Unless you are severely emotionally repressed, you can identify with relative ease the fact you are angry. It is not so easy, however, to identify the underlying feelings, self-statements, self-talk and evaluations which are occurring at the same time as the emotion.

Examples of such underlying evaluations are: "Dave is not returning my phone calls right away. The jerk!" Or: "Who does Carol think she is, acting like she knows everything?"

These underlying identifications and evaluations represent the *cause* of the emotion. The emotion itself (in this case, anger) represents the *result*. The ideas and evaluations refer to what you think; the emotion refers to the result of what you think.

Finding out what you feel (the emotion) and why you feel it (the underlying thoughts, evaluations, ideas) constitutes psychological introspection. If you want to be mentally healthy, in touch with reality and free of psychological problems, regular introspection is a requirement. Introspection is to mental health what brushing one's teeth and flossing are to oral health. Without introspection, your mind, along with your ability to manage it, slowly decays.

The goals of psychological introspection are first, to identify the emotion and, second, to identify the specific evaluations, thoughts, or judgments which gave rise to the emotion. The evaluations can be accurate or inaccurate, rational or irrational. In other words, perhaps Dave is a jerk or perhaps he is not; it depends upon the facts and the circumstances. Perhaps Carol really does think she knows everything, or perhaps you are presuming you can read her mind without proof of what she's really thinking; it depends upon the facts and the circumstances. In order to know reality objectively, you obviously must stop and think, and not blindly accept your feelings as truth.

Needless to say, the task of introspection is often easier said than done. You may be able to easily identify your anger, or your happiness, or your envy, or your sadness, but you still do not always know the cause—that is, the ideas, evaluations, and self-statements—underlying the generalized emotional state.

How, then, can you make the process easier? One method is to consider the generalized definition of the emotion. If you know the generalized definition, then you can often determine what specific thoughts caused the emotion.

Anger, for example, is generally defined as an evaluation that an injustice has taken place, that somebody has done something wrong or unfair when it was under his power to do otherwise. Now apply this generalized definition to a specific situation.

Joe: "I am angry. I do not know why. What does anger mean? Anger means a belief that an injustice has occurred, that somebody has done something wrong or unfair when it was under his power to do otherwise. Has anything like this happened? Let me think. Am I angry at my girlfriend? No, it's not her. I'm really happy with how she treats me overall. I was a little irritated when she arrived late for the movie yesterday, but she had a good reason and that's very unusual for her. Am I angry at my boss? I don't think so . . . He's not my favorite person in the world, and I think he's gruff, but I can't think of anything he's done that is unfair. Wait a minute . . . I know why I'm angry. I'm angry because we had to cancel our plans to go to the beach, because of the hurricane. I feel it's so unfair. I've been looking forward to a break for months; now, when I finally can get away from work, I have to cancel it. It's just so unfair!"

Notice how Joe discovered the cause of his anger by first examining the generalized definition of anger. He scanned his mind for instances of what he considered injustices, until he discovered one. Just as knowing the general definition of anger helped Joe discover what caused his anger, so too can it help him discover his error: "The weather is not a person. Only human beings have free will, so only human beings can be just or unjust. The weather can neither be fair nor unfair. The weather does not have a mind, or the ability to make choices. Nobody is making the weather bad just to ruin my vacation, out of spite. The weather just *is*; it just exists and its patterns are outside of man's control. Frustration and disappointment are appropriate emotions; but anger is not an appropriate emotion. After all, I knew the risks implicit in a beach trip when I made the plans; I knew this is the beginning of hurricane season. Most of the time hurricanes are not a problem. In this case, one was."

You can apply the same principle, that emotions refer to generalized evaluations, to any number of situations in your life. Here are some definitions to guide you through your introspection. For especially difficult or painful emotions, a competent psychotherapist trained in cognitive therapy can assist you.

Anger. An evaluation or belief that an injustice has taken place, that somebody has done something wrong or unfair when it was under his power to do otherwise. For example: "Patty lied to Joe about her extramarital affair. Even now, she refuses to see how unfair this is. I am angry with her." Or: "The store will not take back the suit I bought, even though they have no sign posted warning that all sales are final. I am angry."

Disappointment. An evaluation or belief that expectations, reasonable or otherwise, were not met. For example: "The seminar did not teach me much about how to use computers. It only covered programming. This was a disappointment." Or: "My doctor did not prescribe any medicine to cure my stomach pain. I thought there were pills for such things. I am disappointed." Or: "I thought that monthly car payments would be cheaper than I learned today at the car dealer. I'm disappointed."

Frustration. An evaluation or belief that a goal or desire has been blocked and is, at least for now, unattainable. For example: "I wanted to finish cleaning the house before the weekend. Now it looks like I'll have to do some cleaning Saturday morning. I wanted Saturday morning to cook. How frustrating!" Or: "I wanted to finish my college degree in four years. But because I changed majors I will have to graduate a year later. How frustrating!"

Panic. The sudden, abrupt evaluation or belief that danger, valid or otherwise, is rapidly approaching or is already present. For example: "The house is shaking. We're in the middle of an earthquake!" Or: "It's 2 AM and I just heard glass break in the window downstairs. We're being robbed!" Or: "They're going to build a chemical plant in our county. We're all going to get cancer for sure! We've got to stop them . . . fast!"

Inadequacy. The evaluation or belief that a person or thing does not, and cannot, live up to a particular standard, rational or otherwise; the person or thing is not suited to the intended purpose. For example: "Bill can't give the speech for our company. He has no public speaking experience. I feel he's inadequate." Or: "That vacuum cleaner won't clean the carpet stains. You need to hire a professional service. I feel that the vacuum will be inadequate." Or: "I can't do anything right. Every time I start something, I fail at it. I feel totally inadequate."

Confidence. The evaluation or belief that a person or thing can potentially, or does already, live up to a particular standard, rational or otherwise. For example: "I feel quite confident that with training, and experience, JoAnn will make an excellent accounts manager." Or: "Fred is an excellent architect. He designed three buildings I know very well. I have full confidence in him." Or: "I am a very good and experienced swimmer. I have won many races. I feel confident I can win this one."

Guilt. The evaluation or belief, rational or otherwise, that you are responsible for a particular event or set of circumstances which are negative or harmful in nature; the belief that you have acted against your values. For example: "I told Martha to turn right onto Evergreen Street instead of left. She ended up lost for forty-five minutes. I feel guilty." Or: "I lied to Jerry, hoping that he would not find out what I did. Now that he did find out, we're both even more unhappy and I feel guilty." Or: "That poor homeless man is so pathetic; and I go home to a comfortable house every night. I feel so guilty."

Pride. The evaluation or belief, correct or mistaken, that you are responsible for a particular event or set of circumstances which are positive or beneficial in nature; the belief that you have acted in accordance with your values. For example: "I came up with the idea for this science project against everyone's skepticism. I held my ground, knowing for a fact the project was possible, and now that it has been successfully completed I feel pride." Or: "I raised my daughter with the best principles I know of, and now that she is a successful physician I feel proud of her accomplishments."

Lonely. The evaluation or belief, rational or otherwise, that you are alone in some context, and that being alone represents a threat of some kind. For example: "Here I am, alone and single, and it's another Saturday night. I'm never going to meet someone to marry. I'm so lonely." Or: "I feel so lonely at work. All this deception and corruption is taking place, and nobody talks about it or even acknowledges it. I'm the only one who seems to recognize it." Or: "I'm old, my friends are dying off, and younger people do not understand me. This is no way to live. I'm so lonely, I hope I die soon."

Bored. The evaluation or belief, rational or otherwise, that no challenge suited to your interests or abilities is available, either immediately or in the foreseeable future; the evaluation may be applied generally or to a particular situation. For example: "I am bored with this history class. I already know everything being discussed, as well as everything planned for the rest of the semester." Or: "Retirement isn't working out like I thought it would. I can't be happy living strictly day-to-day. I need a longer-range purpose. I'm bored without one."

Jealousy. The evaluation or belief, accurate or otherwise, that somebody else has some object, relationship or quality that you want, and that you are unable to get it yourself, at least easily or in the near-term. For example: "Ted has a new Porsche. I wish I could get a new car as nice as that." Or: "I wanted to date Marcia. Now I see that she's going out with Bill." Or: "Success seems to come so easily to Brad. I wish I knew his secret. Maybe I'll figure it out someday, but I sure don't know it now."

Envy. The evaluation or belief—often inaccurate—that somebody else has some object, relationship, or quality that you want, and that is, by its very nature, outside of your ability to obtain no matter how hard you try; furthermore, you believe that some kind of injustice is the cause of this discrepancy. For example: "Success seems to come so easily to Brad. He's always had it so easy, and I haven't. He's just a conceited jerk." Or: "The rich are privileged. It's not fair for them to have so much more money than the rest of us, even if they did earn it honestly. Their share of the human pie is too large." Or: "Bill and Marcia are going out with each other. *I* wanted to date Marcia. Well, if I can't have her, he shouldn't have her either." Or (examples where envy is rationally based): "I am confined to a wheelchair because I was injured by a drunk driver in a hit-and-run accident. I will never have a chance to be physically active again like my friends are. I feel envious of them." Or: "The doctor in my HMO cut corners and now, as a result, I am dying of cancer which might have been prevented. I envy those who can expect to live full lives."

Anxiety. The persistent evaluation or belief, rational or irrational, that your well-being is endangered or threatened in some context. For example: "People are going to laugh at me and I am going to make all kinds of mistakes in my speech; I feel paralyzed with anxiety." Or: "I feel anxious that the plane will crash, and I will die." Or: "I don't know how to handle life, like others do. I can't survive or be happy because I don't know the secrets for doing so. I feel anxious most of the time."

Happy. The evaluation or belief that some event, circumstance, or incident which represents a positive value to you has occurred or developed. For example: "My daughter is engaged. Her fiancé is a wonderful man, and an ideal match for her. I'm so happy!" Or: "I just made a million dollars. I'm rich! I'm happy!" Or: "Frank has agreed to invest in my new business. So we can get started immediately. I'm very happy."

Sad. The evaluation or belief that some event, circumstance, or incident which represents a negative value to you has occurred or developed. For example: "The doctor says I cannot have children. I always wanted to be a mother. I'm so sad." Or: "My best friend died last year. I'm still sad whenever I think about him being gone." Or: "My candidate lost the election. I worked so hard for him, and still believe he could have done good things. I'm sad."

Confusion. The evaluation or belief, correct or otherwise, that a logical contradiction exists in some context. For example: "Just last week I saw Tom and he looked so healthy. Now he's dead of a heart attack at age thirty-eight. How can this be?" Or: "You're a woman and you don't want to ever have a child? I'm confused. I thought women had mothering instincts." Or: "You tell me that you want to continue dating me, but you don't return my phone calls and you never initiate a date. I'm confused by the mixed messages between your words and your actions."

Cynical. The evaluation or belief, correct or otherwise, that a person, or group of people, cannot or will not act consistent with a particular ideal, set of principles, or set of standards; the standards or ideal may be rational or irrational. For example: "Everyone is out for his own interests in this world; the world can never be a good place." Or: "You can't trust men. They are all callous, evil exploiters." Or: "Judy is never going to change; she will always be pretentious, smug, and deceitful." Or (a case where cynicism is clearly rational): "The Nazis [or Communists] are corrupt at the core; it would be hopeless, dangerous, and wrong to try and compromise with them."

Pessimistic. The evaluation (rational or otherwise) that events, in some context, will not go well. For example: "I don't expect us to have a good time on vacation. The weather forecast does not look favorable." Or: "I can't foresee a good candidate emerging from these presidential primaries; I'm pessimistic." Or: "I'm pessimistic about finding a good wife."

Optimistic. The evaluation (rational or otherwise) that events, in some context, will go well. For example: "I'm optimistic you'll do very well on the test." Or: "Our marriage will, I believe, be a happy and long-lasting one." Or: "We're going to win the contest; I can just feel it. I'm optimistic."

THOUGHT DISTORTIONS AND HOW THEY CAUSE MENTAL PROBLEMS

Mistaken assumptions, or irrational underlying ideas, cause most psychological disorders.

Too many such assumptions exist to confine to one chapter—or even one book, for that matter. Nevertheless, here are some of the most common erroneous ideas that people experience. As you read about them, ask yourself which mistakes in thinking *you* most frequently make.

Distortion # 1. The unwarranted generalization. Falsely or hastily viewing an event as always or never occurring. Examples: "You always tell me what to wear." "You never help me around the house." "You are always late. You never show any concern for anyone except yourself."

The source of the error: Some generalizations are true; but generalizations require proof. And in the heat of emotion, people are prone to make generalizations without sufficient attention to fact.

Some generalizations are, of course, valid. The sun does rise and set every day. Sufficient intake of poison always leads to death. All people were born, and all people will one day die. We know these generalizations are true due to a combination of empirical observation and logical analysis.

Just because we have established that some generalizations are true, however, does not mean that all generalizations are true. Is your mother truly always telling you what to wear? Or are there instances where she refrained from doing so? Does your husband really never help you around the house? Or can you think of exceptions where he helped out in less obvious ways? Are your generalizations fact-based—or purely emotionally based?

The alternative: Train your mind to be aware that generalizations are not true without factual evidence and logical argumentation to back them up. Think before you generalize. You owe this precaution to yourself, most of all. When you make unwarranted generalizations to your spouse, for example, she will remember them and continue to assume that you really believe them even though you only said it during an argument. You also look foolish if you try to assert something that is not backed up in fact; you look foolish because you have shown that you are not a careful thinker. You also show a lack of respect for yourself when you make statements you are not prepared or able to back up.

Distortion # 2. The myth of force. Falsely believing that if you try hard enough you can get others to change, even if it means using physical coercion, or emotional intimidation, and even if they do not want to change. Examples: "You have a messed-up personality. You're in denial. Go to therapy or else!" "I can make her quit drinking." "If I nag him enough, he'll be a more loving husband."

The source of the error: To force or intimidate someone is not the same as getting their agreement. To force, intimidate, or defraud someone into doing something will not gain his loyalty or his agreement. In fact, it will lead to just the opposite when he finds out you lied, or when he finally becomes wise to your manipulations and he rebels against you. Force, fraud or intimidation only "work" in a superficial, shorter-term way; and even then, what is obtained is of no value. Nothing of value can be obtained through such means. If you give a teenager a car without requiring him to pay for or maintain it in some way, he will not treat it responsibly. If you demand that your wife change her personality and go to therapy, her mind will not bend under such pressure, even if she should change.

The alternative: Instead of trying to force or intimidate people to do things, it is better to refuse to participate in the activity with which you disagree. If you are worried about your spouse's drinking problem, do not nag him about the drinking. Instead, refuse to go out with him when he drinks, and refuse to call his boss to make excuses when he's hung over. If your best friend has an emotional problem but refuses to see a professional, do not berate her for this fact. Instead, when she calls you in an emotional crisis, stay detached and say, "I'd like to help you, but I really think you ought to see a professional about something this serious." And then refuse to discuss the matter any further. If the friend accuses you of "selfishness," then you know you're on the right track. With people of value to you, avoid the false alternative between micromanaging them and helplessly doing nothing. Instead, refuse to participate in their dysfunction.

Distortion # 3. The myth of self-sacrifice. Falsely believing that if you sacrifice for others, they will (and should) sacrifice for you. Examples: "I gave up my career for you; you should give up the idea of having kids for me." "I always put my needs second to others'; why is everyone else so damn selfish?" "I loved, and loved, and loved him; but he still beats me up. Isn't love supposed to be enough?"

The source of the error: We have all been taught the wrong morality. Literally all traditional and modern moral codes stress, in varying degrees, the alleged virtue of self-sacrifice. Only acts from which you gain absolutely nothing are virtuous, according to this twisted code of ethics; the more you personally gain (financially or otherwise) from an action, the less virtuous the act. Since we all gain from earning a living, providing food and shelter for ourselves, and looking before we cross the street, to say nothing of living the good life, then none of us can be totally virtuous!

Obviously, as more pragmatic people realize, such a philosophy is impossible to practice consistently. Even an extreme self-sacrificer such as Mother Teresa probably derives *some* selfish pleasure and gratification from assisting starving people. Consequently, under the ethics of sacrifice, there are no true saints. Yet the "ideal" of self-sacrifice is not merely impractical, and illogical. It is also sinister. Because of its logical contradictions, it creates feelings of unearned guilt and inhibits (and in some cases, even destroys) an individual's need and right to pursue happiness and live life to the fullest extent possible. It makes people think they must either live like Mother Teresa, and be a saint, or pursue a more selfish existence but pay for it with a constant state of guilt. In fact, the morality of self-sacrifice is the deeper cause underlying most mental disorders, particularly low self-esteem. What is low self-esteem, after all, but the chronic feeling that, "I am incapable and unworthy of living life to the fullest."

The alternative: The alternative to self-sacrifice is: refusing to sacrifice yourself to others or others to yourself. "Sacrifice" means giving up something more important in favor of something less important. To give up having children because your husband does not want children is a sacrifice on *your part*; forcing or manipulating him into having a child represents a sacrifice on *his* part. The logical thing to do in such a situation is to divorce your spouse and try to find someone who shares with you the desire to have children. The same principle applies to other major life decisions such as career and overall lifestyle. You will never make yourself—nor another—happy by making yourself miserable. Martyrdom is not the ideal.

Is compromise ever appropriate? Of course. If you want to see one movie and your spouse wants to see another, to go along with his choice does not necessarily represent a sacrifice, at least not if you can trust him to let you make the choice some other time. If you really love your spouse, furthermore, you *selfishly* enjoy seeing him happy. The same idea applies to other relatively minor life situations such as where to vacation, where to eat out, and what color carpet or wallpaper to buy. Rejecting self-sacrifice does not rule out reasonable compromise between consenting, rational, and fair-minded adults. The rejection of self-sacrifice does, however, mean that you need not feel guilty for refusing to have children if you choose not to do so, for refusing to follow your father or mother's career if you don't want to do so, or for opting to live a comfortable life in the United States instead of becoming an international social worker. Rejecting the notion of self-sacrifice as the essence of goodness *does* mean going against what virtually all religious, political, and intellectual leaders preach. The rewards, however, of living by a rational, practical code of ethics are incalculably superior to the depressed and anxious states which dominate so many people's lives—including the lives of those who preach self-sacrifice.

Distortion # 4. The infallibility myth. The false belief that you should be above all error, even honest errors in judgment; in short, the belief that you can and should be all-knowing. Examples: Pretending to know the person someone else is talking about instead of simply saying, "Who are you talking about? I don't know of this person." Feeling depressed and powerless after making a mistake, even a small mistake, instead of cheerfully and objectively trying to discover the cause of your error.

The source of the error: A mistaken idea of excellence. Excellence does not require infallibility. In fact, excellence in any context would be impossible if we were all infallible. Think about it. If you were infallible, and all-knowing, by nature, then what value or achievement would there be in discovering electricity? Or inventing the printing press? Or curing cancer? Or inventing a microchip? The very idea of "achieving" something implies that work was involved, and that a unique person made a discovery that was not initially obvious—nor even conceivable—to anyone. If all of these inventions were knowable to everybody the moment they were born, then what would be the purpose of living? What reason would there be to get up in the morning if there were not an endless list of challenges requiring solution? Would living in the moment, without any need for longer-range planning or purpose, really be such a great life?

The alternative: Too many people complain, "If life were only perfect . . . ." By "perfect" they usually mean a state of existence in which everyone is infallible, and where nothing has to be earned. In truth, such a life would be boring. Of what value is achievement if there is nothing to achieve? How can anything be rewarding if no effort on your part is involved? Is something for nothing really the ideal—or is it just an escape hatch for those who do not want or have the confidence to live life to the fullest, with full freedom and full responsibility? A life without any need for effort would not have the "lows" of hard work; but it would not have the "highs" of pride, joy, and sense of accomplishment, either. Value without effort is a contradiction in terms. The presence of one implies the presence of the other. You cannot feel happy unless you worked for your happiness; and there is no point working unless there is some happiness to be gained. Such is the nature of reality. And reality is not such a bad place.

Distortion # 5. The myth of skepticism. The false belief that there are no absolutes, that nothing is certain, that everything is optional and there is no right or wrong. Examples: "Nothing is certain in this world." "Who am I (or you) to judge?" "You have your reality and I have my reality."

The source of the error: The deeper causes of this error require an involved philosophical discussion not possible here. The shorter answer is as follows: Certainly is possible. All knowledge starts with the sense organs. Even abstract generalizations (e.g., "The sun rises every day" or "All men are mortal") require sensory observation before becoming generalizations. Furthermore, it is a contradiction to claim, with absolute certainty, that absolute certainty is impossible. Consider the following exchange:

Skeptic: Nothing is certain. Absolute, objective knowledge is impossible. What's true for you may not be true for me.

Observer: Are you *absolutely* certain about this fact? Are you objectively certain that objective knowledge is impossible?

Skeptic: Yes. . . I mean no. Oh, shut up!

The alternative: The alternative to skepticism is common sense and a respect for serious, objective science grounded in scientific principles. Just because life can at times be difficult or complex is no reason to conclude that certainty is impossible. Yet this is what most of today's intellectuals, including many psychologists, teach their students and patients. Psychologically, such an idea represents a death-blow to self-esteem. Without the premise that certainty is possible, that knowledge is possible, you cannot hope to cure an anxiety disorder, a clinical depression, or any other psychological syndrome. Even common sense tells you that certain facts are self-evident—the color of the sky, the existence of the moon, the laws of gravity, and so forth. Truths are not always simple and self-evident; but truth does exist. Anyone who claims, as truth, that truth does not exist is a self-evident, self-contradicting fool. Even though common sense is not enough, you are better off with only common sense than with a pseudo-scientist who claims that the notion of objective truth is a myth.

Distortion # 6. The adversarial/conflict-of-interest myth. The false view that people are fundamentally at odds with one another, in the very nature of things. Examples: "Doctors and patients are natural enemies; doctors need patients to be sick in order to make a living." "Pure free enterprise is impossible. Business people, to survive, have to exploit others."

The source of the error: The error in this myth is the failure to see that people have a rational self-interest in *not* sacrificing others. Doctors, it is true, would not exist if there were not sickness in the world. But doctors would also not exist if there were not cures, as well. Doctors have a rational self-interest in not only making money, but providing cures as well; otherwise they would go out of business. Sickness existed long before the practice of modern medicine, a relatively new phenomenon. Cures are what make modern medicine so popular, and cures are what doctors have a truly selfish interest in providing.

The same is true of business, and free enterprise, in general. In a laissez-faire free enterprise society (where, keep in mind, there would be no possibility of government subsidies, special favors, or special interest groups), businesses, it is true, would be totally free to charge what they pleased. But they would also be totally responsible for producing the best possible product at the lowest possible price. Nobody, including businesses, could have their cake and eat it too. If Company A started to lose money because Company B came out with a better, cheaper product, Company A could not go to the government and ask for special favors (such as subsidies, or anti-trust lawsuits against Company B) so it could stay in business. So long as Company A *earns* its # 1 status, it thrives; but the minute another company earns the # 1 status, then Company A has to adapt, and possibly lose business. Such is the nature of existence, and the only appropriate standard of fairness.

These ideas are not relevant solely to the field of economics. They are also relevant to everyday people, and their emotional states, because economic issues obviously affect everyday lives and emotions. Many clients seek psychotherapy because of job stress, stress which is sometimes caused by downsizing and other economic transitions. If employees understand that change is in the nature of a free economy (or, in our present situation, a *semi*-free, highly regulated and subsidized economy), then they will take the attitude: "Some opportunities are ending, but others are opening as well. It is up to me to find the openings. I might actually end up better off than I started." If they take the adversarial, conflict-of-interest view, however, they will conclude: "It's all hopeless. My rights are being violated. Life stinks." The first attitude leads to realistic optimism, hope, and welcoming of change. The second attitude leads to further depression, anxiety, and sometimes even hatred directed against ethnic groups, foreign countries, the rich, or other easy targets. Economic conditions—and, more importantly, one's attitude toward economic conditions—have a very significant impact on mental health. The more you understand rational economic concepts, the better you will cope with the real world each day.

The alternative: To become mentally healthy, adopt the idea that conflicts of interest are not in the nature of things. Follow your rational self-interest to live life competently; others will inevitably benefit, even though their benefit is not (and should not be) your chief concern. Allowing others to live by their rational self-interest will afford you benefits as well. You have choices at the grocery store because farmers and grocery store owners are each seeking their own interests in the pursuit of profit. They benefit from the fact that you work in your job and can afford to buy their products. You, in turn, benefit from the fact that they have chosen their respective careers and you can have the unprecedented convenience of the modern grocery store. (Individuals from former Communist countries, upon visiting the United States, marvel at the grocery stores we take for granted). Apply the same general principle to countless other situations, professional and personal, individual and social. Watch how your mental state changes from cynicism and anxiety to happiness and calmness.

Distortion # 7: The myth of entitlement. The false idea that because you want or need something very much, you ought to have it. Examples: "After all the help I gave you moving, you should now invest in my business." "I need your time right now; you should give it to me."

The source of the error: Agreements must be contractual, clear, and voluntary to everyone involved. This applies not only to business affairs, but personal matters as well. If you helped a friend move, you have no right to expect help from him in return unless he agreed to it ahead of time. Of course, you are not obligated to participate in a one-sided friendship, and if he expects you to do things for him without reciprocating, then you should reconsider your friendship with him. But it is also possible that while he values you as a friend and wants to reciprocate your favor, he does not necessarily want to invest in your business. He is not obliged to keep an "agreement" which only existed in your mind and to which he never consented.

Even more fundamentally, the myth of entitlement is rooted in the ethics of self-sacrifice. "I sacrifice for you, so you should sacrifice for me," is often the underlying idea in feelings such as, "I need your time now; you should give it to me." If the ethics of self-sacrifice were rational and valid, then such an idea would make sense. The problem is that self-sacrifice is neither a moral nor practical way to live your life.

The alternative: Instead, you should pursue your own self-interest without sacrificing the rights of others to do the same. Do not demand that people give you their time or money against their will (a sacrifice of them to you); at the same time, do not demand yourself to give your time or money against your will (a sacrifice of yourself to others). Accept and give support to loved ones who have earned your trust, and earn their trust in return. But never think in terms of blind obligation or duty, either for yourself or others. Have the courage and independence to reject traditional morality that says you must sacrifice for others. In the process, you will become a happier and more moral individual.

WHY EXPRESSING YOUR FEELINGS IS NOT ALWAYS THE SOLUTION

Expressing your feelings is not the solution to all of your problems.

Knowing the cause of your feelings is what matters.

Feelings are nothing more than automatic, split-second thoughts. For example, if you feel the emotion of anger, you might be experiencing the automatic thought, "Joe should not have talked to me that way." Your judgment that Joe talked to you in an unreasonable manner created the generalized emotional state that most of us call anger.

Feelings, unlike conscious thoughts, represent a "knee-jerk" response that you cannot consciously control. You do not, for instance, simply decide, "I am going to feel angry," and then *will* yourself to do so. A feeling, by definition, happens automatically. In this sense, feelings are not under your direct control.

Even though feelings are not under your direct control, they do have origins in conscious thought. If you feel anger at Joe for talking to you the way he did, this emotion presupposes that you possess some idea as to what constitutes "reasonable" communication. At some point in the past, you either made a conscious decision about what is "reasonable" and what is "unreasonable" communication or you, by default, accepted someone else's standard (your mother's, a teacher's, etc.). Either way, emotional experiences—such as anger—are the consequence of various assumptions, thoughts, ideas, and principles formed or accepted by you in the past.

Many people are not aware of the fact that emotions and feelings are the consequence of thoughts and ideas. Various people believe that feelings arise from "God," from their spiritual "karma," from society, or from other entities or influences, especially parents and other authority figures.

Let us consider how these popular theories measure up (or fail to measure up) to the facts.

No evidence or logic supports the notion that feelings come from God or "karma." One can only accept such explanations on blind faith, making them irrelevant to the subject of psychology or science. The instant you allow yourself to go on uncritical faith, facts become irrelevant and logical discussion ends.

Consider the idea that feelings are "socially constructed," a popular notion among today's intellectuals. Social "construction" has no particular meaning, and certainly no basis in fact. Although society does exist, society is really nothing more than a collection of individuals in some geographic or other context. Millions of individuals, the vast majority of whom you will never meet, cannot force—or "construct"—you to think in a particular way. Granted, they can be highly influential, especially if you do not learn to think for yourself and to critically and objectively evaluate what people say. But the fact that it is difficult to think independently and critically does not mean it is impossible to do so. Even in a totalitarian dictatorship, wrong and miserable as it is, you can think what you want in the privacy of your own mind. Society influences an individual, but does not ultimately have to *determine* an individual. People can try to persuade you, and they can even point a gun to your head, but you are always free to think what you choose.

The same principle applies to family members, especially parents, who can play an enormously important role in shaping a child's thinking. Despite parental influences, children are free to think differently and form their own conclusions if they choose. Independent thinking among children becomes particularly evident in the teenage years. Some young adults are more intellectually and psychologically independent than others. In reality, too many young adults either let their families or their peers do their thinking for them, instead of making their own judgments. This sad fact, however, does not mean that it is impossible for individual human beings to think independently and form their own conclusions. The world is full of individualists on both large and small scales.

Your thoughts and emotions can be very concrete, such as, "Sue is an unlikable person," or very wide and abstract, such as, "Life ought to be happy and I ought to strive for happiness in my life." These thoughts and premises are always subject to change, provided that you first see facts or good logical arguments for changing them. Part of a psychologist's job is to help you identify what these subconscious ideas and premises actually are. If you identify any ideas and premises you want and need to change, then a good therapist can help you find methods for doing so. The more fundamental and abstract the subconsciously held idea (for example, "Life can never be happy and happiness will not be possible for me"), the longer and more difficult the change process will be; and, of course, you must be motivated to change.

Your feelings, then, are not the consequence of mystical influences. Nor are they the result of other individuals "forcing" you to feel or think a certain way. Feelings, in reality, represent nothing more than the manifestation of thoughts, assumptions, beliefs, ideas, and premises—valid or invalid—which exist in your mind. With effort and motivation, you *can* change them if necessary.   ⊕

Chapter 4

Self-Confidence

SELF-ESTEEM REQUIRES WORK, NOT WORDS

Lauren Murphy Payne, a psychotherapist and author of the children's book, *Just Because I Am: A Child's Book of Affirmation* says, according to *USA Today* (10/24/95), that kids need to know they're valued as individuals. And how does she define "value?" Says Payne: "The value of each human individual is separate from their accomplishments, tasks, possessions. The value is intrinsic, and it's a birthright."

This is precisely the viewpoint, so representative of today's educators and psychologists, which is destroying children's chances for genuine happiness and fulfillment. You cannot divorce a human being from his accomplishments. You cannot divorce mind from action, body from soul.

No matter how many credentials you hold, you cannot pretend that any individual exists outside the context of his objective actions, behaviors, and demonstrated character traits; to do so is to claim that the individual's mind or "spirit" exists without a body. Mind and body exist simultaneously, and interactively. What you *do* is as much a part of your character or "soul" as what you think and feel.

Nor can you say an individual has a "birthright" to happiness, as Payne implies. Happiness and self-esteem must be earned. How does one earn these values? Through one's ongoing accomplishments, one's continuing efforts, and one's constant initiative to apply oneself to a rational goal that is of interest to him or her. Phony, fawning affirmations of "you're good, you're good" will not build self-esteem, not even in a child. A child needs to be told he's good only when he demonstrates he *is* good, so that he can see the factual evidence behind the affirmation. Facts, not words, make self-esteem and happiness possible.

All individuals certainly have a birthright to *pursue* happiness, to live their lives free from the imposition of force by others who seek to prevent that pursuit. But this is nothing like saying that an individual has a right to happiness itself.

Payne and others like her fail to distinguish between cause and effect. They ignore the cause of self-esteem (initiative, planning, individual goal-setting) while looking solely for the effects (sense of personal happiness, affirmation, feeling good about oneself). In psychological shorthand: they want something for nothing.

By ignoring the nature of cause and effect, Payne seeks to establish effect without cause. She hopes to make kids feel good about themselves without making them work for it. This, of course, is logically impossible.

Writers like Payne do major damage to the field of psychology and the self-esteem movement. Increasingly, conservative individuals are (quite understandably) pointing to the consequences of such ideology in today's schools and saying, "See? I told you so! Self-esteem is baloney."

Payne's notion of self-esteem, the now widely accepted view, is in fact baloney. The conservative alternative? "We need to stop being so selfish, and return to obedience to God, family and nation." We all know what *that* means: a return to the "good old days" which never existed; a return to a state of widespread denial of self. Surprisingly, even many "liberal" thinkers are starting to take such positions, suggesting that a Puritanical backlash is underway. In such an intellectual climate, even an atheist is tempted to say, "God help us all!"

Notice that both the conservative and the modern viewpoints are anti-self. Just as the conservatives destroy the self by favoring blind obedience to authority, the fawning feel-good types obliterate the self by favoring blind obedience to loving oneself. The conservatives want you to love family and country whether they have earned it or not; the moderns want you to love yourself whether you have earned it or not. Each view discards objectivity, facts, and reality. Consequently, both views must be discarded as futile and irrational.

The antidote? The following alternative ideas:

Self-esteem is a *consequence*, not a cause. It's not free; you can't have it for nothing.

Do not wait for self-esteem to "happen" before you set out on life's adventures. Self-esteem only develops as the result of conscious, decisive, and consistent action on your part.

Don't let anyone tell you that because you did not get all the nurturing you needed as a child, that you cannot develop self-esteem and be happy as an adult. Virtually nobody got all of the nurturing and reassurance they needed as children. Past is past. Acknowledge it—but move forward.

Plan rational, exciting goals, based upon your dreams and aspirations but also grounded in reality. And then pursue those goals and dreams, without letting anyone else's doubts or negativity get in your way.

Intelligent, thoughtful action comes *before* self-esteem—not the other way around. This is the true secret of success. There is no other solution, no mythical magic secret.

Putting the cart before the horse—that is, expecting self-esteem without conscious action—is the single biggest mistake I see people make, including (and especially) the most intelligent of people. It is the basic cause of most psychological disorder: the cause nobody wants to hear, but most suspect is true. Why not accept this fact, act on it, and enjoy a lifetime of results.

PSYCHOTHERAPY, SELF-INITIATIVE, & SELF-CONFIDENCE

Psychologist Michele Weiner-Davis writes of psychotherapy: "Therapy should be looked at as a problem-solving process, and it should be just that. Therapy should never take the place of solid friendships, fulfilling lives, or a belief in your own wisdom."

Weiner-Davis is absolutely correct.

A good therapist can offer you something most other people cannot: psychological information on how to explain troubling emotions, better manage stress, and obtain an objective perspective from somebody not involved in your personal life.

No therapist, however, can offer you a substitute for friendship; or romance; or self-initiative; or, most importantly, belief in your ability to use your mind, and your rational judgment, properly and effectively.

Too many people approach psychotherapy the way religious people approach prayer. Religious people pray to God for solutions to their problems, and then passively await the problems to resolve themselves. Many psychotherapy clients approach a therapist on the same unspoken premise. When asked what they want to see happen as a result of therapy, they have no answer. Or, they have a very vague answer, such as "happiness" or "self-esteem." They believe that a psychotherapist will somehow be able to bestow these things, in God-like fashion, upon them. They will spend endless hours—years, if necessary—engaged in open-ended conversations with therapists about their childhoods, about their victimizations, or about the neuroses of their friends and spouses. They are happy to spend the time and the money, because they trust—they have *faith*, like a religious person—that their problems will somehow go away. Such is the mystique of contemporary psychotherapy, at least in the minds of too many people.

What happens when these open-ended, expensive conversations fail to make everything all better? The therapy client may become depressed. He might blame himself for the therapy's failure. Or he might claim it as further evidence that he is not "meant" (meant by whom?) to have a happy and fulfilling life. Or he might blame the therapist. Maybe if he just found the therapist with the right degree, from the right school, of the right age, with the right social connections, or the right number of letters past his name, then maybe everything would work out . . . .

What is the alternative to approaching therapy in such a passive, mystical manner? Learning the skills of *self-initiative* and *self-confidence* in your own judgment.

What is self-initiative? What rules or principles does a self-initiating person follow? Upon what ideas, and self-statements, does self-initiative depend? Here are a few:

1. I alone am responsible for making my life happy. Others can help me, if they choose and if I want them to, but the fundamental responsibility is still mine.
2. I must follow up ideas with action. Ideas are crucial and necessary, but if I fail to test their truth or falsehood in reality, then I will get nowhere. In fact, I will be worse off; I will have betrayed my ideas, which is worse than having no ideas in the first place.
3. I must allow myself to make mistakes. Mistakes are part of the process, and are even good because they point out what I do not know and add to my storehouse of knowledge.
4. I will treat obstacles as opportunities. If I reach a roadblock with one of my goals, I will not say, "Uh-oh, it's all over." Instead, I will say, "There must be a better way

to reach my goal and I will not give up until I find it." Nothing worthwhile is accomplished easily; otherwise, everyone would be doing it.

5. I will never condemn myself for selfishness, so long as I am not violating anyone else's rights. I am not violating another person's rights by pursuing my own happiness, so long as I do not impose physical force on them or lie to them. I am also responsible for the consequences of all my actions. Beyond these basic boundaries, I have no obligations to anyone. I may have certain obligations to friends, children, or other loved ones, but these are obligations I presumably chose freely. Nothing chosen represents a duty.

6. I will not wait for "motivation" or "self-esteem" to spontaneously arrive. These qualities are consequences, not causes. They happen *after* I select a goal and stay with it for awhile—not before.

7. The past is past. It cannot inhibit me in the present unless I let it. Maybe I did not get the support I needed as a child. Maybe I was even abused as a child. Either way, the fact that I was a victim in my childhood does not mean I have to remain an angry, helpless, bitter victim as an adult. Quite the contrary. If I continue to act like a victim now, then I am only magnifying the injustices of my past. The best revenge, if I am seeking revenge, is to live happily and well.

8. Nobody is determining the outcome of my life, except for me. (At least, nobody has a right to). My life is not "meant" to be happy or tragic, unless I myself mean to make it such. Yes, there are many things outside of my control: natural disasters, the era or country in which I am born, my genetic make-up. But the existence of such things in no way proves the existence of some higher force running everything in the universe, either in my favor or against me. My attitude and my actions will shape my destiny more than anything else.

What about confidence in your own judgment? What ideas and thoughts lead to self-confidence? Consider the following self-statements:

1. I will accept nothing blindly. I start with my senses (sight, hearing, smell, taste, touch), and analyze with my own reasoning abilities. I can accept the advice of experts, but only if I know them to be honest, intelligent, and reliable. I should look for actual evidence of these qualities before trusting any "expert"—and *not* judge an expert solely on credentials or popularity.

2. The majority can be wrong, and often are. Let the facts, as I see and understand them through a process of reason and logic, be the final judge of truth. Never, ever, let pressure from my peers or larger groups sway my decision making. Only let facts and logic sway my decision making. If my own independent judgment conforms to the majority, fine. If my own independent judgment is accepted by literally nobody else, that's OK too. The important thing is that I have concrete evidence and sound arguments to make my case, to myself and to others if appropriate. I will change my case only if new facts become available to contradict it, or if I become aware of an argument that I cannot answer and must agree is better

than mine. I will maintain an open, but always critical, mind.

3. Beware of advice-givers, especially those who do not know me real well and offer me advice in an unsolicited manner. Advice-givers are generally telling me what *they* would do in a given situation. But is it necessarily what I would do? Consider the source: that is, the advice-giver himself. What are his values? What are his preferences, likes and dislikes? What is his track record for decision-making in his own life? Do his methods work? Does he apply his methods to his life honestly and consistently? Is this someone I want to imitate? Do he and I possess the same desired outcome—the same definition of happiness? Shouldn't I know these things before following his advice?

4. I will try not to fear the responsibility of making my own decisions. Yes, decision-making can be scary, especially if I am not in the habit of doing it and if I have not yet established a track record for myself. But at least if I make a mistake it's *my* mistake, and I am free to do something entirely different the next time. Life, like any other skill, gets easier over time. I have to start with small steps (that may feel like big steps), and then gradually get better and better at my own pace.

5. If someone I have good reason to trust and respect criticizes me, my first response should be: "What facts, if any, exist to validate this criticism? What facts, if any, contradict this criticism?" Remember that in all cases facts, evidence, and logic determine truth, not merely opinions. My goal is only to know the facts, and to reason with my own mind about them. The opinions of others-in-general do not interest me. The opinions of certain individuals, who have earned my trust and respect, should interest me; but even in those cases I still think critically and do not accept what they say blindly.

6. I should not put other people's feelings above the truth. If I disagree, I should say so, so long as the other individual is open to rational discussion about the disagreement. I need not fall into the traps of either withholding my thoughts out of shyness, on the one hand, or aggressively and with hostility seeking to impose my thoughts on others. Neither way is healthy, and neither way works. When I disagree or I do not understand, I can say so.

SOLUTIONS, NOT EXCUSES

Psychotherapy is not merely an intellectual exercise.

Good therapists do not simply help their clients talk, think, and feel. They also encourage their clients to experiment, work, and act.

Does your therapist give you homework between sessions? "Homework" might include self-help reading, journal keeping, or making a small step to improve your life, such as calling a potential romantic interest for a date or looking at the help-wanted ads for a new job. Good therapists remind their clients that most psychotherapy takes place outside of the therapy office. An hour per week of thinking and talking is not enough to bring the changes you want in your life.

Many therapists focus too much on the past, and on childhood experiences. If your therapist makes this mistake, ask her to help you focus on the present and the future. Ask her to help you see what requires changing in the here-and-now.

Too many therapists will indulge you (however unintentionally) in the false belief that just because your parents treated you badly you are incapable of achieving happiness as an adult. Ask your therapist to help you find an alternative to perpetual victimhood. Ask him to help you find *solutions* to current problems rather than make excuses for why you cannot overcome them.

Still other therapists overstate the influence your childhood experiences had on your personality, and understate your capacity for changing your unhealthy thinking, emotions, and behaviors within a reasonable period of time. Remember that your childhood is not your destiny; your attitude, and your choices, represent your destiny.

Does your therapist want to help put you in charge of your own life, as quickly as possible? Or does your therapist want to develop a personal relationship with you? Many therapists actually believe that it is the therapist-client relationship, rather than the identification of solutions to problems, which causes psychological improvements. They think you need a "mommy" or a "daddy," instead of independence, initiative, and self-worth.

Imagine if a doctor or an attorney took this approach. Instead of diagnosing your medical problem and prescribing a treatment, the doctor would develop a relationship with you and hope for the best. Instead of informing you of your legal rights during a divorce, an attorney would develop a relationship with you and hope for the best. Likewise, the psychotherapist who forms the relationship with you has nothing specific or objective to offer you—beyond, perhaps, a listening ear or a kind word you could almost as easily, and far more cheaply, obtain elsewhere.

Beware of therapists who persist in talking about your childhood. Beware of therapists who encourage endless expression of emotions without helping you think rationally about those emotions. Beware of therapists who commit you to twice-weekly sessions before seeing how quickly you progress. A good therapist does not seek to rush you; but neither will he underestimate your ability to heal quicker than may at first seem possible.

Set goals, as concretely and objectively as possible, by which you and your therapist will determine "improvement." Ask that your therapist help you with this goal-setting task; *this is the skill for which she is paid.* Do not be afraid to challenge your therapist with such questions as, "Could you please explain what you mean by that? I do not understand." Or: "Could you help me understand why it is necessary for me to see you twice a week, instead of weekly or twice a month? Could we evaluate my progress one session at a time, please?" Or: "Can you give me more guidance about how to move forward with my life? I understand my past was less than ideal. But it is the present and the future that concern me."

Do not let your emotional vulnerability prevent you from asking reasonable questions of a therapist. Do not fall prey to the belief that expressing your feelings, over and over, is all that's needed to improve mental health. In truth, ventilating your feelings, while important, will never by itself be enough to make you well. Emotional over-indulgence, in fact, can actually create new problems. If you focus on negative facts or replay negative images often enough, you can become even *more* depressed, helpless, and immobilized.

As an experiment, try for the next 60 minutes to make yourself think solely about gloomy, miserable things, and how hopeless life really is. At the end of the 60 minutes, ask yourself how motivated you feel to improve your life. Therapies which encourage depressed people to wallow in their miserable emotions, without a recipe for hope and progress, clearly cannot work.

Emotionally vulnerable people often recognize that they need to do more than express their sad feelings or make excuses based upon unhappy childhoods. Their rational, intelligent minds tell them they need to set goals, take action, and to recognize that life holds enormous opportunities if they are willing to work for them. They recognize that victimization in the past makes it all the more urgent to move beyond victimhood in the present. After all, if they remain paralyzed, helpless, and angry for their whole lives, the victimizers have really won.

All too often, their hearts tell them to remain with the therapist who will make excuses for them, indulge them, and focus on the past rather than on the often difficult reality of the here-and-now. Their hearts tell them that they need to "work through" their negative emotions, even though neither they nor their therapist make any attempt to define what "work through" actually means. Their hearts tell them to stay put, because it's easier, and safer, and at least they do not have to work very much.

Too often the heart wins, and, despite the unprecedented number of mental health professionals in practice today, the outbreak of mental disorder continues to spread throughout our society.

A woman once made the following comment, in trying to decide between two therapists. "I know the first therapist will try to help me by telling me what I want to hear. This will make me feel better when I leave the office, but my life will remain the same. I know the second therapist will help me, by telling me the truth, whether or not it is what I want to hear. I do not always feel better, at least right away. But I actually can *become* better by being reminded of the truth."

Before choosing a therapist, carefully consider the importance of therapeutic approach and philosophy. Do not only listen to your emotions; listen to your head, and decide with your head. Do not only think of short-term relief; think of long-term consequences as well.

Remember that the therapists with the greatest respect for you will also be the ones who speak the truth to you. Remember, too, that the truth may hurt at first; but it also builds the emotional muscle you will need to better function in life, and to attain happiness.

Good therapy does not result in victimization; it results in empowerment. Good therapy does not twist reality to fit with your emotions; instead, it helps you to emotionally cope with and thoroughly enjoy living in reality. Therapists who truly respect you do not keep you in childhood; they help you grow up.

Shop carefully.

SELF-ESTEEM CHECKLIST FOR PARENTS

Teach your child to respect private property. Do not tell your child, "You must share your toys with others." Instead, tell him that he should share only if he desires to do so. Why should your child hand over his property to some bully who has no respect for the rights of others? You must be clear on this point, if you want him to develop self-esteem and confidence as an adult.

Teach your child to respect the rights of others. If you see your child violating another individual's rights, do not simply chastise her for being "selfish." Explain to her: (1) the rights of individuals are important; and, (2) if she does not respect the rights of individuals, then there is no way that she can expect the same in return. Appeal to her own sense of self-interest.

Teach your child to be an individualist. This does not mean rebelling for the sake of rebelling, or following arbitrary rules. It means teaching your child to think, and to use his capacity for reason and logic to solve dilemmas. Living in reality—and being happy—ought to be the standard by which right and wrong are judged.

Teach your child to think long-range. If your child asks you about a dilemma, do not simply tell him what to do. Encourage him to weigh the "pros and cons"—the long-term as well as the short-term. If he asks you, for example, "Is it wrong to cheat on my math test?" you can reply: "Think about how you would feel if you got an A, and everyone complimented you, and deep down you knew you didn't earn it." Let your child reason this out for himself, and encourage active discussion.

Show your kids a healthy romantic relationship. There is probably no other single factor as important in raising a child. If you are married, or are in a romantic relationship, use this as an opportunity to show your child how two adults can love each other and resolve conflicts in a peaceful, rational manner. It's their job to be kids—it's your job to be adults.

Don't stay in a hopeless marriage or relationship solely "for the children." You are not doing your child any favors if you are miserable. All you are doing is teaching him to fake reality and life. You and your partner owe it to your children and yourselves to make reasonable efforts to resolve conflicts before breaking up. Psychotherapy can be one means of achieving this goal.

If a divorce is unavoidable, then continue to be parents. Ending a marriage does not end the
responsibility for working together as parents. It is your job—not the child's—to
arrange visitation and transportation. While it is certainly desirable to obtain your
child's input about her wishes, it is never appropriate to place the full burden for this on
her.   ⊕

Chapter 5

Difficult People

WHAT IS PERSONALITY?

What is personality? Why is personality important?

Personality represents the sum total of your ideas, convictions, and values, as expressed in both your emotions and your consistent behavioral habits. Personality is your essence or "soul"—not in the mystical sense, but as the logical consequence of the ideas you hold and the extent to which you practice those ideas, more or less consistently, in daily life.

If you believe, for instance, that the world is a treacherous place, that certainty is impossible, that existence is too complicated to be understood, you will have a different personality from someone who believes that the world, though complex, is capable of being understood and that the human mind is capable of grasping objective truths. If you believe that happiness requires continuous growth and effort, your personality will differ from someone who believes he has a birthright to happiness. If you believe that your life is controlled primarily by genetic or mystical forces, your personality will differ from someone who believes destiny is a matter of choice, not chance.

Your personality does not develop in a vacuum. Nor is it the result of purely genetic, physiological factors. Personality is the global consequence of your convictions, convictions so implicitly and deeply held that you may not even be conscious of what they are. Without question, the ideas and events you were exposed to in your early and late childhood were crucial to your later psychological and intellectual development. Nevertheless, as an adult you possess the ability to identify these convictions you have "absorbed," subconsciously, and identify whether or not you agree with them. If the ideas are rational and correct, then fine; if they are irrational and incorrect, then you need to replace them with new ideas and work on automatizing the rational ideas until they become "second nature" to you.

Example: Imagine that you were raised with the idea that the world is a treacherous and malevolent place, and that disaster looms around every corner. The idea was hammered into your head over and over again by your elders, because they sincerely subscribed to this concept and could not help but encourage you to think the same way. As an adult, you experience frequent anxiety attacks and fits of depression which prevent you from following through on your goals. Intellectually, you believe that happiness can and should be the norm, and indeed you even see evidence that others who think and act on such a premise are indeed happy and relatively free of anxiety. You recognize that another way of thinking and living is possible; but you are paralyzed, at times, by the stale thinking of your childhood that says: "Risks are unacceptable. Don't take chances, even small ones. Just stay safe, and secure. Security is the most important thing. It would be a disaster to lose, or to take a chance and have it blow up in your face. Just do what you have to do and let God take care of the rest."

Although your childhood experiences played a large role in shaping your current personality, you also are free to think and act differently now that you are an adult. Even though the stale thinking will take a long time—perhaps years—to fade into the background, you still possess the free will to learn new thinking habits. You *are* able to replace the stale thinking with new, more optimistic, and more realistic approaches. Before telling yourself, "I can't go to college because it will take too long," you make yourself investigate the facts of college financing and look, objectively, at whether the long-run payoff is worth the years of work (and whether the years of work might not at times be fun as well). Before letting yourself feel all the dangers of taking on a new risk, you make yourself identify the positive factors and possible outcomes as well. Before leaping to the conclusion that your automatic, negative, knee-jerk responses represent the whole of reality, you learn to make facts, and not immediate feelings, your method of making evaluations and decisions. You may need the help of a professional and loads of self-initiative; but you can still change your personality, gradually, over time, and as necessary.

Regardless of childhood experiences, conflicts between conscious, intellectualized beliefs and subconscious, emotional feelings and behaviors are commonplace. You may, for instance, agree on an intellectual level that you do not have a birthright to happiness, and that you have to make your own happiness. At the same time, on the emotional level, you may feel resentful that you have to work and set long-range goals, and may in fact procrastinate because of your frustration that life does not proceed easily and effortlessly.

Such contradictions between intellect and emotion lie at the core of most psychological problems. One major goal of psychotherapy and psychological knowledge in general is to help you identify such conflicts and resolve them. If you fail to resolve contradictions between what you think and feel, between what you believe and what you do, then you are much more likely to suffer from anxiety, depression, stress mismanagement and other psychological symptoms. Contrary to what the Freudians and psychoanalysts will try to tell you, the *principles* of personality change are not that complicated; the work of reapplying those principles, over and over, day in and day out, are what make psychological change so difficult.

THE PASSIVE PERSONALITY

The passive individual, consciously or subconsciously, sees life as something to be experienced rather than something to be achieved. He does what he has to do to survive and follow the mainstream, but does not exercise a great deal of initiative in any area of his life. He does what he is told, and rarely seeks to assert himself or challenge an unjustified authority in any way. He finds himself attracted to more dominant types of personalities, who are content marrying or doing business with a passive personality, often because they feel less threatened by someone who will not challenge them.

His method of obtaining knowledge is through what others say; "others" usually means the mainstream, as represented either by the media or simply by what the majority of people in his family, community, or nation seem to be thinking and doing. He is very threatened by the prospect of being the center of attention or controversial, even in the most benign or minimal of contexts. He may or may not believe that certainty is possible; but he does believe that certainty is, at least most of the time, outside of his reach. He takes for granted that self-proclaimed experts know more than he does, even if he is not aware of whether they have earned the status of expert. Indeed, the idea that the experts may be wrong is scary to him because if the experts are wrong, then upon whose judgment will he rely? Certainly not his own, because this is too scary.

Reality, to the passive personality, is a scary but potentially manageable place. He may be religious or atheistic. He may place his trust in scientific and educational institutions, or he may place his trust more in local community or traditional institutions. The common denominator in all passive personalities is that they place their trust elsewhere, outside of themselves: knowledge, to them, is to be passively received, not actively gained. Whether the issue is which movie to see, what house or car to buy, whom to marry, or what philosophy of life to follow, the passive person wants a reassuring and comforting authority to tell him what to do. He is more concerned that his doctor went to an Ivy League school than having to evaluate the doctor objectively through rational criteria of his own choosing. He is more concerned that the most popular newspaper rate a new movie highly than whether or not the movie shows promise of reflecting his own criteria for a good movie.

Although usually not conscious of his motive, he wants to escape the responsibility of judgment, not because he believes judgment is impossible, but because he grants little or no respect to his own judgment. He sleeps well at night, knowing that the universe is a more or less benevolent place because somebody else is at the helm of his existence.

"IT'S ALL YOUR FAULT!"
HOW TO DEAL WITH DIFFICULT PEOPLE

Joe is an angry person. He makes demands on everyone. His boss is afraid to treat him like other employees, because Joe threatens to sue the company. Joe's emotions rule his personal life too. His wife and kids constantly "walk on eggshells" trying not to hurt his feelings or say the wrong thing.

Joe stands ready to tell people how he suffers and how unfair life is to him. He acts as if everybody else must reimburse him for his loss and pain. He talks frequently about wanting a "level playing field," or a "fair deal." Who is to pay the price for his level playing field, regardless of the sacrifice to themselves? His wife, his kids, his co-workers. The world, he believes, owes him restitution.

Have you ever known anyone like Joe? Have you, yourself, perhaps felt like Joe at times? Joe's behaviors and emotions are characteristic of the victim mentality.

The victim mentality refers to the conscious or subconscious viewpoint that life owes you a living. In reality, it is *other people* who end up providing the victim with a living. The "other people" may be family, friends, co-workers, or even society-as-a-whole. The "living" the victim expects can be material *or* spiritual. In other words, the victim might demand unearned wealth, unearned love/approval—or both.

Many people feel and act like Joe only occasionally. Some feel and act like Joe on a consistent basis. Psychologists label the latter group "borderline" personalities. Mental health professionals and other individuals who know borderlines understand that they can be the most difficult types of human beings imaginable.

Borderlines are not necessarily wrong about everything. Sometimes individuals *do* experience victimization. People can be victims of theft, rape, murder, political dictatorship, or physical/sexual abuse in childhood, to name a few examples.

Most genuine victims do not develop borderline personalities, however. If they did, the world would be full of borderlines; yet borderlines represent the minority even in psychiatric offices.

Even more interestingly, many people who do not experience genuine victimization do, nevertheless, develop borderline personalities. This finding suggests that something other than environmental factors shape the development of such a personality. What could it be?

One possible answer: an individual's underlying premises, thoughts, beliefs, and values.

What does a borderline actually believe, and feel? He usually experiences a persistent sense of violation or unfair treatment. He is chronically angry, continuously scanning the horizon for more and more evidence of injustice. Sometimes there is actual evidence of unfairness, and sometimes there is not—but this is not the point.

The point is that to the borderline, his anger is itself the reality. He does not allow himself to see a distinction between emotions and objective facts—at least not with respect to his anger. He deeply believes that his angry feelings, and his angry feelings alone, represent the truth. Reason and objectivity are thrown out the window.

How Do Borderline Personalities Develop?

People often develop borderline personalities as a result of giving up too much for others. Borderlines usually start out as self-sacrificers. They sacrifice for others and then feel resentful when the sacrifices do not pay off.

Consider the case of Sue. Sue's boyfriend gladly accepts her many kindnesses, but he rarely (if ever) does anything in return. Rather than pursue a rational option—such as discussing the problem with him, or withdrawing some of her kindness, or even breaking off with him—Sue instead becomes angry. She complains to her friends, all of whom give her sympathy and readily agree the boyfriend is a jerk.

Instead of accepting responsibility for not letting herself remain a victim, Sue wallows in the victim role and starts to feel there's no way out. She breaks up with the boyfriend without giving him a chance to reform. She repeats the cycle in future friendships and relationships, cutting people off at the first sign of disagreement. The longer she fails to understand her own role in making herself a victim, the more the victim mindset becomes part of her basic personality.

Envy and the Borderline

A typical core emotion for the borderline personality is envy. Envy refers to the deeply held belief that another person's gain is always your loss. "If Frank earns a million dollars, then I am poorer because of it." Or: "If Mary meets the love of her life, then my chances of doing so are diminished." Or: "If Jack is successful in a field where I want to be successful—then he is invading my 'turf' and he must be stopped."

Are such feelings rational? Of course not. They all rest on the false premise that another person's success represents a loss to you. Not true! Life is not a zero-sum game. There is no finite "success pie" from which everyone must struggle for a slice. If for some reason you are not successful, it's certainly not because Frank or Mary or Jack *were* successful. It's actually good they were successful. Perhaps you can learn something from them.

Most of us experience envy at times. If we are healthy we can quickly identify it, challenge it rationally, and not let it run our lives. In the borderline, sadly, envy festers and grows.

How to Spot a Borderline

How can you identify a borderline personality, or someone with victim mentality tendencies? Such people are chronically demanding, arrogant, and—above all—*angry*. They act as if they expect life to be a one-way street, in their own direction. Ironically, they often condemn "selfishness" in others as a way to invoke guilt, and then they cash in on the concessions of the guilt-ridden.

Borderlines are also notoriously insecure and touchy. They demand that others accommodate their feelings, usually without much reference to objective reality, facts, or reason. Their unspoken attitude: "My feelings are the truth. Who are you to question them? What's that? You have feelings too? And what if our feelings conflict? I don't want to hear about it."

How Not to Handle a Borderline

What is the biggest mistake you can make with a borderline? To compromise with him; to concede his irrational viewpoints. To adopt, in effect, the following attitude: "I won't give him everything he's demanding, but I'll split the difference. I won't give in to his crazy or unfair demands all of the time; I'll give in ten or thirty percent of the time. After all, he has had a rough life and I should give him something."

Such a policy of appeasement will only make things worse. Why? Because once you concede the validity of the borderline's irrational expectations, then she will expect you to meet *all* of her demands *all* of the time. Borderlines are all-or-nothing people. They think in terms of principle, but their principles are not rational. Once a borderline senses you are willing to concede even one inch to her whims, then she will expect total surrender thereafter.

Compromising with a borderline communicates to him that his unfair demands are, in fact, rational and just, but that you are only going to respect them ten or thirty percent of the time. The result is that the borderline—who feels you should respect his feelings and demands all of the time—becomes more enraged and envious than ever. He'll feel like you're an inconsistent hypocrite. In a sense, he's right.

You, in turn, will think: "Gosh, here I am trying to accommodate him, and he's just getting more angry. How unreasonable! Here I am trying to be nice, and he's just being ungrateful."

Double-check your assumptions and your definitions. "Reasonable" implies logical consistency. If you give in to the borderline's demands thirty percent of the time, you are not being consistent. Instead, you are communicating to her that she is right in principle but you are not going to act on the right principle consistently. This would be like telling your local grocer, "You are right, in principle, to charge me for food. But I am only going to pay for the food every other time I shop here. The rest of the time I will take it for free." How do you think he would respond?

Remember, a rational individual expects that neither person should have to sacrifice in any relationship. "Rational" means voluntary give-and-take in which neither party forces or intimidates the other into doing something he would not otherwise do.

The borderline does not approach relationships rationally. The borderline feels she is a victim simply by virtue of existing; that it is the job of everyone she encounters to help right this wrong, even if it involves sacrifice and misery on their parts. "I'm miserable, so why shouldn't everyone else suffer a little bit too?" is her unspoken rationalization. Life becomes one big payback scheme in which you become the slave to her every hurt feeling.

To attempt compromise with such a person is to court disaster.

How to Handle a Borderline

If you cannot compromise with a borderline, then what should you do? Be realistic. Face facts. Accept, first of all, that any kind of close relationship with such a person is probably impossible. Borderlines are usually pathetic individuals, and it may seem cruel to deny them intimacy and closeness. But why should you be miserable for their sake? You are not your brother's keeper—and you are especially not a borderline's keeper!

Besides, it may take many abandonments before the borderline has any chance of "hitting bottom" and perhaps beginning to realize that he is the cause of his problems. Be brave. Simply tell him that his demands are unreasonable, unfair, and wrong. Moral disapproval, though out of fashion today, is still a very powerful method for convincing people to change their irrational behaviors and beliefs.

Brace yourself for a policy of tough love. Challenge the borderline's basic beliefs. Tell him, "I understand you feel the way you do. But your feelings seem to imply that I owe my life and my time to you; that I should sacrifice for you; that your needs give you a claim to part of my life. That's not true. I do not owe my life to you, any more than you owe yours to me. If I *want* to spend my time with you, I will. But I can't and won't do it on the premise that either one of us is duty bound to the other."

In short, you let the borderline know in no uncertain terms that *guilt will not work with you.* He can call you selfish and mean until he's blue in the face. You must not budge.

Such a policy will, at first, send your borderline friend into a rage unlike anything you have ever seen. But through it all you must remember that you are helping him. After the anger subsides, if there is a drop of reason and goodness within him, he may recognize that you at least have a point. He might start to think and act reasonably, at which time you can shower him with positive words and behaviors.

It is also possible that he is so far gone, psychologically, that he will not listen to reason and will become even more entrenched in his mistaken views. If so, this would be very sad—even tragic, because borderlines, like alcoholics and drug addicts, often possess great intelligence, promise, and potential. But you cannot take responsibility for the borderline's refusal to listen to reason. Just because he refuses to enter the lifeboat does not mean you must sink along with him.

Borderline personality syndrome is the psychological equivalent of cancer. It can be fatal, and often is. It can cause psychological, spiritual death. Just as it makes no sense to blow cigarette smoke into the lungs of a cancer patient, it also makes no sense to appease the borderline and tell him (or imply to him) that his irrational beliefs are valid. If you care about a borderline, then don't enable, appease, or sanction the irrational ideas and behaviors which make the problems possible in the first place. Instead, challenge him to live a healthier, happier, and more rational life.

The choice, in the end, is up to him.

DIFFICULT PEOPLE IN THERAPY

Borderline personalities can benefit from mental health therapy—but only the *right* kind of therapy. The wrong kind of therapy only worsens the borderline's problems by enabling the unhealthy behaviors and reinforcing, however unintentionally, the mistaken ideas and beliefs.

Many therapists incorrectly believe that borderlines must have their feelings "validated." Validation essentially means to agree with the borderline's anger. "You're right," the validating therapist will state or imply. "Others should understand you and make accommodations for you. Everyone else is selfish and evil. You deserve a level playing field."

Some psychologists even give borderline clients a personal "bill of rights," with such feel-good provisions as "the right to be understood," "the right to be heard," "the right to be accommodated," and so forth.

While indiscriminate validation usually helps the borderline feel better when she's in the therapy office, the moment she leaves the office she will greet the world with even more antagonism, envy, and hatred than before she entered it. Why? Because her expectations and demands are, if anything, even more unrealistic and unfair than ever, thanks to the overly gratuitous therapist.

In ineffective therapy, neither counselor nor client ever consider the questions: "What if others don't want to have anything to do with you? Does your 'right' to all these nice things impose an unwanted obligation on them? And why is it that nobody wants anything to do with you in the first place? Could you possibly be doing something wrong?"

The borderline needs validation—but not in the sense many mental health professionals understand the term. The borderline does not need to hear, in effect, "There, there, your feelings are right."

Instead, the therapist should agree that any objective victimizations (physical or sexual abuse, theft, murder, robbery, fraud) were wrong, and that it's OK to acknowledge their existence aloud. After all, people genuinely victimized often spend years in denial, feeling they cannot call a spade a spade, and repressing their perfectly rational emotions about the victimization.

The victim also needs to hear, however, that it is OK to move on with his life: to not let the victimizer continue to win; to not become paralyzed by anger. The victim needs to learn the idea, in short, that the best revenge is living well.

The borderline can also learn that rational self-interest is healthy and proper—but that other people's 'rights' to act in their own self-interest must be equally respected. Fred does not have to see a certain movie just because his girlfriend demands it; nor should his girlfriend see a certain movie just because he demands it. Fairness is a two way street. Relationships can involve sensible compromises, but should not be about sacrifice and misery.

When both partners (in any endeavor, personal or professional) recognize these basic principles, a spirit of voluntary, give-and-take benevolence results. Example: "You don't have to see the movie I want to see. But I'd like it if you would. In exchange, I'll see the movie you want to see tomorrow. Is it a deal?" This approach works much better and makes more sense than: "You selfish brat! See the movie I want to see."

It is precisely the absence of such voluntary good will that makes the borderline's life so unhappy and demoralizing. He needs to accept responsibility for his own contributions to the lack of benevolence in his relationships. In his quest for victimhood, he alienates almost everyone. Until he accepts and acknowledges this fact, he will fester in his own anger and never move forward.

It can be very hard, and even impossible, to teach the borderline rational ideas and values. Emotions of envy and anger keep getting in the way of progress. Both client and therapist must be extraordinarily patient; and even patience and hard work do not guarantee success with borderlines. Worse yet, borderlines tend to fire therapists who do not tell them what they want to hear, or who set any kind of limit or expectation on them. They often elicit sympathy from each new therapist about how "mean" the prior therapist was.

Any therapist who works with victim-oriented borderlines must search his soul for his own beliefs. Borderlines are brilliant at forcing unexamined principles to the surface. Many of us feel, for example, that it is wrong to be selfish and live for ourselves, even if we accept full responsibility for ourselves. At the same time, we all expect and demand the freedom to choose our own careers and live by our own values. We take vacations where we choose, we decide how many children to have, and we don't like it when others try to impose their choices on us. Many of us condemn self-interest, in the abstract, while nevertheless practicing it in daily life.

The borderline senses this contradiction and demands that the therapist take a stand, one way or the other. By picking fights with a therapist over issues such as payment, scheduling, or demanding immediate attention at inappropriate times, the borderline forces the therapist to confront the questions, "What do I owe this patient? Professional help—or unlimited attention? A two-way street—or anything she desires?"

If mental health treatment has any chance of success with borderlines, therapists must develop a coherent set of strategies so the borderline will hear—and see—the same healthy message as he shops from therapist to therapist. Therapists should not be quick to accept one-sided accounts by borderlines (or anyone) as objective truth. They should evaluate the borderline's claims critically and, if possible, talk to other individuals in the borderline's life. They should see obnoxious borderline behavior as an opportunity to teach (through example) the client how to think and act more fairly, rationally, and benevolently.

The victim-oriented borderline needs to learn that a true "fair deal" is one in which *neither* party must sacrifice for the other. The borderline insists she should not have to pay for her session? Then the therapist should politely and non-defensively reply that he cannot work for free and they have to discontinue their work together. The borderline shows up at the office when a therapist is seeing another client? The therapist will have to politely and calmly refuse to see him. The borderline lies to the therapist and does not expect this to be a problem? Then he must understand that the therapist has the right to lie to him as well.

If borderlines are to learn genuine self-respect, they must work with therapists who demonstrate genuine self-respect. They must learn that life is a two-way street.

Lack of access to others and the limits others place upon them are central to the anger borderline personalities experience. By making unreasonable demands, borderlines alienate people. Eventually these people abandon them, usually without explaining why. The more they experience abandonment, the more borderlines come to view themselves as victims. It's a truly vicious circle.

The value of a professional therapist is to show (not merely tell) the borderline that personal boundaries exist and are fair, benevolent, and rational to all parties. If a therapist "caves" to even one tiny unreasonable demand, then the borderline's problems will only grow worse.

Therapy must be part of the solution—not part of the problem.

ENTREPRENEURS OF INTIMIDATION: THE AUTHORITARIAN PERSONALITY

Have you ever encountered an arrogant, bossy "know-it-all?" Have you ever experienced the unpleasant reality of living or working with somebody who embodies the expression, "My way or the highway"? Do controlling people who think they know what's best for you drive you crazy?

If so, then you have a good idea of what the authoritarian personality is like.

The authoritarian personality seeks an unnecessary and unrealistic degree of control over circumstances and people (especially the latter). As far as he is concerned, his mind—and his mind *alone*—represents the standard of reality. He is less concerned with objective reality than he is with imposing the subjective reality of his wishes and desires upon the rest of the world. He wants the world to operate his way—not because his way is demonstrably better, but merely because he wants it.

The authoritarian person does *not* feel that: "Reality is what it is; if I want to command some part of it, I need to respect its basic nature and laws, including the rights of other individuals besides myself." Instead he feels: "I *will* get what I want. The end justifies the means, just so long as I get what I want. It's a catastrophe if I don't."

Authoritarian personalities come across as defensive, "high-and-mighty" and taking the "my way or else" point of view. It can be difficult to see that, at the core, the authoritarian is a pathetic and weak individual. Declaring war on reality and expecting the impossible of self and others, after all, is no easy task—and eventual defeat is certain.

To date, the American Psychiatric Association has not identified a diagnostic label for the authoritarian personality. It's probably just as well. A diagnostic label might create the impression that the authoritarian personality can neither take responsibility for, nor exercise any control over, his problem. Such a mistaken impression would only serve to increase the aggravation and suffering of a great many people—including the authoritarian personality himself.

Examples of the Authoritarian Personality

First, consider an extreme example. A man abuses alcohol. He verbally and physically beats up his wife and children on a regular basis. He feels that his will should always be done, no matter what. He does not concern himself with evidence, facts or logic. To him, being "right" is not an objective standard which must be validated by factual evidence. Something isn't true because the facts support it; rather, something is true *"because I say so"*—which really means: "because I feel and want it to be true." He believes that it's demeaning to have to present evidence to back up his points, even if he knows he has evidence. People, he feels, should take his word on faith. If other people have minds of their own, it does not matter very much to him. In such an environment, it is easy to see how the man's children and even his wife will be too intimidated to stand up to him.

Consider a less extreme example. A woman works for a big corporation. She's new to her job as a manager of fifteen people. Her predecessor was highly respected, quite competent and loved by most of the staff he left behind. The woman feels much of the time like she's in "over her head." She also feels that she might not be able to become as competent as the man she followed in her job. Instead of accepting that she has these feelings and trying to find ways to rationally cope with them, she shuts them out of her consciousness whenever they come up (even if they come up after work hours when she could introspect about them or discuss them with a friend or counselor). She tells herself, "It's weakness to feel these things. Don't be weak. Set a good example for these employees and, above all, let them know who's boss. They need to know that what I say *goes*."

She says this to herself over and over, but it doesn't seem to work. She refuses to try other methods of anxiety management such as exercise, writing in a journal or talking to a counselor. Her anxiety grows stronger each day. She starts to intimidate some of her staff because the anxiety causes her to be gruff and even rude. As a result, she does not always get the help from them she needs because they are afraid of her and keep their distance. One day she becomes so angry over not having the help and support she needs from her staff that she picks up a stack of files and throws them at her secretary's desk. Instantly she becomes known as "the file throwing dragon lady."

When Reason & Emotion Collide

Sometimes authoritarian personalities hide behind the concepts of "rationality" and "objective reality." They might claim, intellectually, to follow these perfectly reasonable standards. Psychologically and subconsciously, however, they feel and act counter to these principles.

In many cases, the authoritarian personality does not fully recognize his conflicts. To make matters worse, people around him are too intimidated to confront him with his inconsistencies. It then becomes a vicious cycle. The more intimidating he acts towards others, the less others will open up to him or confront him about his flaws. The less his close associates confront him about his flaws, the easier it is for him to continue rationalizing, evading or simply remaining ignorant about his internal conflicts. Only a lone brave soul can break the cycle by confronting or challenging the dictator, but lone brave souls are in short supply. Even when one appears, there's no guarantee that the authoritarian will be open to reason.

Control & Self-Loathing

The authoritarian personality seeks to control others and reality to an impossible degree. In her effort to gain unrealistic control, the file throwing dragon lady lost the respect of those she needed most. Why do otherwise intelligent people pursue such an irrational, self-defeating course? Many reasons are possible. Fear and self-loathing usually lie at the root. The belief that you, as an individual, are small and worthless can go hand-in-hand with the belief that mankind in general is small and worthless. If everyone is so awful, then they obviously need to be controlled.

Of course, the contradiction in this line of thinking is inescapable: "If mankind is so awful, then by what means are *you*—as a member of mankind—going to make the right decisions to control others?" The authoritarian personality never wants to look at this question, however, because it would force him to face his own internal contradictions.

In all fairness, sometimes one person really *is* superior to others in certain respects: not in the sense that he is intrinsically more worthwhile, but superior in the objective sense that he learns more quickly, is mentally sharper and has more skills than most people. Consequently, the more competent individual becomes frustrated and impatient with those around him when they are not equally competent. "I'm surrounded by idiots," is his dominant feeling.

Instead of learning to accept reality, and that most others will always be slower than he is, the authoritarian type becomes angry, hostile and seeks control. For example, he'll try to do things for others instead of delegating tasks. He'll assume an employee won't do the job correctly, so he undermines the employee's morale by doing tasks for him. He treats his kids the same way. In the process, they never develop self-confidence or competence—and then he wonders why he's surrounded by "idiots."

In the most extreme cases, authoritarian personalities can become violent and dangerous; Hitler, Stalin, Mao, or a rapist-murderer all come to mind. In many cases, however, authoritarian personalities are not physically dangerous. Their "rule" is more psychological than physical. Even in Hitler's case, the rule started out as psychological and ideological. Hitler did not merely seize power; he was elected. People allowed themselves to feel guilty and sheepish at his constant insistence that they serve the "public good"—which translated, of course, into serving him. By the time they allowed themselves to see *him* for what he was, it was too late.

Placing Feelings Above Facts

What lies at the root of an authoritarian personality? Pure subjectivism: the notion that feelings are all that matters. In this respect, authoritarianism resembles other personality syndromes—such as the borderline personality.

"My mind answers to nobody, not even objective reality," is the silent premise behind most of the authoritarian's actions, thoughts, and behaviors. He might never admit it, even to himself. Intellectually, he might assert that only God possesses the truth. Or that "societal forces" contain the truth. Or even that "objective reality" contains the truth. But his habitual approach to grasping reality is to go mainly with what he *feels,* even when feelings conflict with facts. What distinguishes the authoritarian personality is that his particular feelings are ones of wanting to control others.

Can the authoritarian personality be changed? Or, more accurately, can he change himself? It's very difficult, at least with the extreme cases. But in the realm of personality change, motivation is everything. If an authoritarian recognizes his irrationality and sincerely wants to work on changing his ineffective responses and behaviors, he will certainly make some progress. Unfortunately, the authoritarian is among the least likely to seek or engage in any form of therapy or counseling. He sees therapists and counselors as charlatans—not because they consistently fail to meet some reasonable standard, but because they might challenge a view or feeling of his which is not in conformity with reality.

The authoritarian does not like the prospect of being challenged, and he knows a good therapist will challenge him. Just as he cannot tolerate error in others, he cannot tolerate it in himself. So it's easier to not place himself in situations where the error could be exposed and he might experience embarrassment. Even if embarrassment is not his major concern, he does not want to face the fact that he might be wrong. Errors are intolerable. So he continues to engage in the pretense that he is infallible—and that everyone else *should* be infallible.

Irrational Beliefs

Many people are only partially authoritarian. They have strong authoritarian tendencies but are more reasonable at other times. Some individuals are authoritarian at work, but not at home (or vice-versa). For such people a significant degree of change is possible if they can fully acknowledge their problem. They need to learn to pay attention to their feelings and watch for mistaken assumptions and hidden, irrational beliefs such as the following:

1. "It's a catastrophe if things are not done my way; no other rational options exist;"
2. "Errors are intolerable and always disastrous; failures are forever;"
3. "Other people must be shown what I see as the right way whether they want to be shown or not, and whether their ignorance harms me or not;"
4. "Life must be at peak performance at all times; things must always be at 100 percent, or perfect—and any slight deviation from this standard is a catastrophe which cannot be tolerated or acknowledged."

Blind, Unthinking Adherence to Principles

Authoritarian personalities tend to cling to remote abstractions irrespective of the facts.

They like to appeal to "principle." They feel, "I will stick by this principle no matter what. To question it would be to tear down my universe. I won't allow it."

This attitude stands in contrast to the rational person. The rational, non-authoritarian individual sees no reason to question his principles over and over; but he is still willing to challenge them from time to time to make sure the principles are correct, or to integrate new knowledge.

The authoritarian's blind, unthinking adherence to principle is one reason you often find them in cult-like settings. They think that they can hide behind cult "morality" and rationalize away their thinking errors by saying, "Well I'm moral and nobody else is."

In fact, authoritarians make a mockery of morality. They do not attempt to apply their moral principles to the specific context of a situation. They rarely if ever give the benefit of the doubt, even to people who clearly deserve it. Morality—they feel—is an end in itself, rather than something which is practical and supposed to advance your life. They would rather blindly adhere to a principle even when solid evidence suggests, (1) the principle might be wrong or, (2) the principle might not apply in this context—further thought required.

Authoritarian personalities frequently and often prematurely cut people out of their lives—*not* because the person did something objectively wrong, but simply because the person dared to question them. Authoritarian personalities are the most thin-skinned people alive. They cannot stand competition. They are entrepreneurs of intimidation, more than they are genuine achievers.

It's sometimes hard to see this clearly, because authoritarian types use their intelligence or physical strength to intimidate people who are unlikely to ever view them as vulnerable. Yet you will not find a more vulnerable person than the authoritarian personality. Authoritarians can only possess the power that others grant them (i.e. spouses, children, co-workers—or voters, in the case of Hitler). They totally depend upon others' non-thinking, and non-questioning. All you need to do is calmly and logically question them about their contradictions and evasions, and they start to fall to pieces.

How Rational, Assertive Communication Can Help

Authoritarian personalities are sometimes physically violent. If they are violent, we look to government authorities or our own self-protective measures to restrain them. Violent or not, authoritarians flourish the extent to which individuals around them suffer from low self-worth and low self-esteem. A society filled with independent and individualistic people will not give in to a Hitler. Only a society, family or group filled with self-sacrificing martyrs who see suffering as their inevitable (and perhaps deserved) fate can succumb to a dictator.

The same principle applies on the individual, everyday level. You need not tolerate sarcastic or hostile behavior from your boss, for example. You almost always have *some* choice, even if it does not seem that way. You can either allow yourself to feel like a victim, or you can start looking for a new job. Or you can resolve to challenge him more, with rational communication. Benevolent, assertive communication can work wonders in many types of situations, and can be an excellent way to at least temporarily defuse an authoritarian-type personality. Here are just a few examples:

"I know that you are my boss and of course you have expectations of me. But you are often sarcastic and demeaning. I'll give you examples if you like. This is not very motivating. I'd appreciate it very much if you would try to talk to me in a different way. Constructive criticism and positive feedback are more motivating. You'll get more out of your employees that way."

"I recognize that sometimes it's not possible to be on time. What bothers me is not that you're occasionally late for our appointments. What bothers me is that you make no acknowledgment of it. You don't say you're sorry, or even a simple, 'I'm late.' This shows a lack of respect for my time, even if it you don't mean it that way."

"I'd really like to help you move. But this weekend is not a good time for me. I made plans which cannot be changed because a lot of details are involved. If only I had known a few weeks ago of your move, it would be different."

"Please don't talk during the movie. I realize you're just having a good time, but it's disturbing others around you."

"I know you want what's best for me. But *I* have to decide what's truly best for me. Since I'm the one who has to live with my decisions, it only seems fair that I get to make them myself. Don't think I'm not listening to what you're saying, even if in the end I choose a different course."

Such communication styles represent the only alternative to either "rolling over" like a victim or fighting the authoritarian personality's hostility with more hostility. People often don't want to try rational communication. They feel it's too much work. Or they fear it shows weakness to be reasonable and benevolent. Or it's "cold" to be rational. None of these excuses are valid. If you don't deal with authoritarian personalities in a calm and measured way, then failure is certain. If you do, then success is not guaranteed, but the odds increase significantly.

Taking Responsibility for the Problem

The "curing" of authoritarian personalities is two-sided. First, the authoritarian personality must identify and challenge her irrational views and behaviors. Next, she needs to begin work on changing them. In short, she has to accept that she is authoritarian, see why it's irrational and self-defeating, and be fully committed to changing the automatic responses and behaviors she has internalized over time.

People in the authoritarian's life must not succumb to fear and intimidation. Although the authoritarian syndrome is an individual problem, it cannot flourish unless significant others allow it to do so. It's hard to be authoritarian or unreasonable for very long if others simply will not let you get away with it! The more the authoritarian personality is challenged with reason, strength and benevolence on a daily basis, the harder it will be for him to get out of control.

Some cases are indeed hopeless. With the violent authoritarian, for example, rehabilitation is often impossible, and jail or court orders remain the only solutions. The best way to spot a hopeless case is someone who shows no indication, regardless of the consequences, of admitting his problems so that he can change them.

The authoritarian needs to understand that it's in his own self-interest to change, and that *he* will benefit the most once significant others are able to trust and respect him. Respect and trust from others, after all, is necessary for making money, raising a family and finding romantic fulfillment. It is also much easier on one's mental health to live with realistic (though high) expectations than it is to live with impossible ones. Once the authoritarian internalizes these core rational beliefs, he can start on the road to a happier, more productive existence.   Ⓣ

Chapter 6

Excessive & Obsessive Behaviors

HOW IRRATIONAL BELIEFS
CAUSE DRUG ADDICTION

According to the cognitive-behavioral school of therapy, illogical, non-factual beliefs play a major role in the development of the urge to abuse alcohol, drugs, and other sources of addiction. The purpose of cognitive-behavioral therapy for the substance abuser is to change these illogical beliefs so that the individual will gradually experience a decrease in (and, if possible, elimination of) the urge to use.

What are typical examples of irrational beliefs that help cause substance abuse?

Here are a few:

Life without using is boring; I can't have fun unless I use drugs. Such a view rests on the popular but mistaken idea that fun and pleasure must be mindless and short-sighted. Individuals who can enjoy seeing a good movie, reading a good book, or having a stimulating discussion with a respected friend are much less likely to develop substance abuse problems than cynics who sneer at the "nerdiness" of such activities. Genuine pleasure need not result in a hangover.

I cannot control my usage; I am powerless over it. This idea ignores the existence of free will. The fact that it is not *easy* to control an addictive behavior does not mean that it is metaphysically impossible to do so. Human beings possess free will, and even psychologically troubled people can still access this free will, if they choose. Free will represents the choice to think (or not to think), and the corresponding willingness to act on one's conclusions and judgments. Free will requires a commitment to face reality on a 24-hour basis. Drug and alcohol abuse represent the opposite choice: the choice to escape reality (or attempt to do so) on a regular basis.

Most addicts I have met can identify one or more situations in which they felt like using the substance, but chose not to do so. Such exceptions to the addictive rule can represent the beginning of recovery. What often undermines progress in fighting addiction is the unrealistic idea that one setback (or relapse) wipes out all earlier progress. People will berate themselves for their relapses, and completely ignore the successful exceptions where they worked hard, and succeeded, at not using. Instead of viewing a relapse as a regrettable occurrence which can be turned into a learning experience, addicts will often use the setback as a rationalization to start using again since "it's all hopeless anyway."

I can't relax without drugs. Vast numbers of people have found ways to manage stress and relax without using drugs or alcohol. The billions of dollars made in the entertainment and vacation industries should be proof enough of this fact. Most psychotherapists, furthermore, know of relaxation techniques to help calm the mind and the body. Using drugs or alcohol merely to relax is just an excuse.

Having this drug problem means I am a fundamentally bad person. If the purpose of your life is to pursue and achieve happiness, then you are actually a good person for attempting to do so. The problem is that drug and alcohol abuse does not bring happiness over the long-run—or even in the short-run, because full enjoyment of life requires the complete and active use of your mind. You cannot fully experience life in a stoned, dull, and constantly "hung-over" mental fog.

Tragically, too many addicts have absorbed the Puritanical idea that pleasure is evil. In so doing, it is only natural that they rebel against such a mistaken, irrational idea by sneaking some short-term pockets of "pleasure" wherever they can. Yet these anti-Puritan rebels have accepted the basic premise of their opponents, the premise that to seek pleasure in life is wrong. If seeking happiness in life really were wrong, then it would make sense to try and escape from reality as drug and alcohol abusers do.

The antidote to addiction is to adopt a guiltless philosophy that life should be happy, that life should be about gratification without escaping reality. This approach allows you to accept responsibility for finding reasonable, and not self-destructive, means for achieving your goals and desires.

I do not need to stop using; it's not hurting me. This belief seems credible only when significant others (parents, spouses, kids, co-workers) enable the problem by protecting the addict from the consequences of his self-destructive habits. Instead of forcing the addict to take responsibility for the consequences of his addiction, loved ones may assist him in remaining a substance abuser. They may make excuses for the abuser. They may call his boss to say he has the flu when he really has a hangover. They may stop at the store and buy the addict a six-pack. They may buy into the idea that addiction is literally a disease, and that the abuser is not morally responsible for any of his behaviors while using. It is difficult to overemphasize the role of enablers in extending the life of an addiction.

I can't control my anxiety/depression without drugs. Anxiety and depression are caused by mistaken beliefs, by ideas grounded in myth rather than in fact. (Examples: "I have a right to happiness; I should not have to work for it;" or, "Only bad people seek happiness in this life;" or, "Disaster is always around the corner.")

Discovering and changing these beliefs is not easy and often requires professional assistance from a competent therapist. But you cannot ultimately control, or even effectively manage, such problems by shutting down your mental capacity altogether through drug abuse. Quite the contrary: you need to increase your mental self-awareness, identify your feelings, and then discover the mistaken ideas which cause those feelings.

You may feel better, at least in the short-run, by using drugs instead of facing up to the basic causes of your emotional problems and doing the work required to correct them. But do not fool yourself into thinking that you can control or cure your problems by denying their existence. It will fail every time.

I'm not ready to stop using. The longer you put off a demanding task, the more difficult it becomes to accomplish it. Why? Because in avoiding the task you come to develop a distorted view of it—usually by seeing it as harder than it really is. Think about all the times you put off doing something, and when you finally did it you realized it was not quite so bad as you expected. In fact, you felt gratified because you finally removed another obstacle from your life.

Magnify this feeling a million times, and you will have a clue as to the reward of successfully facing and overcoming an addiction. Taking charge of your mind and your life is the ultimate "high." Only this time, the sense of self-control and mastery over your existence will be real, not fake.

IS THERE SUCH A THING AS "LOVE ADDICTION"?

Q: Is there such a thing as "love addiction?"

A: No.

Love is a response to the perceived characteristics and values held by an individual. "Values" include such qualities as honesty, sense of humor, long-range goals, and personal preferences.

The love response can be either conscious or subconscious. In other words, you may consciously recognize *why* you love your friend or romantic partner; or you may simply "go with your feelings" and never identify the subconscious value judgments underlying your love for the individual. Either way (conscious or subconscious) love always involves a value judgment.

Most individuals who are thought to be "love addicted" are simply relying on inaccurate assumptions in choosing their friends and romantic partners. A battered wife who stays with her husband, for example, continues to love him despite his brutality. Her friends cannot understand why she stays. The root of her problem is that she has not examined her underlying assumptions about the relationship. "I can cure him by continuing to love him," is an example of one such underlying assumption. "Deep down he is good—he just needs time," is another. Until these subconscious judgments are made conscious and then evaluated logically, there is no hope of convincing the battered wife to leave her husband.

The notion of "love addiction" rests on the premise that the choice of romantic partner is outside of one's control. In fact, however, love is very much within one's control. The control lies in one's capacity for examining subconscious value judgments and changing the irrational ones. Unfortunately, because it can be difficult to do this, individuals often conclude they are "powerless" to change their choice of friends and romantic partners. Although it takes effort, you *can* change your subconscious value judgments and learn to experience romantic happiness.

ADDICTION—SHORTCUT TO HAPPINESS?

The addictive experience, according to drug and alcohol addiction expert Stanton Peele, is characterized as follows:

1. Powerful and all-encompassing;
2. Inspires a sense of well-being, such as through conveying an artificial sense of power or control;

3. Valued for its perceived predictability and thus its safety;
4. Creating negative consequences that diminish the addict's concern for and ability to relate to the rest of life.

What is the alternative to the addictive experience and lifestyle?
1. **Long-range goals** to determine one's short-range actions and the overall purpose of one's life: to be a dancer, a novelist, an athlete, a musician, a business owner, a scientist, a professional or technician or craftsman in some other particular field;
2. **Sub-goals** to serve as intermediary steps to the overall purpose: college, graduate school, stage experience, writing short-stories and articles, developing a client base, buying a house, etc.;
3. **Confidence that one's mind is capable of accessing reality**, that there is no inherent "mystery" to accomplishing goals—instead, simply years of hard work and relentless focus; continuous and never-ending additions to one's base of knowledge and experience; passion for achievements, great and small;
4. **Sense of legitimate power** over one's own life and over existence, the kind of power one feels from continuously working on a goal and achieving crucial victories along the way: a novel's or a story's publication, a business expansion, a creative or artistic achievement, a research discovery, buying one's dream house, sending one's child to college.

Drugs, alcohol, or any form of addiction represent an impossible attempt at a short-cut. A short-cut to what? To feelings of power over existence that can, in reality, only be achieved through ongoing productive effort with the help of a long-range purpose.

In occasional, fleeting moments, the addict may feel like the writer, the scientist, the businessperson, or the artist who actually triumphed after years of struggle and effort. But once those moments (those "highs") subside, he must recognize that reality offers no such short-cuts and his effort to achieve values artificially is doomed to failure. This "hangover" effect leads to feelings of depression and malevolence, which in turn make it harder to actually set goals and achieve them. (Or, if the abuser is already setting goals, it becomes harder to achieve the higher goals of which he would otherwise be capable).

When, after months or years, the addiction reaches its climax, and the addict faces the enormity of this reality and can no longer evade it, he will either collapse in despair or begin his recovery from the addiction. It is at this dramatic turning point that, psychologically and perhaps even literally, he survives or perishes.

The addictive process, as just described, applies not only to drug and alcohol abuse. It also applies, more broadly, to other types of addictions: spending, sexual, gambling, and so forth.

Typically, the addict holds (consciously or subconsciously) one or more of the following mistaken core ideas. He holds these ideas emotionally, not intellectually. His intellect would probably dispute them. But on a subconscious level, he feels them nevertheless.

1. **Happiness should happen to me.** It's not fair that it's happening to others and not to me. Happiness is a blessing, not an achievement.
   Rational Antidote: Happiness is always an individual achievement. It is the sum total of countless hours of working towards both long-range goals and smaller sub-goals. It requires continuous effort to be maintained. It is not a state, once attained, which remains in a frozen form, with no further effort required.

2. **I am not meant to be happy.** It's possible for others, but not for me.
   Antidote: The only entity who can "mean" for you to be happy or unhappy is yourself.

3. **I can shape reality by my wishes.**
   Antidote: Nature, to be commanded, must first be obeyed. Existence exists, and no one person's consciousness can change this fact. Telling lies to others, or lying to oneself, cannot change facts. Only conscious, rational, focused actions can change facts, so long as you respect the basic, objectively proven laws of nature.

4. **Live for today; live for the moment only.**
   Antidote: Enjoy the moment, but also set long-range goals and develop a sense of overall purpose. Without purpose, it is impossible to make effective decisions in the present and to enjoy the here-and-now. Think and plan long-range; and live in the here-and-now. It *is* possible to integrate the two.

5. **Knowledge is a mystery.** My mind is impotent to know things, so why even try? If knowledge is not going to come to me automatically, then I give up.
   Antidote: Reason is the method by which you know things. Reason starts with the observation of perceptual facts and grows with the integration of these facts into abstract concepts. Reason is fallible, but with consistent and vigorous use you are guaranteed to always gain more knowledge in the fields that interest you, and as a consequence increased ability and self-confidence.

6. **The noblest, most moral activity I can do is to live for others.** Charity, not accomplishment, represents the essence of goodness.
   Antidote: The noblest, most moral activity you can do is to live for yourself, and those closest to you whom you value the most. By using your mind productively, and peaceably trading with others, you not only achieve personal fulfillment; you also, as a secondary consequence, make the world a better place. Charity is a marginal issue at best. True charity begins at home, by being your *own* keeper, not everybody else's.

The only way to change the mistaken, emotionally held ideas is to (1) bring them into consciousness, and (2) challenge them, repeatedly, with the rational antidotes. A good psychotherapist can help with this task.

WORK-AHOLISM

Q: What is the difference between healthy and unhealthy levels of work? Is there such a thing as "work-aholism?" If so, at what point does work become unhealthy?

A: Work-aholism is not primarily a problem of quantity. It is a problem of *quality*. The number of hours you work does not, by itself, determine whether you are a work-aholic. The way you approach and view your work does.

"Work-aholism" refers to compulsive work. A compulsive activity is one done mindlessly rather than with the fully enthusiastic and motivated use of your mind. It is an activity done blindly, for the mere sake of doing it, instead of knowing why you're doing it and feeling that it serves a valid purpose in your life.

Compulsive workers see the use of their minds as a necessary evil—an evil to tolerate for a time until they can set themselves free and enjoy some "real pleasure." Even if they hold the intellectual view that work and productivity can and should be fun, the feelings they experience beneath the surface are often quite the opposite.

Numerous popular sayings reinforce the sense that work must be mindless, unfulfilling, and dull. For example: "Don't work too hard!" Or: "Live for the weekend." Or: "Take this job and shove it!" Such expressions imply that work must be an ugly duty rather than personally rewarding.

As a rule, some type of painful or anxious emotions lie at the root of work-aholism. To the work-aholic, work becomes a drug. Like a drug, it helps him shut out the emotions he does not want to experience or analyze. Work helps him not think about his marital problems. Or his loneliness. Or the prospect of doing something more challenging, but also frightening.

What can you do to prevent or cure compulsive work problems?

Live your life consciously. Become introspective. Become aware, on a daily basis, of what's going on *inside* of you and not simply outside of you. Part of being reality-oriented and healthy means paying attention to your emotions and your motivations. After all, your psychological state is part of reality. Your emotions will influence you whether you choose to recognize them or not. You need to keep track of your emotions so that they do not end up controlling you. You need to experience your emotions fully so you can live life more fully.

Keep a regular journal of your thoughts and feelings about work so you can scientifically assess, over time, the content of your attitude. Do you tend to experience emotions of joy and happiness and satisfaction in your job? Or do you tend to feel fearful, rushed, and victimized? Are you enjoying the day-to-day process of your work—or do you become so caught up in goal attainment that you fail to enjoy the work itself?

If you find—after four to six weeks of daily journalizing—that your dominant emotional states are anxiety, anger, and guilt, then it's time to take a hard look at your career and your attitude towards it. Ask yourself if you are in the right field. If you are not in the right field, then start working on a plan to ultimately land you in a different place. If you *are* in the right field, then take steps to develop a more positive, realistic attitude about your job.

Though you may sometimes feel otherwise, it *is* possible to learn how to develop a consistent work-loving mentality. Try the following exercise to get you started. Make a hierarchy of what you like most and least about your job. Take responsibility for doing at least one activity in the top twenty-percent of your hierarchy each day, if possible.

Jack, a salesman, made the following hierarchy:

I like most:

Making the pitch to a customer
Spending time with the customer answering questions
Researching new products/services to possibly sell in the future
Talking with other salespeople I respect who may have new ideas

I like somewhat:

Putting together the paperwork for a likely sale
Making follow-up phone calls to stay in touch with a potential customer

I like least:
Administrative meetings with other salespeople in the company (which tend to be "gripe-fests")
Talking with people totally unmotivated to buy, but pressured to see me by a colleague or family member

Once Jack is consciously aware of his hierarchy, he can exercise more control over both his career and his emotional states. He knows, for example, that on administrative meeting days (which he likes least) he had better set aside time for a sales pitch or for talking with salespeople who have new ideas (activities he likes most).

The purpose of a hierarchy is to help you enjoy your work and pursue your career more consciously. Compulsive work-aholics do just the opposite. They hardly ever approach their careers consciously. They drift along, responding only to external crisis, others' opinions, or random feelings. They let their jobs take control of them instead of the other way around. Then they wonder why they feel resentful and unhappy.

Making a hierarchy, of course, is not the single solution to the problem of compulsive work; but it is a very good method to help stay conscious about, and in control of, your ongoing career development.

The opposite of compulsive work is a conscious, active approach to life and job. Work-aholism flourishes when people fail to make the frequent fine-tunings and occasional momentous choices necessary in any career. Take responsibility for your ongoing career success. Identify what you want and go after it on a day-to-day basis. Learn to enjoy the process of work as well as goal-attainment.

Recognize that most of your steps forward will be small, and only a few will be big. Stay conscious about what you feel and make corrections in both your actions and attitudes as necessary. If you don't, you will become compulsive about your work and then it won't really matter if you are "successful" or not.   ☖

Chapter 7

"Getting Help"

DO I GO TO THERAPY TO CHANGE MYSELF OR TO BE CHANGED?

Therapy as self-change is fundamentally different from therapy as being changed. Therapy as "being changed" presupposes the following:

- I must look to the *external* causes of my problems: my genes, my parents, my spouse, "society;" discovering these "causes" will help me better understand why I am as troubled as I am.
- My therapist's responsibility is to make these bad feelings or problems I am having go away; my goal is a sort of psychological "utopia" where depression and anxiety (those twin evils) are eradicated forever.
- Therapy is a medical procedure, most of which takes place in the therapy office. Even if nothing is happening as a result of the sessions, I should simply wait and let the process "do its thing." Objective goals, agreed upon by myself and my therapist, are irrelevant.
- The primary purpose of therapy is to develop a close, intense relationship with my therapist. The hope, in so doing, is that I will have emotional reactions to this therapist that will, somehow, teach me things about myself and my relationships with others. Therapy should always be once or twice weekly, for months or years at a time.

Therapy as "self-change" presupposes an entirely opposite set of assumptions:

- I will look *internally* to the causes of my problems: my subconscious premises, my habits of thinking, my expectations, my methods of communication, my overall outlook on life. I also will look for evidence of what is going well for me, what is better, and the things I do *not* need or want to change.
- My therapist's responsibility is to take me seriously, and to expect that I do the same of myself; to help me develop increased self-reliance, self-respect, and the intellectual/behavioral tools I need to provide myself with symptom relief. My therapist is also in charge of helping me set objective goals as to how we will each know our therapeutic encounter was successful. My therapist will explain to me, as needed, how I can see objective, concrete evidence that I am (or am not) making progress.
- Therapy is not medicine. It is a much more active process than surgery or sticking my tongue out and saying, "Ahhh!" Most of the therapeutic work takes place outside of the office. Psychotherapy is by definition a strictly intellectual, cognitive process. Until I begin to consistently exert the will to apply what I learn intellectually, to the best of my knowledge and ability, then therapy is worse than a waste of time.

- I need a therapist who is self-confident, strong, and compassionate without being selfless. While I must trust the ethics and competence of this therapist, the central purpose of therapy is not to develop a long-term relationship with him/her. My therapist will help me learn to think and act in more self-respectful ways. It is OK to consult with him only as often as he/she and I agree is necessary; it is not written in stone that we must meet once a week, or forever.

SELF-ESTEEM IS NOT FREE

Self-Esteem is a consequence, not a cause. It's not free; you can't have it for nothing.

Do not wait for self-esteem to "happen" before you set out on life's adventures. Self-esteem only develops as the result of conscious, decisive, and consistent action on your part.

Don't let anyone tell you that because you did not get all the nurturing you needed as a child, that you cannot develop self-esteem and be happy as an adult. Virtually nobody got all of the nurturing and reassurance they needed as children. Past is past. Acknowledge it—but move forward.

Plan rational, exciting goals, based upon your dreams and aspirations but also grounded in reality. And then pursue those goals and dreams, without letting anyone else's doubts or negativity get in your way.

Intelligent, thoughtful action comes before self-esteem—not the other way around. This is the true secret of success. There is no other solution, no mythical magic secret.

"WORKING THROUGH"

Q: I certainly don't deny the idea that it's important to change false beliefs and implement correct ones, as you emphasize in *Effective Therapy* and your essays. However, I submit that this picture is insufficient. It leaves out any recognition of how deep the problems which begin in childhood can go, and how difficult such problems can be to counteract.

What, for instance, of children who are severely traumatized by parental abuse early in life, even before they've learned to talk? Are they just "moaning and groaning" (i.e., indulging themselves in useless complaints) if their psyches have been wounded in ways which resist amelioration? I think not. And do such problems require more than verbal techniques? I think yes.

A: First of all, you presume that early childhood trauma necessarily ruins people for adulthood. You take this as an undisputed fact, implying that no proof is required. I hate to break the news to you—but proof is needed here. It's not necessarily true that people are as ruined by their childhood experiences as you seem to assume they are. I know plenty of people who rose above their childhood traumas; and many others who simply don't remember them, and don't care to do so. They're doing just fine.

Secondly, you state that more than verbal techniques are required to help psychologically heal people. I take this to mean that something other than reason—something other than the thinking, introspective mind—is needed for resolving internal conflicts. Exactly what do you propose in its place? If you are a therapist, exactly what do you do to help your clients heal? Primal screaming? Finger-crossing?

You need to state explicitly just what you propose in place of a psychotherapy based upon thought, common sense, and observation of reality. Please don't say that people need to "work through" their childhood issues. This vague, overused term has no meaning unless you define it concretely.

Are people who were wounded psychologically in childhood moaning and groaning simply by acknowledging the fact that this happened? By saying it aloud, perhaps for the first time? By refusing to pretend any longer that what is wrong—sexual or physical abuse, for example—*is* indeed wrong? Of course not. But they are moaning and groaning if they keep stating these truths over and over again, subtly (or not so subtly) making it an excuse for failing to take responsibility, set goals, and live life to the fullest *in the present.*

It's interesting that I rarely hear my clients ask to spend a lot of time focusing on their childhood in therapy. This is almost always the therapist's idea—not the client's. In my practice, I promote the concept of "Solutions, Not Excuses." People often tell me this is exactly what they want and need. Many of my clients see me after previous efforts using traditional psychological approaches—centered on re-living childhood and almost nothing else—have failed at everything, except perhaps putting a pool in their therapist's backyard.

Most criticism of my ideas comes from fellow therapists and humanities intellectuals in general. They hear the way I think, and they say, "It can't be that simple. You're leaving out the complexity." But they never identify exactly what the complexity is. You don't, either, in your question. You say that childhood is often wounding and painful. Of course this is true, and some objective viewing of the past certainly can be helpful. But how do you justify the extent to which most therapists take this? *Who* actually benefits from the years and years of open-ended focusing on the past with little or no feedback about how to change ideas, feelings, and behaviors in the present?

Some people think because I (and similarly minded therapists) hold the psychologically damaged adult responsible for changing his self-defeating beliefs and actions, that we are somehow "blaming the victim" for injustices perpetrated against him by his parents or others. This is simply not true, and there's no basis for thinking it.

I don't blame the victim for what the victimizers did. All I do is accept the fact that what's done is done, and the only person who can do anything about your life is *you,* in the present and in the future. Furthermore, don't extend the injustice by spending the rest of your life seething in hatred and anger about what the victimizer did. Move on, rise above it, and try to keep in mind that the best revenge is living well.

To some, it feels uncomfortable to hold individuals responsible for the improvement of their own psyches. I actually believe it's more respectful and dignified to do so. A therapist who has confidence in the potential of human beings, as well as confidence in the power of reason and thought, can do much to help a suffering person. The same can't be said for a therapist who "helps" his clients to stay victims forever.

THERAPY AS PROSTITUTION

Q: Isn't the personal relationship with my therapist critical to the success of the therapy process?

A: Viewing the relationship between therapist and client as the essence of psychotherapy is the same mistake made by Freud and most of his remaining followers today. Of course the therapy alliance is a personal, highly sensitive relationship. But there is no reason to make this relationship the centerpiece of therapy, any more than you would make your relationship with your accountant the center of the tax season, or the relationship with your mechanic the central feature of repairing your car.

You should hire a therapist to help you with a specific, objective problem (or group of problems). When the problems are resolved (or are at least more manageable), you are finished. It may take one session, or many sessions. But to start off with the assumption that therapy, by definition, should be a long-term, uninterrupted weekly relationship is unnecessary and unrealistic. It's also artificial. To sit for one or two hours a week and pay for a one-sided conversation with somebody is not in any remote sense a substitute for real life relationships. Quite frankly, it's closer to prostitution (without the sex).

FALSE MEMORY & SEXUAL ABUSE

Q: What is the controversy over "false memory" syndrome and what does it have to do with sexual abuse?

A: Memory is a difficult and complex subject about which a great deal still needs to be learned, specifically through the sciences of psychology and physiology which study the human mind and brain.

Nevertheless, we are certain that sexual abuse of children does occur, and that for a variety of reasons some children will not speak up about it until adulthood. In my own experience, sexually abused children are often simply too afraid to speak up prior to adulthood. Adults sometimes do not believe (or want to believe) that the abuse is taking place, especially since it often involves a relative, and prefer to evade the possibility rather than face it. I even know of cases where sexually victimized children later claim, as adults, that they actually enjoyed the feelings of physical pleasure or attention, and when they were old enough to grasp the problems with the abuse they were too horrified to risk acknowledging such emotions aloud.

We also know with certainty that sexual abuse must have some kind of psychological effect on the adult's later life. In my experience, some abuse victims become sexually promiscuous or sexually abstinent for much of their lives. Others, while intellectually committed to a monogamous relationship or marriage, find it difficult to avoid destructive extramarital affairs. Still others recognize the abuse for what it was at a reasonably young age, and move on to lead happy, romantically healthy lives.

At issue in the "repressed memory" controversy is the technique used by some psychotherapists to assert the existence of sexual abuse in a client's childhood without sufficient, or in some cases any, evidence to support the claim. When a psychotherapy client experiences a vague feeling or "memory" of sexual abuse, such a therapist will encourage the client to immediately accept the feelings as factual. No matter how outlandish the memories or how serious and potentially damaging the accusations arising from these memories, the sexual abuse "survivor" is told that she is not responsible for providing proof or validation of her memories.

For example, a therapist will interpret a client's dream or perhaps a romantic problem as an indication that she was sexually abused as a child. The client will search her memory and recall nothing. The therapist will persist, telling the client she is in a state of "denial" and until she allows herself to emotionally relive the repressed memory of abuse, she will never "recover."

To facilitate the process, the client will usually join a Survivors of Incest therapy group where she will be explicitly taught to treat any random feeling that she may have been abused as objective proof that she was, in fact, molested. In some cases, therapy clients have taken parents and other accused molesters to court and won on the testimony that the client suffered from "repressed memory syndrome." In other words: the feeling that you may have been molested is objective proof that you were—and the person you feel might have molested you can be jailed.

While some cases of past abuse are undoubtedly authentic, a growing number of therapists are actively engaging in victimization hysteria. In a daytime talk show cultural climate where victims are often considered heroic and virtuous solely because of their victimhood, we should not be too surprised to see more therapists cashing in on the repressed memory trend, both intellectually and financially.

Repressed memory proponents, breathing new life into the maxim that a little bit of knowledge is a dangerous thing, have stretched the theories of psychoanalyst Sigmund Freud to their ultimate conclusions. If Freud could assert, in the absence of evidence, that all little boys want to have sex with their mothers, then how unreasonable is it for his successors to claim that an odd sexual dream, a random emotional "memory," or a failure to find a romantic soulmate proves that you were sexually abused as a child?

The deeper, more significant error beneath today's repressed memory hysteria consists of a steadily growing acceptance of the arbitrary, or the purely emotional, as equivalent to the logical and objectively factual. One tragic illustration of this trend involves the case of thirty-year-old Eileen Franklin. In 1990, Eileen sent her father to prison for the rape and murder of her childhood friend twenty years earlier. Eileen's claim, supported by her therapist, was based upon the spontaneous recovery of memories after twenty years of "repression" and "denial." Incredibly, Eileen allegedly reported five different versions of her memory to others, and overtly changed her versions to accommodate new factual evidence about the murder as it became available during the trial. In spite of these contrivances, and with the help of remarkable testimony by Eileen's therapist that a feeling of child abuse constitutes, by itself, objective proof of abuse, a conviction for murder was secured.[3]

"If you *feel* it, then it's true." This premise dominates so much of contemporary psychotherapy, it is little wonder that false memory syndrome has become an issue. Although science still has much to learn about the neurophysiology and psychology of memory, the example of Eileen Franklin's therapist shows that some mental health professionals have perhaps even more to learn about the distinction between emotions and reason.

THERAPY BY TELEPHONE

Q: Isn't therapy by telephone a bad idea, since the therapist is unable to see the facial expressions and body movements of the client?

A: According to a cognitive-behavioral therapist, the basic purpose of therapy is to help a person identify and change mistaken thoughts, premises, and behaviors so that emotional conflict and distress can be alleviated.[4] It is not necessary to see facial expressions and body movements in order to help an individual achieve this goal.

In fact, talking by telephone can even be an advantage. People are usually very self-conscious and anxious when seeing a therapist. It makes them feel more comfortable not to face the therapist when revealing very personal facts and emotions to a stranger. In my own experience, clients open up much more quickly when I speak to them by telephone than is the case in face-to-face encounters. Revealing emotions is a crucial part of cognitive-behavioral therapy. Not only does expression of emotions make the client feel better; emotions are the "raw data" the therapist needs to draw upon in order to find out what errors in thinking are causing the psychological conflicts.

To many therapists, especially those trained in traditional, Freudian-oriented approaches, the very notion of telephone therapy represents anathema. Whether they label themselves as Freudian or not, they uncritically accept the Freudian premise that the personal relationship between the therapist and client is the most crucial component of therapy. They do not view therapy as a primarily practical, solution-focused, objective method for resolving conflicts and problems. Instead, they see therapy as a neo-mystical bond between therapist and client, with establishing and maintaining the bond as a therapeutic end in itself. Because his main goal is to emotionally connect with the client, rather than evaluate the client's thinking and behavior, the relationship-centered therapist considers phone therapy too "impersonal" to be productive.

Although a good emotional connection between therapist and client can certainly contribute to progress, over-emphasizing it will result in a much more expensive, longer-term
process than necessary. This bonding also comes at the psychological cost of an unhealthy
dependence of the client upon the therapist (or even vice-versa).

If you are seeking therapy and dislike the idea of phone consultation for any reason, then
simply don't do it. However, do not assume that phone therapy is second-rate. For many reasons, it can be superior to conventional, face-to-face therapy. Furthermore, good telephone
therapy is enormously preferable to mediocre or bad face-to-face therapy. The ideas and
methods of your therapist are much more important than whether or not he can bond with
you and be your friend.

IS DEPRESSION PSYCHOLOGICAL, BIOLOGICAL, OR A COMBINATION?

Q: Is depression primarily biochemical, psychological or usually a combination of
the two?

A: Depression is a syndrome generally characterized by some combination of the following symptoms: low energy, low self-worth, a pervasive sense of hopelessness,
sleep disruption, increased or decreased appetite, physical lethargy, and automatized thoughts and premises which are negative in tone and content.

Although some of the manifestations of depression can be physical (e.g. listless-
ness, low energy), it is impossible to label a problem "depression" without the presence of negative feelings within the person suffering from it. Depressed persons feel
depressed, regardless of what causes the feelings. These negative feelings do not necessarily represent distortions of objective reality. For example, a parent whose child
dies in a terrible accident will experience the symptoms of depression, a depression
clearly derived from observation and experience of objective reality.

More frequently, however, mental health professionals encounter individuals who
suffer from thought distortions of one degree or another—thought distortions
which manifest themselves in depressive states. For example, a man might hastily
conclude that a fight with his wife about money means they are no longer in love and
will break up in the near future. Or, an adolescent might overgeneralize a rejection
by a potential romantic interest to mean that he is never going to find a lover. In some
individuals, even otherwise fairly rational ones, poor thinking habits such as hasty
conclusions or unfounded generalizations can, over time, lead to psychological syndromes such as clinical depression.

In more serious cases, depression represents the psychological dead end of consistently holding mistaken philosophical premises (explicitly or implicitly) for years
or even decades. The most common example is the ethic of altruism, the idea that
self-sacrifice is the standard of moral virtue. A young woman holding altruist

premises, for example, might sense (correctly) that her parents are having marital problems which accelerate when she goes away to college for her first year. Torn between her long-time goal of pursuing an academic career and her need to emotionally support her parents, she drops out of school to be with her parents. After several weeks home she is, not surprisingly, listless, resentful, and depressed.

Only a therapist who understands the irrationality of self-sacrifice—and its inevitable psychological consequences—can help this young woman adopt the belief that her own life and the selfish pursuit of rational values is the only moral and healthy way to live. No amount of medical treatment, not even state-of-the-art antidepressant medications, can permanently relieve this young woman's depression until she comes to understand the futility of self-sacrifice and the necessity of placing her own life first.

Although depression always involves a psychological—i.e. cognitive—component, considerable evidence does exist to suggest that antidepressant medications (such as Prozac, Paxil, and many others) can bring a certain degree of relief to depressed persons. In my own practice, I usually do not refer individuals for antidepressant medication unless: (a) their problem is so prolonged and severe that psychotherapy alone will not be enough, and (b) they clearly understand that antidepressant medication will not solve their cognitive problems for them, and that self-generated, therapeutic work (in and out of the therapy office) remains an absolute requirement for improvement. I tell them, metaphorically, that if the antidepressant works, they will be swimming *with* the current instead of against the current; but that either way they still need to swim, and the therapist is merely their coach.

Philosophically, man is simultaneously both mind and body. While one has to separate the two for conceptual purposes, it is somewhat artificial to view depression as either purely psychological or purely physiological. We certainly know that depression, because of its cognitive-emotional component, is by necessity psychological. But it is also reasonable to assume, especially with expanding knowledge about the physiology of the brain, that certain physiological states coexist and interact with the psychological state of depression.

The coexistence of these physiological states does not imply, however, that one's underlying thoughts, ideas and philosophical premises are irrelevant. Quite the contrary: man's underlying ideas will always represent a major cause of his corresponding psychological and physiological states.

CAN PSYCHOTHERAPY HELP ME?

Religious people often say, "God helps those who help themselves." Well, the same is true for psychotherapy. Before seeking any kind of psychotherapy, make sure to examine your motives clearly. Do you accept full responsibility for your particular problem, and simply want someone to put you in better touch with reality so that you can solve it? If so, then therapy can be very helpful to you, provided that you have a problem or dilemma which you have so far been unable to solve on your own.

On the other hand, if you expect that your therapist will somehow solve your problems for you, and there will not be much work on your part, then you are sure to be disappointed. Therapy is not "black magic." It does not "do" something "to" you. When practiced properly, it is an educational process designed to help you understand the relationship between your thoughts and emotions. Your therapist's job is to help you examine your feelings, and then show you how your feelings stem from either rational or irrational thoughts. By learning to change your thoughts, in therapy, you can change the way you feel and act.

The measure of success for psychotherapy is the degree to which it helps you see reality more accurately and more clearly. Since some aspects of reality are unpleasant, you will naturally not always enjoy psychotherapy—even if the process is working very well. On the other hand, if you maintain a commitment to stay focused on reality—with the help of your therapist—then you will find, over the long haul, that your life is more fulfilling and pleasurable than you could ever have imagined.

FOCUSING ON CHILDHOOD IN THERAPY

Q: How much, if at all, should my therapist focus on my childhood in therapy?

A: Therapy should address one's childhood only insofar as it might have affected one's current emotional condition or problem. Good therapists seek to link childhood to the present in direct and explicit terms.

For example: "Do I tend to give up easily, allowing myself to be influenced by my father's idea that life is hopeless and impossible?"

Or: "Do I subconsciously tend to sacrifice myself for others, on the assumption that selflessness is a virtue and martyrdom is heroic?"

Or yet another example: "Do I tend to associate with people like my hostile and insensitive parents, when in fact I should be consciously looking for individuals with different characteristics?"

Each of these questions implies that mistaken ideas, however subconsciously absorbed in the past, can nevertheless be changed in the present.

Traditional psychodynamic or "insight" therapists, on the other hand, teach clients how to relive their childhoods for the mere sake of doing so. The insight therapist thinks that almost everything the client does is the result of unconscious childhood conflicts playing themselves out in adult life.

"Unconscious" means that such conflicts meet with resolution only through the special talents of a trained psychoanalyst. If the client feels anxious, for example, this means he has not recovered from a childhood desire to sleep with his mother. If a client is depressed, this means he must be traumatized by the fact that his mother abandoned him. If a client does not like to spend money, she may still engage in unconscious struggles with her parents over toilet training. Aside from the bizarre, often arbitrary nature of these claims, psychodynamic therapy additionally requires faith on the part of the client that acquiring such "insights" will somehow solve his current emotional and behavioral problems.

In my own work with clients, I sometimes ask about childhood merely to obtain a better understanding of how the individual's thinking might have been affected by an earlier stage of life. I am very careful to consider the possibility, however, that a person may have already consciously rejected certain ideas from his childhood and will consequently be less affected by them. An adult child of an alcoholic or sex abuser, for instance, may have long since consciously rejected the irrational approach to life represented by her parents. Unlike the fatalistic insight therapist, a good therapist recognizes the relevance of free will and the overriding power of ideas, rather than early childhood traumas, on one's emotional states.

Childhood, *per se,* does not cause emotional problems. Mistaken conclusions formed in childhood will lead to later problems if not consciously corrected in time. Therapist and client should only discuss childhood to discover distorted thinking habits or false ideas still held, however subconsciously, in the present. Discussing childhood *ad nauseam,* for its own sake, is of no value at all. In fact, it might actually lead to an increased and unnecessary sense of self-pity, hopelessness and helplessness.   ⑰

3. Elizabeth Loftus and Katherine Ketcham, *The Myth of Repressed Memory: False Memories and Allegations of Sexual Abuse* (New York: St. Martin's Press, 1994).

4. Michael J. Hurd, *Effective Therapy* (New York: Dunhill, 1997).

Chapter 8

How to Help Your Children Grow Up

DISEASES *DU JOUR:* HOW BEHAVIORAL
DISEASE LABELS HARM KIDS

A dangerous trend in contemporary child psychology involves the tendency to turn child behavioral problems into medical "diseases." Too many mental health providers appear increasingly eager to provide young children and teenagers with such diagnoses. Children who talk back to their parents or who occasionally disobey a rule are said to have "oppositional-defiant disorder." Teenagers who are truant and run away from home have "conduct disorder." If they lie, steal, or even kill, they are victims of "antisocial personality disorder."[5]

Stanton Peele summarizes the current diagnosis hysteria most eloquently: "More children are being persuaded at earlier ages that they have a disease and that this diseased person is *who* they are. We seem rapidly to be creating a future world of people who identify themselves primarily in terms of their diseases."[6]

Countless parents have been convinced by teachers, principals and psychiatrists that their child has the disease of "attention-deficit disorder" or "learning disability," to name the two most common examples. Parents quite logically conclude that the "disease" needs to be "treated." Consequently, they fear placing any limits on their children or attempting to challenge them in any way. Even the most intelligent and well-educated parents will plead with therapists to explain how to "cure" their child, failing to understand the importance of teaching the child long-term goal setting, separation of feelings from facts, and self-responsibility—the real tools of self-esteem.

The consequences of this cruel and unfair disease formulation extend well into the college years and undoubtedly beyond. A college teacher, for example, told me of a case where a student asked to be excused for skipping a class even though he had no good reason. His excuse? "I have a learning disability," he replied. When the teacher asked the student to explain in his own words the meaning of the concept "learning disability," the student merely shrugged, "I don't know. I was always told I had this disease and that there was no use studying; so I believed it." Psychiatrists and educators who flippantly hand out disease labels to the young children should more seriously consider the long-term consequences of their sometimes ill-informed diagnoses.

Disease labels often encourage parents to ignore the fact that children can and do make choices. One of the most popular forms of labeling children is attention-deficit disorder (ADD). The use of the term "disorder" implies an *inability* to pay attention as opposed to an unwillingness or refusal to pay attention. Interestingly, parents of children with ADD frequently tell me that their kids are quite able to concentrate on activities they find enjoyable, such as music or time with their peers.

According to researcher Jane Healy, research on ADD has suggested that so far as learning is concerned, the issue is one of selective attention. Selective attention refers to the ability to concentrate and stay focused on a particular task, such as homework or class lectures. "But selective attention," Healy writes, "has proven hard to measure.

Like memory, it is 'task specific,' changing according to the job the brain is asked to do and the underlying motivation to do it. For example, many teachers who complain that students can't pay attention and listen in class also notice that the same children will concentrate on a computerized video game for long periods of time. In these two situations there are clear differences between both motivational and cognitive factors such as auditory or visual attention, saliency (attention-grabbing quality) of the stimulus, requirements for memory, physical involvement, and the pace of the activity, all of which affect attention."[7] Such factors suggest that ADD is more than a medical disease over which its victims have no control whatsoever.

The problem of disease labeling children does not result from a shortage of government funding or well-meaning professionals. The core problem lies in the mistaken idea that behavioral problems can be labeled "diseases" in the absence of sufficient (or even *any*) physiological data, and without any reference whatsoever to the possible role of human will. Since when, you might ask, did truancy and car theft become "diseases?" Since when did manipulating parents, teachers and other authorities become a "disease?" Since when did staying up an hour past one's bedtime become a "disease?" Because there are no rational scientific principles guiding much of contemporary psychology, there is no telling how far psychiatric opportunists will carry the disease concept.

Today's diagnosis hysteria can be explained by at least two specific factors. Child psychology, like all psychology, is a young science. Researchers in the field of child cognitive development are still in the data gathering stage. Consequently, psychotherapists who work with children have nowhere to turn for objective diagnostic criteria except the American Psychiatric Association's Diagnostic and Statistical Manual (known as the DSM-IV). The DSM-IV serves as kind of a "bible" for mental health professionals, including child therapists. Since the manual uncritically accepts and adopts the disease formulation for child behavioral problems, few therapists see any advantage in questioning it.

The other factor contributing to diagnosis hysteria has to do with the anxiety of parents. Parents with troubled children are naturally quite anxious. They want to apply a label to their child so they can better understand his problem and how to deal with it. It also relieves them of any responsibility in the matter. If the child has a disease, rather than poor judgment and self-discipline, then they can hand all responsibility for the problem over to the doctor.

Since mental health diseases supposedly have nothing to do with free will, then the child need not take responsibility, either. Many therapists, motivated either by a desire to reassure parents or to cash in on the disease hysteria, are quite compliant in providing parents with such labels. It is hard to imagine sending a worse message to a young child or a teenager than this: when you misbehave, it is because you are ill. Simply go to the psychologist for "treatment" and the misbehavior will stop. The psychologist will "fix" you.

Responsibility issues extend beyond the family and the doctor's office. As most Americans now realize, public schools are increasingly out of control. In more and more school districts, teachers and school officials desperately seek measures to control violent and even homicidal kids. Since parents appear increasingly unwilling (or unable) to provide even basic discipline for their children, teachers face an increasing number of behavioral problems. However well-intentioned, applying diagnostic labels to children for cognitive and behavioral problems creates the illusion that parents and children have no responsibility for the problem. Abandonment of responsibility will not solve today's growing problems in public schools.

Parents should remain wary of therapists or teachers who are in a hurry to label their child. The best therapists will want to treat child problems within a family context, and help the child return to a normal (or even better) state of functioning as quickly as possible. The best therapists have no interest in labeling the child. Good therapists primarily want to provide parents and children with new ways of thinking and new ways of behaving so that family members can lead better lives and eliminate any genuine psychological symptoms.

ATTENTION DEFICIT DISORDER— MYTH OR REALITY?

An increasing number of mental health professionals are finally starting to question the notion that there is such a thing as "attention deficit disorder." Attention deficit disorder, also known as ADD, refers to the supposed medical disorder where a child is consistently "unable" to pay attention, sit still, or concentrate for significant periods of time.

The questions have less to do with whether ADD exists as a syndrome—since obviously many children do demonstrate these behaviors—than with whether or not it is proper to label ADD a medical "disorder." Mental health clinicians such as myself, for example, continually hear parents of kids diagnosed with ADD point out that their kids *can* concentrate when and if they choose to do so. The operative word here is "choose." Proponents of ADD seem to be suggesting that kids do not make choices; that if Johnny does not concentrate on his homework or pay attention in class it must be due to a "disorder" rather than a simple choice not to focus his attention.

What objective, physiological evidence do experts offer in support of their view that ADD is a medical disorder? Little to none. It is true that some kids labeled with ADD—which used to be called "hyperactivity"—do calm down significantly when given certain types of medication (such as Ritalin), or changes are made in their diets. But these facts by no means prove that attention is solely the result of physiological factors.

How, for instance, do you reconcile the fact that many kids with ADD pay attention some days more than others? And how do you explain the fact that some kids who display ADD in the classroom show no evidence of such a syndrome when playing a video game, talking to friends on the telephone, or engaging in other intellectually undemanding activities? If ADD kids have a biological inability to focus, then why do they easily concentrate on so many activities?

This is a very serious matter for parents to consider. This is more than a dispute over mere wording or diagnostic classification among health professionals. The real questions boil down to these: Is my child failing to concentrate in school because he has a medical disease which prevents him from doing so? Or is he failing to concentrate in school because he chooses not to do so?

The fact that kids with so-called attention deficits *can* concentrate when they desire to do so suggests that ADD is a matter of choice, not mere biological chance.

This does not mean that ADD-diagnosed kids are faking it. It is fair to assume that at least some ADD kids sincerely find it difficult to concentrate in school (or other activities). In other words, they are not properly motivated to concentrate.

Why? What causes lack of motivation in children?

Countless explanations are possible. Perhaps they do not understand the importance of concentration; perhaps they have not been taught that solving a math problem or learning a history lesson requires patience and persistence, and does not happen automatically.

Perhaps the educational philosophy of the school is misguided; many schools today, especially public schools, emphasize feeling good about oneself and getting along with peers over learning basic conceptual skills such as reading, writing, arithmetic, and independent judgment.

Perhaps the parents, however well-meaning, are not using appropriate and consistent methods of discipline.

Perhaps the child has decided that studying is irrelevant to his well-being.

Perhaps the child is unhappy, due to tensions within the family or irrational fears of failing, not pleasing his parents sufficiently, or embarrassment if he performs poorly in class.

Perhaps the child is disorganized, and while he shows great aptitude in class he has no structured routine for doing homework.

Any combination of these possibilities, or countless other possibilities more relevant to the particular child in question, could be causing the poor concentration in school. *None* of them are indicative or suggestive of a medical disorder.

How can you improve your child's attention span, without resorting to drugs or medical disease labels? Here are a few suggestions.

Limit Television and Video Games. There is nothing intrinsically wrong with television and video games. The problem is that they can become habit forming at the expense of other activities such as conversation, reading, and quiet introspection. Furthermore, excessive television and video games can reinforce short attention spans and encourage a short-sighted, range-of-the-moment mentality. Certain television shows, even educationally acclaimed ones such as *Sesame Street,* tend to favor perceptual imagery over abstract thinking. While there is nothing wrong with perceptual imagery, abstract thinking is essential for learning to read, conceptualize, reason, and think about a wide variety of subjects.

Teach Kids Self-Talk Skills. Kids need to develop the habit of identifying their feelings and asking themselves questions about those feelings such as: "Why do I feel this way? Is it accurate to feel this way? Why am I angry at Mommy? What did she do that made me angry? Should I tell her how I feel? Why or why not?" It is important not merely to teach kids to express their feelings, but also to analyze their feelings rationally, at as sophisticated a level as they are capable. This will help kids learn that feelings and facts are not necessarily the same thing. It will also assist them in the development of impulse control, self-discipline, and overall self-esteem. Kids need to learn early on that it is unhealthy to either (1) repress, ignore, and evade feelings, or (2) act blindly on feelings without analyzing and discussing them first.

Find Out What Interests Your Child. Kids are not born with knowledge of what's out there. It is up to parents to help kids explore their options and interests. Some kids will prefer more individual activities such as reading, writing, coin collecting or working with computers. Other kids will prefer outdoor activities such as bicycling, team sports, or individual sports. Others like music; others want to learn more about the weather; still others enjoy tree climbing or fantasy play. Encourage your kids to make their own individual, carefully thought out choices. Above all, accept responsibility for helping your child discover what interests him; do not expect him to "instinctively" know what he likes to do.

Take Care of Yourself. As a parent, you already know that your job is a 24-hour, never-ending responsibility. Do not let this awesome responsibility interfere with your need to take care of yourself. Let your child see that you possess a life apart from him—that you have certain activities that you choose to do either by yourself or with adults only. Do not be a self-sacrificing martyr and rationalize that this is in your child's best interest; it most certainly is not. Doing too much for your child will not only spoil him, it will make his adult life a living hell as he expects the rest of the world to treat him in the indulgent, unrealistic way that you treated him. It's OK to have your own interests and hobbies apart from your child, even as you accept the responsibility of being a parent.

Give Your Child Choices. This does not mean letting your child do whatever he feels like whenever he feels like it. It does mean letting your child have as many choices as possible—and letting him experience the consequences of those choices as well. If your kid wants to stay up all night watching TV, why not let him do it one time—but also tell him that he must get up at the normal time, go to school, and perform as well as he usually does. If your teenager wants to date a boy you are convinced is not good for her—let her, provided that she comes home when she's supposed to, keeps her school work up to par, and so forth. A parent's job is not to let a child have everything he wants without restriction; nor is a parent's job to run a prison camp. A parent's job, psychologically speaking, is to show the child the nature of reality. The principle that all children must grasp by young adulthood is that *actions have consequences.*

IS ADD A DISEASE OR NOT?

Q: The fact that those of us with Attention Deficit Disorder (ADD) are able to focus on things we find interesting or pleasurable does *not* mean it's a problem with motivation.

Why heap unwarranted, crippling guilt on your patients with ADD? They already have to put twice as much effort into life as everyone else, in order to only get out half as much.

A: You assume that ADD represents either a medical disease or a moral problem, and that no other alternative exists. A third explanation does, in fact, exist.

ADD is a psychological syndrome, not a medical disease. A psychological syndrome results from deeply held but mistaken beliefs or habits. Although a genuine problem, it is potentially under one's control by actively identifying and changing these beliefs or habits. A medical disorder, on the other hand, is only curable through passive receptivity to medication, surgery, or other externally imposed treatments. ADD is classified by the American Psychiatric Association as a *mental* disorder (i.e., a psychological problem); yet the dominant view spread by the media today is that ADD is a medical disease.

ADD refers to an internalized choice to improperly focus one's attention. It is a choice that has become subconscious to the ADDer, but remains a choice nevertheless. Countless causes are possible, as revealed in my years of experience working with ADD individuals. These causes include overuse of television and video games, improper teaching methods, or poor mental and behavioral habits. The most fundamental psychological cause? Low self-esteem—that is, the belief that you are incapable of or unworthy of pursuing values, of achieving your potential, and of living life to the fullest. If you are not convinced, at the deepest level, that you can use your mind and you should use your mind, you will never feel motivated to focus.

The best antidote to ADD? Set both long- and short-term goals; live by *reason*, rather than by faith or emotional indulgence; value your own life on earth above all else (not just as a remote abstraction, but in actual, day-to-day living); and learn practical techniques to better focus your attention on reality, with professional help if necessary. No medicine can do these things for you.

Correlation is not proof of causation: the fact that some people with ADD find that they focus better while medicated does not prove that ADD is a medical disease. Neurological change (e.g. relaxation, calming) brought about by medication may heighten your ability to focus, but is not itself the cause of your choice to focus and think. You acknowledge that people with ADD have to put extra effort into life, in order to get more out of it. This proves that something other than your neurons and genes are performing your thinking and focusing for you. In the end, it is up to you to exercise your free will, to maximize the potential of those neurons and genes and cells inside your brain. Without your choice to think, those cells and neurons are worth nothing.

RAISING A HEALTHY AND MORAL CHILD

- **Human knowledge is not automatic—especially for kids.** Kids are not born with knowledge that adults take for granted. Your child is not born knowing that he should be quiet in public, or that he should eat healthy foods, or that he should think before he acts. Even so, you should still hold him responsible for his wrong actions. If you don't, then how else is he going to learn? If you don't punish or at least correct him for lying or hitting, then how else will he learn that this behavior is wrong?

- **Try to keep perspective.** Your child does not act disobediently just to irritate or embarrass you. She is simply being a child. Childhood is, essentially, a learning process. Children must learn what the limits are. All kids test limits; some will do so more than others. Accept that this is the nature of childhood and, above all, do not take it personally. Instead, try to think of it as an opportunity to teach your child right from wrong.

- **Avoid the false alternative between permissive and restrictive discipline.** Permissive parents reason with their children but do not punish them. Restrictive parents punish their kids but will not reason with them. The only rational alternative is to give your kids the *reasons* as to why they should act a certain way, allowing them (at convenient times) to ask questions. (Example: "You need to go to bed by ten o'clock so that you're not tired in the morning. That way you can better concentrate in school. Any questions?") Children are much more likely to follow rules, even unpopular ones, if you let them ask questions at convenient times. Use punishment only if reason fails.

- **Positive incentives are generally more powerful than negative punishments.** However, do not reward a child for doing what you consider the bare minimum— getting up in the morning, going to school, being minimally civil, and so forth. Save the rewards for actions you consider to be beyond the bare minimum, such as excelling in school, trying extremely hard on a difficult task, or listening to his own intelligent judgment rather than responding to peer pressure. Rewards need not always be concrete and material. Positive feedback, along with constructive criticism, are crucial to building morale and confidence within a child.

- **A family is neither a dictatorship nor a democracy.** As parents, you must have the final say. This is only fair, since you have full responsibility for the child's welfare until he is capable of self-support. However, you should also remember to explain and discuss, not merely command. If a child makes a logical point proving you wrong, you should stand corrected and make the necessary change. This will teach a child the benevolent view that it is OK to ask questions and that reason can work in bringing about solutions.

- **Kids differ from one another.** For whatever reasons, some children are highly oppositional and require a lot of supervision. Others show remarkable self-discipline. Some respond to reason the first time, and some will never listen to reason. If you have a persistently difficult and oppositional child, remember that she needs consistency more than anything else. Try to resist the temptation to control everything she does or punish her for every wrong action; this is impossible and unnecessary. Instead, choose your punishments wisely. Think about what you consider to be the top ten or fifteen percent of offending behaviors, and punish her swiftly and consistently for them. Sometimes, successfully holding your ground with a child on one simple issue—such as bedtime, or homework—can lead to success in other problem areas, because she will develop respect for you and generalize this respect to other areas. With difficult and manipulative kids, respect is often more important than warm and fuzzy feelings of love. Face this fact—and work with it.

- **Avoid medical disease labeling of your child's behavior, such as "attention deficit disorder" or "conduct disorder."** These diagnoses distract you from the fact that your child is capable of making choices and is responsible for his actions. Do everything possible to help him make better choices, rather than blame his laziness or nastiness on some nonexistent "medical disease." Even if a doctor's prescription, such as Ritalin, appears to improve behaviors, it does not change the fact that your child still makes choices every hour of his life. He can choose to scream in the grocery store, or to restrain himself. He can choose to pick up his clothes, or to ignore your requests to do so. Kids make choices, just like adults make choices. In the end, no pill can choose their values for them or make them do their homework.

- **Do not encourage your child to be selfless, and do not condemn him for being "selfish."** Think about it. If you tell a child not to be selfish, you are implying he should *not* act in his own self-interest. This means he should not brush his teeth, he should not study hard in school, and he should not look before crossing the street, since all of these actions are in his own self-interest. Nor should he treat his friends respectfully, since they are of personal value to him and it is in his self-interest to treat them as such. Certainly, you want him to be polite and to respect the rights of others to their own property and time. It will be more motivating, however, if you explain to him why it is in his personal interest to respect the rights of others. For instance, you might say, "If you want the right to keep your own toys, then you have to respect the same right in others. You can't have it both ways." This is a much more logical and motivating argument than, "Don't be selfish! Put others before yourself." Also, it shows that respecting the rights of others does not mean he has to sacrifice his own privacy, property, and happiness.

- **Do not punish a child for what she thinks or feels.** Only punish her for an action, provided you consider the action to be wrong and serious enough to warrant a punishment. You can challenge, disagree with, or express strong disapproval of her thoughts or feelings, but do not punish her for them. If you do, then you will discourage independent thought and make it more likely that she will mindlessly follow any group that will accept her. You will also encourage emotional repression, which leads to psychological and moral problems.

- **You do not harm a child's self-esteem when you constructively challenge or punish him.** Quite the contrary. You are teaching him the nature of reality. As an adult, you know that you have to think and work and make certain rational choices in order to survive and find some measure of happiness. If you want money, you have to go to work. If you want to buy something big, like a car or a house, you have to save. A child is not born with an automatic grasp of these principles. He will not learn them unless you teach him how to think logically and take responsibility, from the earliest age possible. Challenging him intellectually, encouraging him to read, to think critically, and to persuade are crucial tasks. Withholding support from him when he behaves irrationally represents part of this learning process. Don't count on teachers and day-care workers to impart these virtues to your kids. As parents you must do the bulk of the work, if you want your kids to grow up into healthy and mature adults.

SEVEN TRAPS TO AVOID WITH THE DIFFICULT ADOLESCENT

1. **Watch out for unearned guilt!** Sometimes adolescents will try to make you feel guilty for something which is clearly not your fault. For example: "All the other kids have their own telephone; why can't I?" What other parents do is no substitute for your own rational judgment.

2. **Earlier family problems, such as divorce, are no excuse for compromising your standards**— such as school performance, personal responsibility, etc. In fact, children from "broken homes" may require more consistency than other children. Consistency can be a loving reassurance that the family will move on, despite the disruption of a divorce.

3. **If your child does not experience the consequences of his actions, he will be unprepared for the real adult world.** Even in a democracy, adults are held responsible for their actions. The same is true for adolescents.

4. **Do not fall into the trap of giving your adolescent all of the advantages of adulthood without any of the responsibilities.** Let your teenager pay his or her own way wherever possible. Just as there is no "free lunch" for adults, there should be none for teenagers. In this way, the teen will be better prepared to accept adult responsibilities.

5. **Prior sexual or physical abuse is no reason to turn your child into a professional victim.** There is no question that these are very serious issues, and often require some form of mental health intervention. But you are doing your child a terrible disservice if you hold her less responsible for her actions because of the abuse. For example, if you hold her to lower standards because she was victimized, you send her the message that she is somehow less capable as a result of the abuse.

6. **Good parents can have bad children.** There is absolutely no research to prove that parents "make" their children do bad things. It is certainly the case that the way you treat your child will have a significant influence on him; but children, like adults, make choices. Do not blame yourself if you do everything in your power to be consistent and caring, and your child still engages in antisocial or even illegal behavior.

7. **If you seek mental health treatment, make sure you see a professional who agrees with these views.** Interview them. Do not assume that all therapists subscribe to these ideas. You, and your child, deserve a therapist who does.

HOW TO AVOID BEING TOO
PERMISSIVE OR TOO RESTRICTIVE

Adolescence is a time of increased freedom and increased responsibility. When dealing with adolescents, parents and teachers need to avoid being either too permissive or too restrictive.

Permissive adults emphasize freedom at the expense of responsibility. A permissive parent, for example, will allow his seventeen-year-old son to have unlimited access to the family car or to buy expensive clothes regardless of his current school performance. Such a parent will think: "I want my son to have all the advantages I never had."

Such a "loving" sentiment can actually be unfair to the adolescent. It allows him to have the advantages of adulthood without any of the disadvantages. When he enters the adult world, his peers will hold him responsible for his actions and he will feel confused, hurt, and angry. Friends will find him manipulative. In extreme cases, he may turn to substance abuse or other criminal behavior. A permissive approach hinders the development of the young adult's self-esteem.

Conversely, restrictive adults emphasize responsibility at the expense of freedom. For example, a restrictive parent might tell her teenage daughter: "You can't have the car tonight because I say so," or, "You can't have the money for that purchase because I say so." The restrictive parent bases her decisions on emotion instead of reason. The adolescent learns that freedom must be achieved through a manipulation of her parents' emotions, rather than increased responsibility. She may work hard to obtain good grades during a school semester, but her parents will continue to deny her privileges for no logical reason. Children of restrictive parents enter young adulthood feeling resentful, angry or depressed. The damage to their self-esteem is similar to that of children from permissive families.

The alternative to permissive and restrictive parenting is consistency. Consistency does not mean "rigidity." It means the thoughtful establishment of clear, achievable rules by the parents. The degree of freedom given to the adolescent should always match the degree of responsibility he demonstrates. For example: above-average grades lead to unrestricted use of the car (within normal rules); average grades lead to restricted use; below-average grades lead to no use of the car until the grades are at least average again.

Such an approach is neither restrictive nor permissive. Unlike the restrictive approach, it puts the adolescent in charge of her own life at a time when she wants increased independence. Unlike the permissive approach, it is consistent with the nature of the adult world he will eventually confront. Although consistency can sometimes lead to family tension in the short-run, in the long-run the adolescent is free to develop into a mature, responsible adult. Consistency is the key to both freedom and responsibility.

THE FREEDOM/RESPONSIBILITY PRINCIPLE

Exasperated parents often ask themselves this question: How am I supposed to make good parenting decisions? What standards or rules should I be using? The answer is simpler than it may seem. Parents can ask themselves: how much *freedom* and how much *responsibility* does my child currently have?

The guiding principle is this: the more responsibility the child shows, the more freedom he should have; the less responsibility the child shows, the less freedom he should have.

With some children, this runs smoothly with hardly ever having a discussion. With other children, unfortunately, parents must pay strict attention to this principle and never waver from it or let down their guard. If the child asks for more freedom in the absence of sufficient responsible behavior, parents need to turn the issue around: parents need to tell the child that he cannot have more freedom until he first masters the responsibility required for his existing freedoms.

Consider, for example, the sixteen-year-old who wants to be allowed to go to a beach house with his classmates. He insists that he should be allowed to go because the other kids are allowed to go. Parents need to avoid this line of reasoning; it is entirely illogical. Instead, parents must first ask themselves: Has my child been living up to his current responsibilities in a consistent enough way that he has earned such a privilege, at least for one time? This has to be thought out carefully; and it is also helpful to involve the child in this process, provided that he will not be manipulative or rude about it.

The freedom/responsibility principle applies no matter what the child's age. It becomes particularly important in the teenage years, however, because (1) the child has reached a stage in his intellectual growth where he can emotionally manipulate parents, if he wishes to do so; and, (2) teenagers, quite understandably, are generally more demanding of freedom than are younger children; their minds and bodies are approaching adulthood but are not quite there yet. It is normal and healthy for them to yearn for freedom; yet it is also necessary and healthy for parents to set logical limits on them, utilizing the freedom/responsibility principle.

The principle also applies in the opposite direction. Children who accept a lot of responsibility ought to use their freedom as well. And if they do not, the parents should teach the child to stand up for himself and not cave in so easily to others' demands. The parent might even tell the child: "Tell me if I'm being too hard on you. I will try to watch this, but you need to help me be sure that I'm fair to you. Don't suffer silently." Despite today's media attention on the growing number of juvenile delinquents and obnoxious adolescents, there are undoubtedly still many "silent sufferers" who need their parents' attention as well.

There is no substitute for a reason-based approach to raising children. My experience shows that if the parent applies this approach consistently, there will rarely (if ever) be the need for extensive psychotherapy. A good therapist helps the parent learn and apply this approach regularly, if and when difficult problems arise. And since parents may not have been raised rationally themselves, they may indeed be in need of such help. But the important thing for parents to understand is that they *do* have the power, with practice, to raise their children in a healthy, logical, and consistent manner.   ⊕

5. American Psychiatric Association, *Diagnostic and Statistical Manual of Mental Disorders, Fourth Edition* (Washington, DC: American Psychiatric Association, 1994).
6. Stanton Peele, *The Diseasing of America: Addiction Treatment Out of Control* (Boston: Houghton Mifflin Co., 1989), p. 113.
7. Jane Healy, *Endangered Minds: Why Children Don't Think and What We Can Do About It* (New York: Touchstone, 1990), p. 154.

Chapter 9

Toxic Labels

ADULT ADD:
CHEMISTRY OR CHOICE?

Q: I have to disagree with many of your statements. Growing up unidentified, with ADD, was an experience that I would not wish upon my worst enemy. Being shunned by family, peers, and educators due to "laziness" and "day dreaming" behaviors leads to low self-esteem and self-image. Thankfully I am a Survivor and I made it through not only an undergraduate degree, but went on to receive an M.S.

I have been working in schools for over 16 years.

Do I think that ADD can be overdiagnosed? Sure, I think that there needs to be caution when diagnosing any "disorder" or "disability." However, it is my belief that ADD is a spectrum of disability, ranging from mild symptoms to symptoms so severe they are disabling.

How do I know that ADD is real? I live it everyday of my life. I know the fog, and the many tracks of thought that play simultaneously in my mind. ADD does not allow for the filtering systems to function, and thus the behavior that is judged inattentive is in reality the opposite! If you were to look into my brain during a time of perceived inattentiveness, you would not see a blank board; rather you would see a cacophony or storm of thoughts and ideas. I am an intelligent, caring individual and I have (for the most part) turned this disability into an ability! How do I know ADD is real? I take stimulant medication, and this medication lifts the fog, allows me to filter internal and external distractions, while leaving my pulse and blood pressure rate at normal levels. How do you explain this phenomenon?

A: You give yourself too little credit. You assume—in fact, you passionately believe—that physiology is everything. You don't leave room for the concept that human beings have free will. We can exercise the choice to think. We can *choose* to lift the fog by focusing our minds on something important to us. We can set deadlines, to motivate ourselves. We can develop better organizational skills. We can learn to believe in ourselves and trust our minds. We can choose to live life by focusing on reality and actively pursuing values.

You do acknowledge that you have free will, whether you realize it or not, when you state, "I have (for the most part) turned this disability into an ability!" For *you* to turn something like this around, you must have exercised some kind of free will. The pill, you imply, could not have done everything. Yet you contradict yourself when you assert that ADD is a purely physical, brain disease rather than a problem with motivation, self-initiative, and self-esteem.

How we motivate ourselves plays a huge role in attention. For example, most of us were raised with "thou shalts" and "thou shalt nots." "Thou shalt study." "Thou shalt work hard." "Thou shalt concentrate." In one form or another, explicitly or by implication, this is how most of us are taught to motivate ourselves.

These commandments may be true. But *why*? In what context do they apply? *Why* is it in our own selfish interest to follow them? Should we study or work hard for our *own* sakes—or merely because someone tells us we have to do so? Few, if any of us, ever address these profoundly important motivational questions. Because we don't, concentration and motivation can become difficult. It's hard to work under the will of arbitrary commands—even if those commands come from our subconscious minds rather than from a real, live dictator.

It certainly must be painful to be called lazy or shiftless when, deep down, you know this is not who you really are. It isn't fair. People are not always reasonable and fair—even when they mean to be. But this does not justify pretending something is a medical disease when it really has little or nothing to do with medical problems.

Instead of calling you lazy, your elders should have helped you understand your motivational problems so you could then free yourself to achieve your potential. They should have told you to focus your mind for your *own* sake—not just because they commanded you to do so, or because it made them feel good. Your "laziness" was actually a form of rebellion against their authoritarian approach to child-rearing—only you never knew it.

You say that medication helps you. But it's also very clear that you have done a lot of other things as well. Time after time, you struggled to change your view of yourself. You told yourself, again and again, that you're *not* lazy and shiftless, no matter what other people say. Whether you realized it or not, you adopted a philosophy of individualism. You put the supremacy of your own mind—your own evaluation of yourself—above the arbitrary or mistaken conclusions of others. This is not only healthy; I call it courageous and heroic.

You asked me to explain why the fog lifts when you take medication. Maybe the fog lifts just as much, or even more, because of your own repeated efforts to change your view of yourself and to actively use your mind and talents. I know many people who take medication but continue to focus poorly. Until they look at their own self-image and their own habits, like you did, nothing changes. I even know of some cases where individuals stopped taking medication for ADD and their concentration and performance actually improved! How do you explain *that* phenomenon?

Undoubtedly there are physiological processes, not yet fully understood, which affect the mind and our thinking; but there is more to human life than physiology. The proof lies in any one instance of an individual exercising his choice and will to think—no matter what the circumstances. Life is more than a series of chemical reactions. You are not merely a body—you are simultaneously mind *and* body. When it comes to personal growth and achievement, your psyche and your intelligence and your self-image matter just as much as (and maybe even more than) the configuration of the neurotransmitters in your brain.

Congratulate yourself on the results of your efforts. You have earned them. Stop giving all the credit to the drug you take—and the physicians who congratulate themselves for prescribing it.

MENTAL ILLNESS—
THE FACTS AND THE FANTASIES

Q: You seem to reject the idea of "mental illness" in your book *Effective Therapy* and
your essays. If mental illness is not a valid concept, then isn't psychotherapy a
fraudulent practice?

A: Psychotherapy is an alliance between a professional, objective helper and an individual with personal, emotional, or interpersonal conflicts. A therapist or helper
need not necessarily believe in the idea of mental illness. Many therapists, including myself, view their client's issues as problems in living rather than "diseases."

The idea of mental "illness" is really a metaphor rather than a literal application
of what psychological conflict involves. Psychotherapy has a proper place in a person's life so long as psychological conflicts, emotional distress, or interpersonal conflicts exist. No doubt they always will.

In many ways, a psychotherapist is the secular equivalent of the priest, the minister and the rabbi. It's a universal and natural human need to want to talk about personal problems and find solutions, or a sense of perspective. Sometimes it does not
help to talk with family members or close friends, and a more objective outsider is
required.

Ideally, a psychotherapist helps an individual apply a rational philosophy of life to
human dilemmas and problems. This is why it is very important for a therapist to
subscribe to a rational philosophy, as opposed to an anti-life, anti-mind philosophy
such as Sigmund Freud, B. F. Skinner, and many of the other figures who dominated
psychology's first century. "Rational" simply means a philosophy which holds individual human life and fulfillment as an end in itself, with reason (as opposed to blind
faith or emotion-worship) as the means of knowing reality. A good therapist, if he is
to help his clients, must understand that the human mind is efficacious and capable
of finding solutions.

Particularly important to a rational philosophy is an emphasis on free will. It is
only with an acceptance of the fact that we have free will that we can take responsibility for ourselves and pursue the happiness, achievement, and fulfillment most of
us desire. Most existing psychotherapies rely upon either very different or highly
inconsistent alternatives to the idea of free will. They tell us we are determined by our
childhoods, our genes, our animalistic reflexes, our "past lives," our genders—nearly
anything except our ideas and assumptions. They tell us to rely on the analyst, the
support group's opinions, authority figure directives, the Higher Power—nearly anything except our own capacity to think, reason, and form responsible, independent
judgments.

So much fatalism and determinism exists in the minds of most people, that they
actually need a rational form of psychotherapy to help them see (and learn to feel)
that they are capable of self-determination. Unless the therapist herself subscribes to

a self-determining view—the opposite of the "mental illness" perspective—you can be sure that therapy will contribute to the problem rather than the solution.

Q: Can't medication, such as Prozac, help people with their emotional and psychological pain and suffering?

A: Medical psychiatry and medication do have their place. But as practiced today, these fields greatly overstate their effectiveness. To hear many psychiatrists speak, you would think that Prozac and other drugs had solved the problem of human misery for all time. Reality is quite the opposite. Many people on drugs like Prozac suffer side-effects and a wide range of other disappointments. I know, because I talk to such people on a daily basis.

When medication fails, most psychiatrists refer their patients for psychotherapy. But they insist that their patients keep the faith, and continue to take the failing medication anyway. Sometimes medication eventually ends up helping, but often it does not. Even when it does help, the results are usually temporary.

The other problem with modern psychiatry is that it largely ignores the existence of a conceptual mind and, by implication, the possibility for other methods—reason, common sense, introspection, psychotherapy—to alleviate human suffering. Medical psychiatry proceeds on the incredibly shallow premise that the brain's neurotransmitters must be manipulated by drugs, and that there is no other way to achieve happiness. If we can just rearrange these neurotransmitters and other brain chemicals in the perfect way, the theory goes, then mental health can be achieved. How unrealistic—and how anti-human!

The medical viewpoint ignores the fact that we have concepts and premises and ideas which are influencing our moods in a much more fundamental way than brain chemistry. It also evades the fact that we have free will, and that (with effort) we can choose to change our beliefs and attitudes and, as a consequence, our emotional states.

Human beings have minds as well as brains. We possess souls: not in the ghostly sense of minds or spirits detached from the body, but in the rational sense of minds acting in simultaneous unison with the body. If you believe, at the core, that life is good, that your mind is useful and competent, and that you deserve happiness, then you will tend to feel serene and productive. You probably won't need Prozac. If you have internalized the widespread view that you are guilty simply by reason of being born (the Original Sin or collective guilt doctrines), then you will tend to feel neurotic and compulsive. You can take Prozac to reduce the symptoms, but nothing will permanently cure you except identifying and, where necessary, changing your core beliefs.

Until more mental health professionals understand and recognize that ideas, not brain chemicals, are the most fundamental movers of the human spirit, the psychiatric field will remain (at best) mediocre and misguided.

Q: Does having a mental problem, such as kleptomania (compulsive stealing), mean that the individual is not responsible for his actions?

A: A kleptomaniac needs to be held responsible for his stealing in the same way as someone who does not fit this label. In fact, the knowledge that he will be held responsible can help the kleptomaniac from acting on his compulsive desires. You're less likely to steal if you know you'll be punished for it—particularly if you're a kleptomaniac rather than a hard-core criminal.

At the same time, just because the kleptomaniac is morally accountable for his actions does not mean he is without inner psychological conflict or turmoil. Kleptomaniacs, unlike criminal personalities, experience a conflict between the act of stealing and their chosen value system. In other words, they feel what they are doing is wrong, but they do it anyway. Why? Perhaps to gain attention; perhaps to relieve stress; perhaps to simply get something they desire even though they know they're going about it in an improper way.

A criminal, on the other hand, actually believes he's entitled to the stolen property and views his theft as kind of an entrepreneurial game or challenge. He values the "challenge" of stealing and enjoys getting away with it as much as (if not more than) obtaining the stolen object itself.

Although the motives and psychological experiences of the common criminal and the kleptomaniac differ, the end result is the same from a social and political point-of-view. Each violates another's property rights and consequently needs to be held responsible. If your car or television or money is stolen, for example, you don't care why the thief stole it. You don't care if the thief is a kleptomaniac or a hardened criminal. You simply want justice, and that's entirely appropriate.

Liberal psychiatrists who say that the kleptomaniac is "mentally ill" and therefore should not be held responsible for his actions are dead wrong. They completely evade the reality of free will and choice, even in the context of psychological distress. Pleading for their patients in court, they simply act as if free will does not exist— despite the fact that many people with psychological problems heroically use their free will all of the time. Consider, for example, the smokers or drinkers who end their addictions with little or no professional help. Or people who conquer their depression through determination and persistence, as some actually do.

Similarly, ultra-conservative types who claim that immoral behavior such as stealing can never be an indication of a psychological problem are also dead wrong. They overlook the fact that some people who commit wrong acts do experience genuine remorse and guilt and conflict over their behavior. Not everyone who commits a criminal act is a die-hard criminal personality. Some thieves might actually benefit from professional psychological help, so long as the psychologist does not make improper excuses for their behavior.

We tend to approach this issue—whether it's kleptomania or another type of psychological problem—from a false "either-or" perspective. We assume that the choice is between: (1) mental problem with no responsibility whatsoever (the "bleeding heart" view); or (2) responsibility for actions and no mental problems whatsoever (the ultra-conservative view).

In actuality, psychological problems do exist; but the individual is still responsible for his actions whether the problems are present or not. Consider the cases of infamous serial killers, such as Jeffrey Dahmer or Charles Manson. Can anyone seriously argue that these men did not have mental problems and deep psychological conflicts? At the same time, can anyone seriously argue that these men are not evil and should not be held criminally responsible for their actions?

Immorality and psychological problems are not mutually exclusive. Evil might be the ultimate consequence of failing to address one's psychological conflicts over time. Evil could be the characterological tumor which grows from a long period of uncorrected, initially undetected psychological conflicts.

If the mere presence of psychological problems rules out holding people responsible for their actions, we would have to throw out the concept of justice and personal responsibility altogether. We would have to abolish laws against physical violence, fraud, and theft, and live in a state of literal anarchy so as not to hurt the criminal's feelings or "self-esteem."

Obviously, such an approach is dangerous and insane. Criminality and psychological problems are interconnected; but criminals must still be held accountable for their actions. What makes much more sense is to teach people how to be introspective and mentally healthy from an early age—and to consistently uphold, as an absolute, the right of everyone to be free from the initiation of force, fraud, and theft. It's unlikely that theft and crime will ever disappear altogether. But under the right social, ethical, and psychological conditions, they could diminish to a minimum.

Q: I believe that all human emotions are "pro-life" in the sense that man has evolved them over time. Emotions—even unpleasant ones—are not illnesses. They are evolution's way of motivating us to take the actions necessary to achieve our values. What do you think?

A: I have known people who perform obsessive rituals, such as washing their hands dozens of times daily even if they are clean. I have known people who binge on junk food and then force themselves to throw up. Still others I talk to feel compelled to kill themselves, even though their lives are full of promise and opportunity. These individuals may know their actions and feelings are irrational, but they still feel emotional compulsions to do these things. Should they conclude, "Well, my emotions are pro-life, even my unpleasant emotions"? Obviously not. Yet if your assertion that all human emotions are pro-life is correct, then it must be logical for them to do so.

I agree that emotions are not illnesses and in today's society we have "medicalized" things which are not in fact medical. But just because emotions are not illnesses does not mean they are always desirable, either. It's better to feel happy and joyful, for example, than to feel sad and morose.

Suffering is neither a virtue nor a value. Sometimes pain is the cost of pursuing values; sometimes, too, it can pave the way towards a previously unknown solution. But suffering is never an end in itself. One should do everything possible to make suffering the exception, not the rule; to make it unimportant; to find the silver linings in the clouds, if they exist.

I am also troubled by the underlying premise of your question. You appear to assume that emotions are determined by forces other than the individual's own mind, by something other than the person's perceptions, observations, and evaluations over time. You refer to the concept of "evolution." If by this you mean that individuals who learn to effectively manage their emotions are more likely to survive and flourish, then I have no problem with what you are claiming.

But you seem to be claiming that some unnamed entity ("evolution" or whatever else) somehow determines what large numbers of individuals feel. I disagree. I see people as ultimately beings of self-made soul. Human emotions are not hopelessly and helplessly determined by collective forces or mystical entities or anything else. Although general trends among people can be identified, psychology is, in the end, an individual matter. People can change their ideas, their values, and their behaviors when they see reason to do so. They can evolve into healthier, happier individuals in the course of a single lifetime. They need not submit passively to the kind of collective psychological evolution you seem to be describing.   ⊕

Chapter 10

Stupid Things Kids Learn from Ignorant Adults

ONE PLUS ONE EQUALS
WHATEVER YOU *FEEL* LIKE

Peggy McIntosh, the director of Wellesley College's "Seeking Educational Equity and Diversity" (SEED) program, chastises schools for asking children to give correct answers to mathematical problems, grammar exercises, and history questions. She claims that the emphasis on right/wrong answers is a "culturally oppressive" idea and is "unfair" to minority children.

McIntosh, and other theoreticians like her, offer no empirical evidence for this assertion. They merely take it as self-evident truth. (An interesting approach for individuals who apparently do not believe there is such thing as objective truth). As an attempt to justify, although not prove, her claim, McIntosh describes the struggle of a young girl to learn the answer to 5 + 2 + 6. The little girl did not properly grasp the mathematical principles for solving the problem, so she consequently got the answer wrong. While most educators would attempt to teach the child how to get the problem *right*, McIntosh instead complains that the child is victimized by "a win-lose world in which there's no way the child can feel good about the assignment." The implication: a child can, and should, feel good about doing a math problem before actually solving it. In other words, a child should be able to feel the psychological rewards of competence and success without having to do any of the work!

McIntosh goes on to claim that "excellence" is a dangerous concept for schools and argues that schools need to stop giving out "gold stars" and other honors because, she insists, such honors reflect a white-male, biased approach to education. She believes that instead of trying to teach children how to distinguish objective (provable) facts from falsehoods, schools should shift their focus to teaching kids how to be "cooperative," accepting and "equitable."

If this sounds radical, consider that McIntosh is actually somewhat behind the times. Her philosophy of education is quite compatible with that of educational philosopher John Dewey, whose views have been influencing most American public schools (and many private schools) throughout the twentieth century. Both Dewey and McIntosh emphasize the importance of turning children into unthinking, conforming citizens with good interpersonal skills rather than into objectively intelligent, independently reasoning individuals. The flawed ideas of Dewey and McIntosh have been particularly prevalent in the last two to three decades. Note that by every known measure of educational performance, and by every conceivable barometer of parent-teacher observation, American education dramatically deteriorated in quality throughout the twentieth century, especially in the final two to three decades. This fact is quite logical because as individualism declines, so do competence and success.

McIntosh merely represents the most extreme version of a point of view that has dominated American education (especially public education) for decades. Do not be fooled by her references to racism and fairness. Her real enemies are objective truth and objective knowledge; and, unlike most education officials or professors, she has no difficulty admitting this fact outright.

If we accept the common sense observation that some children perform better than others, then we run the risk of hurting some children's feelings. To McIntosh and those of her ilk, this risk is intolerable. It is better, in their eyes, to simply ignore the notion that there is objective knowledge, that some individual children show more intelligence in certain areas than others, and that some children apply themselves more diligently than others and consequently attain better results in school.

To counter the false views of McIntosh and those like her who dominate today's education departments, one must recognize that there exists another form of discrimination and prejudice previously ignored: *discrimination against the objectively superior and intelligent.* What about the rights of kids who work harder, and consequently do better? How fair, and equitable, is it to tell these kids that they are on the same level as a child who does not do his homework or pay attention in class?

What does it do for classroom morale to tell the superior kids that they are no different in performance from the kids who are not doing well? Even if some poor performers are learning disabled (a claim for which there is seldom any hard, neurological evidence), how fair is it to tell superior performers that they are on the same level as the poor ones? To spread such Pollyanaish deceit amounts to evading obvious facts in favor of wishful fantasy—and, as any good psychologist will tell you, nothing could be more harmful to a kid's self-esteem.

Some kids perform better than others, for whatever reasons, known or unknown. This remains a fact, and there is no need to punish superior kids by lying to them that they are "equal" when they can plainly see they are not. Nor does it help the lower performing kids, who should be emulating the superior performers' work habits rather than staying stuck at the level of mediocrity. Yes, each child should be seen as an individual with unique abilities and interests; but it does not logically follow that one must deny the fact that some kids show more ability than others in certain areas.

As Charles J. Sykes, an outspoken critic of this non-objective, deceitful approach to education, writes, "learning basics [i.e. objective subjects] can be hard and might entail both effort and disappointment. But basics also imply a set of standards outside of the child himself, a standard that is uncompromising and to which the child must accommodate himself. This, of course, is anathema to the democratic, child-centered [Dewey/McIntosh] classroom."

In other words, teaching children that $1 + 1$ *does* equal 2 and that Western civilization *did* accomplish more than primitive savages who huddled in caves and tents for centuries, implies something far deeper: the fact that reality exists independent of consciousness, wishes, and desires. That feelings and convictions are not necessarily the same as objective facts. That objective facts are not identified by blindly following some authority (real or imagined) who says what's true; nor are they identified strictly by how one feels inside. Rather, objective facts are determined by observation of reality and the integration of facts into conceptual abstractions. Or, to put it in another way: some kids perform better than others, and some kids are quicker at forming more sophisticated concepts than others.

We have reached the literal dead end of the Dewey/McIntosh/non-objective approach to education. To the McIntoshes of the world, ignorance does not matter so long as everybody is *equally* ignorant. This is, in fact, the only way to make non-objective approaches to learning "work." If equality, and not objective truth, becomes the ultimate goal of education, then it will not be hard to convince kids that there are no correct and incorrect answers—even to the question, "What does 1 + 1 equal?"

In a world where 1 + 1 equals whatever you feel like, then we are all "free" to be equally stupid. Only in a world where there are objective truths, truths which exist whether you feel like it or not, is there any possibility of achieving the satisfaction and happiness that comes from discovering what those truths are. Those who are willing and able to discover those truths deserve our respect, admiration, and gratitude. Those who seek to obliterate the existence of objective truth, so we can all wallow in each other's mediocrity, deserve our contempt.

SESAME STREET—JUST CHILD'S PLAY?

Is *Sesame Street* really as good for children as educators and politicians claim? Most people would presume "yes," but the fact of research studies (not commissioned by the government or others with a vested interest in continued funding of the show) suggest quite the opposite.

1. New research on the developing brain suggests that many, perhaps even most, preschoolers' brains are not adequately suited for the "sounding out" method of learning words that *Sesame Street* encourages.
2. Many researchers now believe that early pressure by *Sesame Street* to remember letters and their sounds may cause learning problems for some children, especially children in the socially disadvantaged groups the show is intended to reach.
3. *Sesame Street* overemphasizes letters and numerals and underemphasizes the language and thinking skills necessary to make them meaningful.
4. Research studies show that bad readers view reading as "sounding out the words," while good readers view reading as "understanding what the words and sentences say." Unfortunately, *Sesame Street* encourages the "sounding out" method of learning to read.
5. *Sesame Street* also subordinates meaningful dialogue to brain-grabbing visual events, noises, and slapstick comedy. This emphasis is particularly troubling for disadvantaged children and children with reading difficulties, who need verbal and not merely visual strategies for processing information.
6. Although children who have watched *Sesame Street* get better at pointing to pictures in response to vocabulary words, this type of recognition-level test cannot be taken to mean that the children use the words in their own conversation. In fact, children whose

parents encourage them to watch the show demonstrate the lowest overall vocabulary scores in studies.

7. The presence of rapid, minute-by-minute alterations in context which characterize the show—from a pirate ship to a city street, a barnyard to a cartoon of letter symbols—is directly antagonistic to the active and sustained work on connecting ideas that is needed to understand written text. *Sesame Street* sacrifices in-depth learning and understanding to attractive perceptual sequences.

8. Research reveals that children do not follow *Sesame Street's* content as well as most adults think they do. One researcher observes that, "too often the children simply failed to follow the material being presented from one sequence to the next. The necessary time for mental replay was not allotted, and there was insufficient repetition."

9. Less intelligent children, the disadvantaged audience *Sesame Street* was originally intended to reach, actually remember less from exposure to the show than other children.

10. Research evidence suggests that *Sesame Street* discourages the development of good reading skills, intellectual persistence, and visualization procedures, especially if used as a substitute for reading and intelligent conversations with adults.[8]

WHEN DOES PHYSICAL PUNISHMENT BECOME CHILD ABUSE?

Physical punishment, in general, is not appropriate for children.

For one thing, it can easily turn into abuse. Child abuse occurs when an adult releases his frustrations and anger upon the child. In other words, the child becomes part punching bag, and part recipient of a punishment.

Initiating physical force against a child implies that force is preferable to reason. Do you really want your child to grow up with this idea? It's true that very young children are not always capable of reason, and certainly not very willing to use it. But this does not justify initiating force against a child. Plenty of other alternatives for punishment are available—and positive incentives should be attempted as well.

I have interviewed hundreds of parents and they consistently tell me that hitting does not work very well—at least if "work" means raising a mentally balanced child who learns to rationally restrain himself from doing wrong things.

Is physical force or punishment *always* wrong? No, there are exceptions. If your child is in a physical fight with another child, you will have to use force to pull him away from the fight. When he refuses to go to bed, you may have to pick him up and make him go to bed. If he is about to do something harmful or wrong—such as touch a hot stove or throw food at his sister—you certainly can and should use physical force to restrain him. A smack on the wrist or a pull on the shoulders may be the only option you have under such conditions.

There may also be situations where your child hits somebody else for no reason—in other words, for a motive other than legitimate self-defense. In these cases it may be appropriate to hit or smack your child in return, simply to show him what it feels like. You have to be very careful, of course, to make sure that the hit or the spank is restrained and the child does not become a punching bag for your own anger or frustrations. You also have to be absolutely certain that the physical force your child initiated against another was completely unjustified. If either of these criteria cannot be met, then err on the side of caution and simply don't hit or spank your child.

It is true that the threat of physical punishment can be motivating in a way. It sometimes seems appealing when compared to the permissive approach of many families today where there are few rules or limits of any kind. But force is still not a good substitute for ideas, reason, and explanation. Force does not tell your child *why* something is wrong; it only tells him that he should be afraid of doing something arbitrarily deemed "wrong."

As a child gets older, the reasons for being good become increasingly important as tools of motivation and self-discipline. You need to instill reason and thought within his mind as early as possible. Otherwise, how can he or she become a thinking, ethical adult?

Fear, at least by itself, is not a very effective motivator over the long-run. Many people who grew up under the threat of being whipped by the belt largely abandon ethics once they are adults. Look, for example, at the serious ethical problems some of today's leaders of the baby-boom generation demonstrate. Many of these baby-boomers were probably raised by the belt or the whip. Since they never became very skillful at rational self-restraint, it's not surprising some of them grew up to become deceitful and impulsive.

"But little kids can't reason." This is the most common rationalization in favor of the belt or the whip. Of course little kids can't reason like adults. But this does not mean they are mindless. We underestimate children, especially young children. If you watch them carefully, you will see that they often know exactly what they are doing. They may not be able to grasp more complex concepts such as "justice" or "right" and "wrong," like adults do. But in many ways they are just like adults, trying to get what they want in the fastest and easiest way possible. Even if reason won't work on the verbal level, you can still motivate them through positive and negative incentives—punishment chairs, kind words, nice faces, disapproving faces, play time, and so forth.

If you want your child to become psychologically and ethically healthy, then avoid the use of physical force. If you want him to understand that it's wrong to initiate force against others, then don't initiate force against him—unless it's a clear retaliation for his own violent behavior or simply to protect him from self-harming behavior.

THE MYTH OF UNCONDITIONAL LOVE

Q: Don't children need unconditional love? Shouldn't a parent always tell a child, "I will not always agree with your actions, but I will always love who you are?"

A: Children do not, in fact, need literal unconditional love. *Literal* unconditional love would
mean that parents accept everything a child does, blindly, all in the supposed interest of
the child's self-esteem. If the child lies, for instance, a parent practicing unconditional
love could not show anger or hurt at the child's behavior; nor could the parent tell the
child that lying is wrong, and why. If all love is unconditional, after all, there is no such
thing as right and wrong.

Children *do* require a patient, highly tolerant form of love because of the many, many
holes in their knowledge prior to their complete intellectual and psychological development.
This type of love, however, does involve limits and conditions. If your child helps you clean
up the kitchen and drops a plate, for example, you will feel temporary irritation with him. In
such a situation, it makes total sense to tell him afterwards, "I was aggravated when you
dropped the plate, but I never stopped loving you."

If your child does something deliberately malicious, however, such as stealing a toy from
a friend or initiating violence (outside of clear self-defense), then you should wholeheartedly
withdraw your approval, at least in that particular context. You should tell him why you dis-
approve of his action, and why you are disappointed in his choice to act that way. You can
make it clear that you will forgive him only if he shows resolve not to repeat the behavior in
the future.

The last thing you need to teach your child is that he will (and should) always be loved
regardless of his actions. A child needs to learn the distinction between innocent errors of
knowledge (such as not realizing how easily plates can break) and willful, destructive
actions (such as lying, violence or theft).

A child certainly needs a patient parent who understands that children are not born with
adult knowledge and need time to acquire it. Yet, precisely because children are not born
with knowledge of right and wrong, it is up to a parent to teach the child such concepts: not
merely through lectures, but through concrete, consistent conditions and consequences.
Sometimes such lessons are difficult for both parent and child, and may require a temporary
withdrawal of affection and closeness between them. In the long run, such an approach is
kinder to the child because it will help him learn to think in terms of correct principles and
beyond the immediate whims of the moment. Without such training, a child is likely to remain
a child, psychologically, throughout his adult life.   ⦿

8. For sources of research, see Jane Healy, *Endangered Minds* (New York: Touchstone, 1990).

Chapter 11

School Violence:

An Interview by

Joseph Kellard

SCHOOL VIOLENCE:
AN INTERVIEW BY JOSEPH KELLARD

Q: Many people, sociologists and psychologists among them, blame the rash of shootings by kids in schools on the violence depicted in video games, movies, and TV and on the prevalence of guns in America. What do you think is the most fundamental cause that unites all of these incidents, and to what extent, if any, do depictions of violence in the various entertainment media play in them?

A: Only a profound and all-encompassing hatred of existence could motivate such a crime. Many student killers in recent years demonstrated elements of these motives, but not with the ruthless consistency of the Littleton, CO, terrorists.

The hatred of life and existence that these young killers exhibited—and their determination to bring the rest of the world down with them—is unspeakable. Morally, it simply does not get any worse than this. Yet crimes motivated by such hatred are happening with increasing frequency in public schools.

In the case of the Colorado disaster, the young men clearly hated anything remotely associated with life: achievement, happiness, and valuing of any kind. Notice the reports we're hearing that the killers hated competent athletes and competent students. The only thing they "valued" was the hatred of any and all earthly values. This is known as nihilism.

Look, too, at how one of the killers shot a female student when, having been asked by him if she believed in God, she insisted, "Yes." One need not be religious to experience horror and revulsion over this event.

What could motivate such an act? Only one thing: hatred of valuing as such. It was not religion or belief in God that the gunman wanted to snuff out. It was the fact that his classmate valued something—*anything*—which the killer felt he had to destroy. It was her integrity—even at gunpoint—which he felt had to be eliminated, ruthlessly and on the spot. It was the best within her—her independence of spirit, a sign of loving life—which he could not tolerate.

This nihilistic hatred of life and of values unites all tragic incidents like this one. Without it, no such tragedies would be possible. Not all the guns or violent movies in the world can convince somebody to terrorize a school if he does not possess this profound and all-encompassing hatred of existence; if he does possess it, not all the censorship or gun control laws on earth will change his mind.

Q: You published a letter in the *New York Times* that noted how these shootings occur only in public schools, and that they have something fundamental to do with the violence that occurs in them. Why do you regard kids who attend public schools, as opposed to private schools, as prone to be (more) violent?

A: Think about the ideas children learn in today's public schools. They are usually taught, at least implicitly, that there is no right or wrong. There is no good or bad. They learn that hatred—even when deserved, as in the case of violent criminals—is always a sin. That the superior students must be held back for the sake of the feelings of the inferior—as demonstrated by such public school policies as test norming. Or that selfless charity, rather than self-interested achievement and love of life, represents the essence of morality—as evidenced by community service requirements.

Increasingly, the intellectual and psychological atmosphere of most public schools is not so much geared towards love of life and training of the mind as it is towards duty, selfless service, and protecting the feelings of others at any price. How dreary and uninspiring, to say the least!

Under dictatorships, government schools are overtly used to train students to be good citizens—that is, slaves of the state. Our own public schools serve the same kind of purpose, only in a more subtle and hypocritical way. Students learn not so much how to achieve, reason and think for themselves, but rather how to be politically correct and serve others. The school agenda is set not so much by teachers and parents, but by officials in Washington, DC. As goes Washington, so go the schools. Principals and school officials are under pressure not so much to teach kids the basics, as to please the bureaucrats and politicians in Washington who finance and rule their schools.

Parents neglect or ignore their sacred responsibility to actively monitor their child's education; instead, they passively leave the job to the government, an entity to which they trust few other things. Socialized education, like socialized medicine or socialized anything is "free;" people tend to value things less when they are free, and take less responsibility for them. Parents (and teachers) who do try to take on the system are faced with an unaccountable bureaucracy, and have no way to effect change outside of writing a letter to their congressman.

Private schools are not immune to the effect of bad ideas. But they are relatively immune from the effect of political edicts. They are also much more compelled than public schools to be rational, effective, and get the job done. Kids attend private schools because parents carefully chose them—and feel good enough about the schools to write out tuition checks. If private schools fail, they go out of business; if public schools fail, they get more funding.

Fear of lawsuits and a pervasive, fawning attitude of "non-judgmentalism" make it difficult if not impossible to expel bad or lazy kids from public schools—at least, until they open fire or set off bombs. But by then it's too late.

Q: What do you tell the people who say: "But there are millions of kids who attend public schools and have been raised with the same teachings as the murderers in Colorado, while they live basically normal lives and commit no harm against others or themselves." If public schools are perhaps incubators for the breeding of violent kids, why aren't more kids murdering their schoolmates and others?

A: Schools—public schools or otherwise—cannot totally mold kids. Some kids are more intellectually honest than others. Some exercise their free will better than others. Some have better family influences which help them rise above the worst elements of the public schools. Some will squeeze the best education they can out of the public schools or, failing that, motivate themselves to learn elsewhere.

The problem is not that public schools are turning all kids into murderers. But more public school kids are turning to murder than ever before. Why? In part, because public schools increasingly tolerate and even actively spread the idea that there is no such thing as right or wrong, except what you *feel* inside.

Children, like adults, will always have free will. You can teach them right from wrong, and they are still free to do wrong if they choose. But it's much easier for kids to rationalize the doing of wrong—especially on the grotesque scale we saw in Littleton, CO—when they are taught that there really is *no such thing* as right or wrong in the first place.

Q: In America, fame and celebrity, coveted by many at any cost and often short-lived, falls on seemingly anyone today—from an intern who writes a best-selling book simply because she slept with our nation's president, to the depraved people on Jerry Springer's show who are willing to verbally and physically abuse one another to be "somebody," if only for a moment. To what extent do you see the mainstream media's focus on these violent acts in schools as inspiring kids to copy them at their own schools for instant fame? And what does this say about fame in America?

A: The mainstream media are not so much the creators of today's culture as they are the manifestation of it. Keep in mind that television networks find it hugely *profitable* to air "The Jerry Springer Show" (and similar horrors, such as the interview of Monica Lewinsky). Why is it profitable to air such garbage? That's the real question.

The popularity of such shows does not prove that most Americans have degenerated into Jerry Springer's guests, or to a Ms. Lewinsky. If they had, our country would be in a state of complete civil collapse unlike anything human history has ever seen. Economically and culturally, there is still much tremendously and awesomely good about our culture, so we can't be that far gone.

What we are witnessing today, and for some decades now, is the virtual death of hero-worship. Great majorities of people don't seem to want to look up to heroes anymore. Instead, they want to look down to their inferiors. The average person does not watch "The Jerry Springer Show" and feel, "Gee, those people are just like me." The average person watches "The Jerry Springer Show" and feels, "Gee, it could be worse. At least I'm not like those clowns."

Tragically, people no longer want to admire; they would rather sneer. Consequently, the morale and mental health of both the individual and society-as-a-whole has suffered gravely.

This cynical, negative psychology is the dominant mindset into which most of today's kids, like the rest of us, are inducted. Only the unusually savvy and independent-minded will fight it. This nihilistic mindset is enough to drive the most troubled elements to open fire on an entire school. Most kids don't go this far, of course; but many kids are closer to the psychological cliff than their parents want to believe. One reason for this is the dominant hatred of beauty, heroism, and success which permeates our culture right now.

"Copycatting" of violent crimes may be a real risk. But I don't know what can be done about it. The real problem is not the copycatting. Nor is the real problem a quest for fame. The fundamental problem is that there are a growing number of children who feel so hopeless and cynical about life that they want to end it all—their life *and* your life!

Q: What is the most important thing that Americans must do to dramatically reduce the violence in this nation, particularly violence committed by young people?

A: Short-term? Close down the U.S. Department of Education as soon as possible. Get the federal government completely *out* of education. Most of the irrational ideas in the public school system trickle down from the top, from those wrongheaded intellectuals and hapless policy wonks in Washington, DC.

At the community and local levels, public school teachers and administrators should be left relatively free to be more rational and common sense-oriented in running the schools. They need to be left as free as possible to operate schools the way private schools are—teaching kids how to read and think, and expelling those who refuse to learn.

Longer-term? Completely privatize the schools. Pass laws like some of those currently under discussion with Social Security. Allow parents to obtain tax-credits for schools of their choice, and to set up tax-free education savings accounts when their children are born (or even sooner). Allow parents to home-school, as record numbers are doing today. Phase public schools out of existence—or at least let them compete with private schools in a fair race. It won't be hard to predict the winner.

Stop making schools the responsibility of everyone-in-general (meaning: politicians). Instead, make them the responsibility of the people who run them and the parents who pay money to send their kids there—as with any other commodity in the marketplace.

As a family therapist, I constantly encounter parents with the "somebody should take care of it attitude" about their kids' education. Parents who would never in a million years drop their kid off at the doctor's and ask little or no questions about what the doctor is doing, take this very approach with their children's education. They treat the medical condition seriously, while almost ignoring the intellectual condition altogether.

More fundamentally, people need to make their priorities clear and *face reality*. It's not possible to have something for nothing. The "free" public school system—the system of socialized education—has failed, as it had to fail. When responsibility and freedom are taken away from people—especially for something so profoundly important as the training of the young mind—negative and even catastrophic results will follow. If the state of today's public schools is not sufficient proof for this assertion, then what will it take? How many more young minds must be quietly crushed—and young bodies overtly killed—before we accept the reality that socialized education has failed and that it's time to change?

Most of all, parents need to think honestly about the wrong ideas which schools—and even parents themselves—are sanctioning. Think about who *does* and *does not* benefit from the politically correct ideas that: there is no such thing as right and wrong; there is no objective reality; feelings are just as powerful or even more important than rationality and facts in comprehending the external world.

Certainly the rational, and the good, do not benefit from this moral relativism. Certainly the superior athletes and the superior students do not benefit; they have the most to lose when the idea of moral relativism takes over. They only stand to lose when the intellectual atmosphere is stifled so that the inferior won't have their feelings hurt. They only stand to lose if the bullies, the druggies, and the lazies who refuse to think and work are kept in school (by law) because "everyone has a right to an education."

The bullies and the life-haters and the little Nazis, on the other hand, only stand to gain from the spread of moral relativism. If they join irrational groups or act in bizarre ways, who are adults to stand in the way? If they want to build bombs in the school basement or their parents' garages, they can count on most parents and teachers to look the other way, saying to themselves: "Who am I to judge? Who am I to assert myself? Maybe he's just doing what's right for him." Goodness knows, the schools can't expel the druggies and the bullies and the little Nazis; their parents would sue!

How can these irrational trends and tendencies *not* lead to resentment and psychological conflict in many kids? How can they *not* lead to outright violence among the worst elements, sooner or later? To stop the violence, we need to end the public school system—and all the ideas which make it possible.

Q: Speaking now of violent crime in general, why is it that a significantly disproportionate number of violent criminals are males? And do you reject theories such as that it is because of their so-called "aggressor" hormone: testosterone, or, as certain feminists believe, that it is something deterministic in a male's being, or, that it is a displacement for the pressures he feels for his traditional responsibilities as a male?

A: Ultimately, why a person becomes violent is much more a consequence of the individual's values, beliefs, and philosophy of life than of the individual's gender. There is nothing in either a man's or a woman's gender which makes violent, criminal behavior inevitable; nor is there anything about a person's gender which makes violence impossible.

Generally speaking, men are taught from childhood to be aggressive, while women are encouraged to downplay or disregard anger and aggression. As a consequence, when a man becomes angry, it is more likely that he will overtly show his anger than a woman would.

Men are also less likely to engage in introspection about their feelings. Women are more likely to talk things out with family and friends, or even keep a diary to help them manage emotions such as anger. Since men often reject these outlets, they might turn to violence as a first and only means of expressing their anger.

Gender may be a factor in criminal behavior, but it is by no means a determining one. Furthermore, men can learn to express their anger in more rational, less aggressive ways while women can learn to express their anger in more overt, rational ways. Nothing in the nature of either males or females makes such change impossible.

Q: Finally, of all the cultural commentators that I have heard talk about this tragedy in Colorado, I don't believe I have heard one of them say that a fundamental cause of violence in America's youth comes from our public schools. The only such criticism comes invariably from religionists, who believe that so long as God and prayer are kept out of public schools, violence in them will continue. To most Americans, however, the connections between violence and public schools that you have made are totally alien to them. Why is this so?

A: For all its flaws and contradictions, American culture is still essentially reason-oriented. Being reason-oriented means having a high regard—indeed, even a reverence—for the pursuit of knowledge. Most Americans see education as a basic requirement of life, which in an advanced society it certainly is. Consequently, they view education as a moral and political right which should be accessible to everybody. It seems inconceivable to them that the government stop providing a guaranteed education to everyone—even if it's increasingly apparent that the "education" may be doing more harm than good.

If you argue for privatized schooling, what most people hear you saying, in effect, is: "Education is not that important. You don't have to have it; it's a luxury." Americans need help understanding that it's precisely *because* education is so important that the government needs to get out of it.

Government, by its nature, is an agent of force; this is why it is valuable and necessary for keeping the peace, prosecuting violent criminals, upholding legal contracts, and defeating foreign invaders. It does not belong in the classroom, however, because the mind does not think under force or compulsion or political correctness; schools cannot teach young minds effectively under such conditions.

Today's public school system has, to a very great extent, become a vehicle for flaky, irrational ideas which would perish if forced to survive on their own in the marketplace. Its one-size-fits-all structure is appropriate for the military or the police force, perhaps, but not for the complex and deeply personal process of learning.

About the interviewer:

Joseph Kellard is a newspaper editor, reporter and freelance writer living in New York. He also publishes a cultural-political e-mail newsletter. For more information, Mr. Kellard may be contacted by e-mail at jkaxiom3@aol.com.   ⊕

Chapter 12

How to Grow
Up Romantically

WHY LOVE IS, AND OUGHT TO BE, *SELFISH*

Contrary to the so-called wisdom of the ages, romantic love is not about sacrifice. True love and sacrifice are utter opposites. While occasional, short-term compromises are necessary in all forms of human relationship, a romantic partner never asks you to sacrifice yourself for him; he never wants you to do something that is a violation of your very self. He would rather let you go altogether than see you take an important step—such as having children, or giving up your ambition—just for him (or her).

Never confuse love with sacrifice. If you do, you will be subjected to the same disillusionment and despair that has plagued most marriages and other love relationships throughout all of human history. Today's high divorce rate is merely the climax of the vicious and false view that love is sacrifice.

It need not be this way.

David Seabury, a clinical psychologist, eloquently illustrated this point in his book, *The Art of Selfishness*.[9] "Never marry because someone loves you," writes Seabury. "It is not an adequate reason, and sometimes a bad one. If he is possessive and jealous, he doesn't love you. He only wants you. He needs to own you to inflate his ego. Having you as a slave gives him power. If you satisfy his greed, you'll regret it all your days. Possessiveness and jealousy are signs of predatory animality, hangovers from the cave."

All too often individuals mistakenly label such "greed" and possessiveness as *selfishness*. Precisely the opposite is true. Individuals with self-respect and self-esteem do not want to possess you. They want to share the experience of life with you, side by side, as psychological and intellectual companions. Your lover will lose respect for you if he sees you can be owned like a dog or a cat or an object.

Seabury continues: "Marry only when the other person seems lovely to you. Marry when you love, not when you would sacrifice for him, or wish to possess him. When those twin evils, self-denial and possessiveness, enter a human relation, hell comes with them, and love flies out of the door. If you married on the basis of self-sacrifice, you would consistently pick out the poorest character on earth to wed, for that would be the greatest denial. The laws of love are, in fact, one of the proofs of the idiocy of self-denial as a way of life. To relegate your intuitive and primary desires to the background makes marriage into prostitution. To let anything but the reality and integrity of your love lead you into marriage is sheer crime.

"Never step into wedlock to please another person. You defile love if you do, and if your marriage doesn't then end in divorce, it should. The true, deep drive of the mate impulse will rise someday, somewhere, to make a compromised relationship into an agony. Never let the fate of anyone else stand in the way of love, or you will come secretly to hate and destroy the person for whom you sacrificed your chance for romantic happiness. Let anyone, be it father or mother, son or daughter, and—yes—husband or wife, share with you the consequences of the coming of love into your life. Go with your love and to your love. But don't go halfheartedly, waiting until you or life are ready. Just don't start anything if you can't see it through."

None of this is to imply that love is only based on feeling. Remember: Just don't start anything if you can't see it through. Romantic love, while selfish, is also an all-or-nothing proposition. Those who ignore this fact (as most have) do so at their own peril. One must understand and *think* carefully about the reasons for loving an individual, in the realm of romantic love more than anywhere else. All too often, poets and philosophers have relied on platitudes about sacrifice and selflessness—so-called "virtues"—as an excuse for not thinking carefully about why one wants to enter a particular romantic relationship. "Love knows no reason," the poets and philosophers have wailed for centuries. Love had *better* know reason, if it is to survive and flourish. In its perfect form, romantic love is the fusion of unyielding reason and unbridled passion.

Again, I quote David Seabury: "There is one basic rule in love: 'Be yourself, always.' Start by being so, it's your only protection. Do nothing to win a man or woman that is contrary to yourself, for you'll only win trouble if you do. She, or he, who doesn't like you as you really are, will come to hate you secretly when the facts are discovered.

"Never become an appendage to a marriage partner. Keep your native hungers, your intellectual values. Never let a man put you in the home and keep you there, or a woman tie you to the home as one chains Fido to his kennel. You belong to life first, to your partner only insofar as he or she doesn't try to possess you.

"Most important of all, never marry a person who can't remain a sweetheart, and with whom you wouldn't want to be, even if you didn't have the protection of marriage. There is always the danger that a man will become a husband at the expense of being a man. If he loses identity in this relationship, he will in the end lose the relation. If he becomes submerged in quasi-companionship, acting the dutiful slave because a woman dumps her problems on him, and society shoves him into the hopeless position of the burden-bearer, he'll end by being an unwanted echo." (I would only add that in today's world, where both men and women vigorously pursue careers, this risk is shared equally.)

To a very great extent, the future of the human race depends upon the ability of individuals to form satisfying, happy and long-term romantic relationships. There are no "family values" without solid, authentic love relationships to nurture them. Do not be fooled into thinking that a return to the "good old days" will solve our problems. It is true that there are more divorces and unstable relationships today than ever before. But this simply means that in the past individuals kept their miserable feelings to themselves and sacrificed even more than they do today.

The only solution starts with your own, individual life. Abandon the view that sacrifice is the root of all good. Sacrifice and selflessness—especially in romantic relationships—is in fact the root of all that is miserable in the lives of so many.

HOW SELF-SACRIFICE
DESTROYS ROMANTIC HAPPINESS

Many marital problems are caused by the idea that good spouses sacrifice for one another. When one romantic partner says to another, "You're selfish," he or she may really be saying, "You don't sacrifice enough for me." A truly healthy spouse does not want a selfless, sacrificing partner. She cannot love someone who does not derive self-ish joy from being with her. She understands that genuine, voluntary love and self-less duty are a contradiction in terms.

Remember the scene in the movie *Titanic* where Rose jumped off the lifeboat to stay on board the sinking ship with her lover, Jack? Notice that Jack did not want Rose to sacrifice her life for him. On the contrary, he even lied that another lifeboat was waiting for him so she would go ahead and save herself. As her lifeboat descend-ed from the deck and she looked back up at her lover, Rose *voluntarily* decided that she wanted to stay on the doomed ship with him after all. When they reunited in an embrace, Jack did not praise Rose for her "sacrifice." He understood that nothing like guilt or charity or "community service" motivated her decision. He was clearly over-joyed that she valued him enough to stay with him. By staying with Jack to the end, Rose made the ultimate *selfish* decision. Romantic love (and romantic theater) does not get any better than this.

Integrity and honesty represent the two most important requirements of any romantic relationship. Self-sacrifice makes these virtues impossible. If a partner con-stantly worries about pleasing his spouse, even at the expense of himself, then how can he possibly keep his word over the long run? If he promises his partner the moon, how can he ever deliver? If he loses sight of the fact that a rational commitment should benefit both partners, and be a two-way street, how can either one remain happy in the long run?

The conventional, traditional ethic of self-sacrifice is perhaps harder on a marital relationship than any other single area of life. Nearly everyone enters a romantic partnership with some form of expectations, either conscious or subconscious. If these expectations are based upon the widely-held idea that good and loving people sacrifice for one another, chances are excellent the couple will end up in a therapist's office or a divorce court unless they challenge this mistaken idea. Self-sacrifice, by destroying the individual's sense of self, ends all possibility of romantic happiness.

The antidote to self-sacrifice is a philosophy of mutual self-respect and mutual self-interest. Each partner respects himself enough to treat his spouse with honesty and esteem, provided the esteem is earned. Neither one ever makes a promise he is not prepared and willing to keep. Neither one ever hides the truth from the other on the assumption that, "I don't want to hurt his feelings." Honesty, although sometimes painful in the short run, is the only thing that works in the long run.

Instead of always hurting the one he loves, he treats his partner with respect and honesty. After all, if his spouse is the most important person in his life, does it not serve his own self-interest to treat her with the respect she has earned? And if his spouse has not earned any respect, then why is he still with her?

Love based upon respect is also conditional. You cannot love your spouse if he becomes a drug addict, if she lies to you, if he consistently ignores you, or if she does not keep her word. Rational relationships represent a form of spiritual contract, in which each partner gains, emotionally, from the character, talents and virtues of the other partner. Only the irrational idea that selfless, unconditional love is the ideal could lead people to tolerate deceit and disrespect in the name of "preserving the marriage" or "keeping the family together."

Unconditional love is not the ideal form of romantic union, no matter how many self-help books, popular songs or religious leaders say otherwise. The best proof for this assertion lies in the number of unhappy relationships based on such a premise.

Selflessness in relationships leads to the very opposite of its intention. Instead of benevolence and compassion, it breeds resentment, despair and even hatred. Because continuous self-sacrifice (sometimes called "co-dependence") places one at war with reality and human nature, it leads the sacrificer to resent his "loved" ones and possibly turn them into victims. The next time you read in the newspaper about a man who murders his wife, his children, and then himself, consider it an illustration of the "ideal" of self-sacrifice taken to its ultimate, consistent conclusion. Millions of others suffer the consequences of the same philosophy, on a smaller scale, each and every day of their unhappy lives

It is impossible to respect or love someone who always sacrifices for you in a fawning, Pollyana-like manner. It is also impossible to truly love another without fundamental respect for yourself. In earlier eras, people kept their misery to themselves and stayed in loveless marriages for decades, often with the help of secret extramarital affairs. Today, couples openly divorce when they can no longer stand the psychological stench of mutual self-sacrifice, dishonesty, and disrespect. Fundamentally, the root problem in both eras is the same: an orgy of self-sacrifice and selflessness.

In order to find true romantic happiness, one must first discover its causes: self-respect, integrity, and rationality.

TEN RULES FOR RATIONAL COMMUNICATION

1. Do not interrupt. Allow your partner to finish what he is saying. When there is a pause, politely ask, "Are you finished?"

2. *Actively* listen. In other words, think about what she is saying. Look for evidence of honest misunderstandings. They are almost always present. Misunderstandings, rather than fundamental differences, are the root cause of most marital quarrels.

3. Do not try to formulate your answer while he is talking. When it is your turn to speak, pause and carefully formulate your answer before stating it. Don't rush things.

4.   Allow time-outs. If you are too emotional to continue, take a five- or ten- or thirty-minute time-out. Take responsibility for re-initiating the discussion at the end of the time-out. Although time-outs can be frustrating, it is more frustrating to try to carry on a conversation when one or both parties are too emotional to think clearly and logically.

5.   Be very careful to avoid saying things you do not mean. Hateful, hurtful statements, made in the heat of emotion, do irreparable damage. Words do have consequences.

6.   Try to remind yourself that you are an adult, and that you are no longer a helpless child at the mercy of adults. You are in this relationship by choice. Nobody is forcing you to be here, and you owe it to *yourself*, more than anyone, to resolve this conflict rationally so that you can be happy with your spouse.

7.   Try to avoid generalized comments such as, "You *always* accuse me..." or "You *never* show me you love me..." Use generalized statements only if you know for a fact they are true. In the heat of discussion, you might *feel* they are true, but feelings and facts are not necessarily the same thing.

8.   Avoid defensiveness. Don't feel you have to defend yourself against enemy attacks, with the person you supposedly love the most in the world as your mortal enemy. Instead, calmly and politely ask for the evidence that you never show that you care, or the evidence that you are not truthful, or the evidence that you do not keep your promises. You do not have to accept assertions without proof, even from your spouse.

9.   If your partner does provide convincing evidence for a criticism of you, act like a grown-up and accept responsibility for the fact you made a mistake. Adherence to the facts of reality is a virtue, and will help your spouse respect you more and improve your own self-esteem. Faking reality, denying that something is true even though you know it is true, represents the greatest sin you can commit against yourself or your spouse. The damage is permanent.

10. Follow this absolute rule: feelings and facts are not necessarily the same thing. You have no right to assert your feelings as truth without valid, logical proof to back them up. Neither does your spouse. If either partner fails to follow this rule as an absolute, marital happiness will never be possible.

IS IT INFATUATION . . . OR LOVE?

To love is to value. It is impossible to divorce the concept of love from the concept of value, and then pretend to call it "romantic love."

Love without reference to reason is no less neurotic than any other emotion detached from reality. Romantic love, if it is to be both long-term and fulfilling, must be based upon known qualities about the individual's character. In other words, you must be able to see clearly the reasons why you love your partner, and why the feelings you are having are not solely ones of infatuation.

Infatuation

What is infatuation? According to psychiatrist Aaron Beck, "The perspective of infatuated lovers is an idealization, or positive framing, analogous to the negative framing which occurs when love turns to aversion. The positive frame produces an idealized image of the lover that highlights the desirable features and shades the undesirable ones."[10]

Infatuation is a form of "selective focus" made possible by an individual's limited (and in some ways superficial) knowledge of the romantic interest.

Despite the fact that infatuation—by itself—is not a sufficient basis for a long-term romantic relationship, it does not mean that such a relationship cannot eventually develop from infatuation. As proof of this, consider the many long-lasting relationships (including possibly your own) which began as intense infatuations. According to Dr. Beck, "Infatuation serves a crucial role: it forges a powerful bond that spurs a couple to commit themselves to a relationship . . . The gratification a couple experiences by being together, sharing pleasures and problems, offers a strong incentive for forming such a partnership and perpetuating these pleasures."[11]

It is important to stress that infatuation is not the same as psychological denial. Denial, in the romantic context, would involve a refusal on the individual's part to consider negative traits in his romantic partner once they became known to him. Infatuation, on the other hand, involves a subconscious tendency to "downplay" the negative traits one suspects to exist in the partner, and to "overplay" the positive traits.

Infatuation occurs in the context of not yet knowing the character of one's partner. In the psychologically healthy individual, infatuation does not involve a refusal to know one's partner, but rather an honest desire to see the best in someone. Denial, on the other hand, would have to occur in the context of knowing with certainty that one's partner has various character traits (dishonesty, maliciousness, etc.) and refusing to pay attention to them.

Infatuation is the hope of a romantic relationship; true romantic love represents the *actualization* of such a hope. Infatuation becomes unhealthy only if the individual loses perspective and begins to evade or deny relevant facts about his partner once they become known to him.

Infatuation versus Romantic Love

The problem of distinguishing between an infatuation and genuine romantic love can be especially difficult. Ayn Rand had some fascinating insights on this issue: "It is with a person's sense of life that one falls in love—with that essential sum, that fundamental stand or way of facing existence, which is the essence of a personality . . . It is one's own sense of life that acts as the selector, and responds to what it recognizes as one's own basic values in the person of another."[12]

But Rand goes on to point out that a sense of life is by no means a sufficient condition for the highest form of romantic love. "Many errors and tragic disillusionments are possible in this process of emotional recognition, since a sense of life, by itself, is not a reliable cognitive guide . . . Love is *the expression of philosophy*—of a subconscious philosophical sum—and, perhaps, no other aspect of human existence needs the *conscious* power of philosophy quite so desperately. When that power is called upon to verify and support an emotional appraisal, when love is a conscious integration of reason and emotion, of mind and values, then—and only then—it is the greatest reward of man's life."[13]

This last statement appears consistent with my idea that infatuation is not a sufficient condition for a genuine romantic relationship. In Rand's terms, infatuation might be viewed as one's attraction to another individual's sense of life—as positive, goal-directed, or benevolent, for example. But it is only through a *conscious* process of character judgment that one can complete the romantic "circle." In other words, one must be willing to consciously integrate the reasons for loving one's partner into one's subconscious, automatized response. If the two are known to conflict, the issue cannot be ignored without potential long-term consequences.

The Nature of True Romantic Love

True romantic love is possible only when each partner has identified his or her personal values and achieved a sense of self-esteem. Self-esteem requires an understanding—at least implicitly—that love requires rationality.

There are many horrible clichés which contribute to the prevalent idea that love and reason are opposites. "Feelings know no reason" and "All you need is love" are two particularly destructive examples. When taken seriously, or held subconsciously, such ideas can lead to one of the most tragic false alternatives of all: the notion that romanticism and reality are incompatible. Therapy offices (and television talk shows) are littered with individuals who have concluded that romantic love cannot be reconciled with the realities of day-to-day living. Such persons believe that if they are to experience romantic love, they must either sacrifice friendship and intimacy, on the one hand, or passion and excitement, on the other.

To individuals who hold such false alternatives, one of three options are available to them in the area of romantic love: (1) a life of isolation and celibacy; (2) a life of cynical promiscuity and superficiality; or, (3) a life of disillusionment and despair, usually in the context of marriage, accompanied by a conviction that one has "settled" and that romance is impossible. Traditionalists bemoan the movement away from celibacy and disillusionment toward promiscuity, while modernists advocate promiscuity as the only logical alternative to what preceded it. Seldom do we hear the case made for the *integration* of romantic love and reason.

Attempting to help my clients see that there is an alternative to the dreadful vision of "romance" portrayed on many television shows and in too many movies is perhaps the hardest task I face as a psychotherapist. Why? Because in order to grasp the nature of romantic love—as an integration of conscious character judgment and subconscious sense of life—requires that one first accept that there are objective standards by which a potential romantic partner can be judged. The combined forces of mysticism and militant subjectivism which dominate today's culture have all but succeeded in destroying the hope for romance many individuals might otherwise hold.

Nevertheless, I am happy to report some success in our romance-starved culture. I will provide two case examples. I recently worked with a man who had been frustrated by a series of intense but short-lived romantic relationships. For six months, I consistently challenged his implicit and explicit premises that sexual passion and love are necessarily divorced. In time, he began to acknowledge that he had chosen attractive partners who "looked good" but did not share his basic value system. Once he began to see how this had hurt himself over the long run, it became much easier for him to reject superficiality and instead "hold out" for a partner who was both physically attractive to him and shared some of his basic values and goals. In fact, the prospect of a sexual encounter—while delayed until he met the appropriate individual—became much more exciting to him.

In another case, I saw an eighteen-year-old male who was literally obsessed with his very troubled girlfriend of four years. Despite her often cruel and deceptive behavior towards him, he felt somehow "responsible" for her well-being and virtually crazed by the idea that she might someday have sexual intercourse with another man. At one point I asked him, "Does she share your basic value system?" He thought carefully and said, "No. She doesn't. That's the problem, isn't it?" Years later, I learned that he broke off with the girlfriend and developed a much better, long-term relationship with somebody new.

Conclusion

Romantic love is essentially conditional and value-oriented. One task of psychology is to help individuals distinguish between infatuation and genuine romantic love. A secondary and related goal of psychologists should be to help individuals challenge their subconscious assumptions that love and reason are incompatible. Only a philosophy which challenges the ancient idea that love is divorced from reason can provide the basis for a proper psychotherapeutic approach.   ⏀

9. David Seabury, *The Art of Selfishness* (New York: Pocket Books, 1937, 1964).
10. Aaron Beck, *Love Is Never Enough* (New York: Harper Perennial, 1988), p. 42.
11. *Ibid.*, p. 41.
12. Ayn Rand, "Philosophy and Sense of Life," *The Romantic Manifesto* (New York: New American Library, 1969), pp. 25-33.
13. *Ibid.*

Chapter 13

Rational Love

TAKING A CHANCE ON LOVE—
HOW TO CHOOSE A PARTNER

Some claim that romance knows no reason. They believe that to analyze a relationship is to ruin it. "Romance is a feeling," they insist. "You either feel it, or you don't." Romantic emotions, according to this theory, have no causes. They just happen mystically, or perhaps fatalistically.

Contrary to this traditional view, romantic love does, in fact, know reason. You love the partner of your choice for many reasons. The reasons may be conscious or subconscious, part of your awareness or outside of your awareness. Your choice of partner—valid or invalid, healthy or unhealthy, or a mixture of the two—represents a complex totality of many evaluations about physical beauty, personal compatibility, and fundamental values. Your perception of your partner with respect to each of these areas determines the type and the degree of your emotional response. Romantic love is never an accident; it is never causeless.

To ensure a happier and healthier relationship, you need to make these subconscious evaluations conscious. You need to ask yourself, and find answers to, the following types of questions:

"What, specifically, makes a romantic relationship work? What principles or qualities are essential to a happy romance?"

"By what standards should I evaluate my current relationship? Or a past relationship that did not work out?"

If you do not evaluate your relationships consciously, then you are leaving the course of your romantic life to chance. Leaving love to chance is, in fact, what most people do; and it is the reason why so many people are unhappy with their spouses.

Are you willing to do the work to achieve romantic happiness? Are you willing to think, and not rely only on your feelings? Are you willing to question ideas you were taught, when those ideas conflict with logic and facts? In short, do you want to be happy? If so, then consider the degree to which each of the following characteristics exist in your relationships, past or present.

Honesty. Honesty represents the most fundamental essential of a happy, healthy romance. People want honesty from their partner for obvious reasons. A liar is hard enough to tolerate in a friendship or a business relationship; in a romantic relationship, dishonesty can be emotionally devastating.

Just imagine how difficult a romantic relationship with a dishonest person has to be. How do you know he really loves you, if his words do not matter? How do you know she remains faithful to you, if she subverts the truth to her wishes? How do you know he really intends to keep the promises he makes to you?

Honesty is the foundation of any romantic relationship. You allow yourself to be vulnerable in your romantic relationship as in no other area of your life. Allowing yourself to fall in love and to make a serious, long-term commitment involves an emotional down-payment of enormous importance. Before making that down-payment, you ought to at least be certain your partner is honest.

Psychological Health. "Honesty" actually means more than simply telling the truth. Genuine honesty means adhering to reality, focusing both on the facts of external reality and the thoughts, feelings, and motivations of your internal consciousness. Psychologically, honesty presupposes honesty with yourself. So do not merely evaluate whether your partner tells the truth. Consider, as well, the following types of questions.

Is your partner introspective? That is, does he spend time identifying his feelings and motives, at least to himself? Or is he emotionally repressed, and evasive? Does he think about his feelings, and rationally evaluate them? Or does he blindly act on impulse or whim, rarely taking the time to analyze his feelings first?

My experience as a therapist shows that dishonesty towards one's partner starts with dishonesty towards oneself. Two types of individuals are especially likely to be dishonest in relationships: the emotionally repressed type, and the impulsive type.

Emotionally repressed personalities do not acknowledge their feelings and motives, even to themselves; consequently, they are more prone to rationalizations and other games of self-deception. Because they do not identify their anger towards a friend, they treat the friend badly or rudely without knowing why. Because they do not identify their fears about getting married, they end up calling off the marriage, or prematurely pushing themselves into having a child, without knowing why. Sometimes they are "driven" by inappropriate or irrational motives. They are unwilling to make themselves aware of these motives and correct them because of their resistance to introspection. Ironically, people who do not pay attention to their feelings and motives end up being controlled by them.

Impulsive personalities, on the other hand, are aware of their feelings and motives but tend to act on them without analyzing them. They are subjective about their feelings, which means they treat their feelings as equivalent to rational, objective facts and sometimes demand that you do the same. If they feel angry, they will act on it before trying to figure out why. If they feel like making a career change, they quit their job before investigating the cost and other consequences of the decision. If they feel like breaking up, they act on the feeling, perhaps later regretting and reversing the decision. They have no problem with acknowledging and experiencing feelings, but they resist and resent the need to rationally analyze them.

Repressives and impulsives represent two sides of the same unhealthy psychological coin. Each tries to bypass the responsibility of identifying and analyzing his emotions: one through denying them, the other by acting blindly on them. Consequently, each ends up harming himself and those around him.

Try to avoid these personality types in your romantic relationships. If your partner is clearly and consistently either repressive or impulsive, and refuses to work on changing it, then you ought to seriously consider ending the relationship. If your partner is somewhat healthy, but merely has repressive or impulsive tendencies (as many people do), then encourage him to identify and work on them, with the help of a professional therapist if necessary.

Integrity and Consistency. People truly worthy of your respect mean what they say and make every effort to fulfill their promises and intentions. In short, they practice integrity: the virtue of consistency between thought and action.

If they agree to meet you at 9:00, they make every effort to arrive at 9:00. If they do arrive significantly late, they are sincerely sorry, apologize, and attempt to correct the problem in the future rather than just ignore it. If they freely make a commitment to see you on a certain day, or to help you with a particular task, they remember to do so. They remember not only because they respect you, but also because they respect themselves. They like to follow through on their agreements and promises because they recognize the psychological rewards of consistency between thought and action.

Such respect towards others flows from a person's respect for himself. Without respect for himself, there is no chance he will treat you well. How can he possibly show consideration for you if he has not first learned to expect this for himself? In looking for a romantic partner you should not only ask, "Does he respect me?" You should also be asking, "Does he have self-esteem, and respect himself?" It is in your own best interest that he does.

People with integrity do not make promises, especially serious ones, that they are unprepared to keep. They do not say they want to have children, just to convince you to get married, and then flip-flop when you later propose having a child. They do not freely and happily agree to a sexually monogamous relationship, and later develop a secret extramarital affair on the side. They do not say deliberately hurtful, vicious things to you and then afterwards use the excuse, "Well I didn't mean to hurt you this badly." Instead, they take responsibility for their actions.

Fairness. Healthy partners expect no less or no more from you than what they expect of themselves. They do not subscribe to double standards. If they are supposed to be on time, so are you. If they are supposed to keep their promises, so are you. If good intentions do not excuse their behaviors, neither do good intentions excuse your behaviors. The happiest relationships are ones where each partner is self-respectful and expects—indeed, wants—his or her partner to be the same.

A healthy partner is not a self-sacrificer. Self-sacrificers expect virtue of themselves, but not of others. They are martyrs by choice, who put up with unfairness, inconsistency, and dishonesty even though they themselves strive to be fair and honest with their partner. They tolerate broken promises, alcohol or drug-related binges, and even extramarital affairs because they do not believe they deserve simple fairness.

A healthy partner is also not an other-sacrificer. Other-sacrificers expect virtue from others, but not of themselves. Other-sacrificers show little regard for the rights of their partners and high regard for the rights of themselves. Instead of cherishing their partner, they insult and abuse their partner, not because of "too much" self-esteem but because of too little. The romantic partner—potentially one's greatest ally—becomes one's greatest enemy.

In a truly healthy relationship, neither partner sacrifices himself to the other; neither one wants his partner to sacrifice, either. Each understands that sacrifice and double standards of any kind are totally at odds with a love relationship. The healthy person respects his own right to happiness, but also respects—in fact, passionately wants—happiness for his partner as well. He cherishes his partner as one of the most, if not *the* most, important value in his life.

Commitment. If you yearn for something more than a brief fling, or an on-again/off-again relationship, then you need a romantic partner who is both able and willing to commit. Before making serious romantic commitments, many people need to "shop around" the romantic marketplace for a period of time. Some will need as little as a few months or a year; others will need decades. Most fall somewhere in-between.

Before allowing yourself to emotionally and romantically attach to another person, make sure this person shares your definition of commitment and is as ready for a serious relationship as you are. Make sure you talk with him about your expectations for the relationship such as dating others, the amount and quality of time together, buying a house or having a child, or staying together to old age, to name only a few examples. Even if you are a perfect match in other respects, you cannot be involved romantically if you seriously disagree about commitment issues. You will avoid much emotional pain if you express your expectations objectively and concretely from the beginning.

Compatibility. Compatibility is no less essential than honesty, self-respect, and integrity. You may, for example, meet a thoroughly honest, self-respecting, and fair person with whom you have little or nothing in common. Yet in order to romantically love this person for a long time, you must also be able to like him. You ought to feel that he or she is someone with whom you would like to be friends even if there were no sexual-romantic attraction. The tired Hollywood vision of couples who despise each other but have great sex represents neither the ideal nor reality: at least not if your goal is a serious, long-term relationship.

Common interests include the way you spend your free time, the types of books and movies you like, where you prefer to take vacations, the types of social activities you enjoy, and the kinds of friends you choose. Romantic partners need not share absolutely identical interests. Oftentimes one partner develops a new interest because of the other partner's involvement in an activity. Too much in common may become boring and unchallenging; at the same time, too little overlap in common interests can lead to endless conflicts and miserable self-sacrifice on either or both sides.

Intellectual compatibility is also important. Whether your partner has the same amount of knowledge as you in a particular area is optional; your partner's general thirst for knowledge and personal fulfillment, however, must be on a level close to yours. You ought to be able to have intellectual discussions with him or her on a level that challenges and excites you. You ought to see your partner as in your intellectual "ball park." Otherwise, while the relationship may be fulfilling sexually (for a time), you won't have much to discuss after the sex is over.

Admiration. Is your partner utilizing his talents and abilities to the greatest extent possible? Is he pursuing a career, or some set of long-range goals, with vigor and satisfaction? Or is he lazy, procrastinating, and immobilized for reasons potentially under his control?

Is she self-directed, self-motivated, and capable of self-discipline? Or does she live by the "seat of her pants," moment-by-moment, on unconsidered whims, urges, or ideas she'll never seek to bring to realization? Is her philosophy of life simply based on dreaming, or on the actualization of her dreams?

The answers to these questions will determine the level of admiration you have for your partner—including whether you will feel any admiration at all. Most people do not realize how important mutual admiration is to a romantic relationship. They tend to assume that so long as the sex is good, or so long as romantic, caring feelings linger, all will be well. During the initial infatuation phase of a relationship, it can in fact be easy to overlook the need to admire your partner. But the issue will inevitably reassert itself down the road. You ignore it at your own peril.

Admiration is necessary for both men and women. A man needs to admire a woman no less than a woman needs to admire a man. Whether engaged in a formal career or in the raising of a child, for example, a woman can earn the respect of her partner so long as she seeks to do an excellent job. Increasingly, a man may choose to raise a child because it is easier for him, at a particular point in time, to interrupt his career than it is for his wife. Many parents of both genders, of course, engage in child-rearing and career-seeking at the same time. It is possible to actualize the essential qualities of long-range thinking and excellence-seeking in many different contexts, including child-rearing and other activities that do not pay a salary.

Admiration for your partner, based upon his or her objective accomplishments, helps sustain romantic feelings throughout the life of a long-term relationship. My experience has shown that it often represents the difference between a lasting relationship and a short-lived one.

Physical "chemistry." Your partner ought to be physically attractive to you. Romantic love and sex, after all, represent an integration of the physical and the mental aspects of human existence. Just as "romance" without reference to the intellectual and moral qualities of your partner would be superficial and shallow, "romance" without reference to the physical and external qualities of your partner would be sterile and Puritanical. Neither approach works, and neither represents the ideal. If long-term happiness is your goal, the physical and mental realms should be integrated, not separated.

When searching for a romantic partner, evaluate him or her physically as well as intellectually and morally. Do so shamelessly, albeit privately. Is she your "type" physically? Does he dress and groom himself appropriately, in a style you like? Is she confident in her demeanor, without seeming pretentious or phony? Is this somebody with whom you can imagine yourself having sex? Allow yourself to focus on these factors guiltlessly. Without the physical and the sexual, you have only a friendship—not a romantic relationship.

Compassion. Compassion refers to an overall state of empathy, warmth, and caring for the other partner. It involves a willingness to listen, support, and "be there" for the other person in times of crisis and in times of ordinary, everyday stress.

Contrary to popular myth, compassion is not selfless. If you really love, respect, admire, and are compatible with your partner, then you logically want to be nice to him, you want to be supportive, and you want him to be no less happy than you are. Because you value your partner so highly, perhaps above all else, the desire to be compassionate stems from a purely selfish need to protect and nurture the one you love. If you do not love your partner this highly, and compassion does in fact represent a sacrifice or a duty for you, then why are you together in the first place? What business do you have calling it a romantic relationship, if the object of your romance does not bring you enormous satisfaction? My experience as a psychologist has shown that the failure to resolve such a contradiction results in the ruin of countless relationships.

Healthy romantic love is not sacrificial. If you do not feel compassionate towards your partner, perhaps you are not getting enough out of the relationship. Perhaps you need to sort out your expectations and feelings and decide if they are indeed realistic, at least for this particular relationship. Or perhaps you need to talk with your partner about what you believe is not working in the relationship, and assess if he is willing to make some necessary changes along with you.

Compassion represents the logical consequence of mutual respect, honesty, and all the other essentials of a good relationship. Without the presence of these essentials, compassion will not be possible. If you believe your relationship lacks compassion, check first to make sure the other essentials are present. Compassion is an effect, not a cause; it is the result of each partner's observation and conviction that the other represents (to him or her) the most important and valuable person on earth.

Try not to be overwhelmed by all the factors needed to make your relationship a happy one. If you live your life consciously, seeking to apply these standards of romantic happiness to each new situation you encounter, then you are far less likely to make mistakes than if you go only on your feelings, as most people do. By bringing thought and reason into the romantic realm, you can experience romantic success just as you may have already experienced career or financial success. You need not become overwhelmed. On the contrary, for a little extra effort you may at last find peace in one of the most fulfilling areas of human life.

MRS. P.—THE CASE OF UNCONDITIONAL LOVE

Mrs. P. presents for psychotherapy because of general dissatisfaction with her life. In her first session with the therapist, she acknowledges not knowing what she wants to change. "I just know I need help," she says. She has been married for seven years. It is her second marriage. Her previous husband was an irresponsible, physically abusive alcoholic. She had three children with him, and several years into the marriage she left him. She struggled to raise her children on her own. She pursued sexual relationships with a number of physically attractive but psychologically disturbed young men who used drugs and introduced her to life in the "fast lane". She eventually remarried (to Mr. P.) when her children were teenagers.

On the surface, her new husband was just the opposite of her first. He was a responsible accountant. He was not particularly ambitious, but he could be relied upon and was never physically violent. Their joint income allowed Mrs. P. and her children to live in a comfortable middle-class environment for the first time in their lives. They became "yuppies".

For the first few years, the marriage was satisfactory for Mrs. P. As time passed, however, she began to see a darker side to her new husband. He was certainly not physically abusive like her first husband. But he did drink a lot on the weekends. While he never appeared intoxicated, he tended to become depressed and irritable when he stopped drinking. He hated to spend money, and hated to see her spend money. Every purchase—from groceries to house furniture—involved an argument; sometimes she won, sometimes he won. Despite such conflicts, she thought to herself: "He's good for me. Without him, I would be too reckless and free-wheeling."

Over time, however, this rationalization turned to resentment. Sometimes she looked at her husband and despised him. He was a highly intelligent man with great potential, but he stayed "frozen" in both his career and his intellectual development. At the age of thirty-five, Mr. P. felt he had come as far as he needed to go. "I'm stopping right here," he beamed as the family moved into a new house. "I have no further to go." This sense of life clashed sharply with Mrs. P.'s belief that one should continually grow and learn. In certain brief moments, she almost grasped the magnitude of this difference in values. But she would talk herself out of it in the following way: "Sometimes he hates life. Yet if I want a good man, I must put up with this. If I want a man who loves life, I'll have to go back to the violent and reckless men I used to date."

Before seeking the help of a therapist, Mrs. P. attempted to keep herself busy so as to avoid thinking about the issue. For a time, this seemed to work. She found a challenging job and concentrated on redecorating the house. Her husband resented any attempt on her part to spend money and preferred that they stay home every weekend instead of going to restaurants, movies, and plays, etc. Mrs. P. became gradually more disgusted with her husband. Consequently, their sex life virtually disappeared. Mr. P. responded with more anger and drinking. In addition to drinking all weekend, he began to drink himself to sleep most evenings. He became more and more critical of his wife and began to lecture her in a stern, paternalistic manner about the need to conserve money. This pushed her even further away from him emotionally. She retreated into her friendships and her cats. She actively considered extramarital affairs.

Despite the marital problems, Mr. P. claims to love his wife. At the same time, he often wishes he were married to a woman whose goals and desires did not cost any money. He rationalizes this contradiction aside, however, by deciding that "a man's duty is to love his wife." It is only during heated arguments that he expresses his intense dislike of her values. For the most part, he tries to ignore this feeling.

In the therapy office, Mrs. P. says: "I am sick of my husband. He disgusts me in every way possible. I never thought that being with a good man could be like this. I tried relationships with fun-loving, irresponsible men, and they were disasters. Now this is turning out to be the same. All I can count on are my cats. My cats love me no matter what. They love me unconditionally. This is the kind of marriage I want."

Assessment:

Mrs. P.'s unhappiness stems from a fundamentally wrong premise about good and evil. In her eyes, her present husband—who is life-hating, but "responsible"—is moral and good; while her previous partners—who were abusive and reckless, but "life-loving"—were immoral. This is a false alternative, because both her present husband and her earlier partners are selfless individuals. In her first husband, a total lack of self-esteem led to a need to drink and control her behavior through physical violence. In her second husband, a total lack of self-esteem leads to a need to drink and control her behavior through paternalistic lecturing and a refusal to allow either of them to enjoy their earnings. In the context of a rational value system, neither man is a model of moral virtue.

Furthermore, Mrs. P. believes that she needs a romantic relationship based upon unconditional love. In fact, she already has one. Mr. P. has made it clear that he would rather have a wife who shares his sense of life. Yet he stays with her anyway, claiming to *love* her. Mrs. P. also recognizes their fundamental value differences, yet evades them in the subconscious hope, perhaps, that "love will conquer all." The truth of the matter, however, is that unconditional love cannot conquer anything. It can only lead to long-term disappointment and romantic ruin. Both Mr. and Mrs. P. fail to understand that romantic love is a profoundly selfish experience. Operating on the premise that love is selfless, Mrs. P. continues to wait for her unconditional acceptance of her husband—however obnoxious he might be—to "do its thing." It never happens.

Therapeutic Change

First, Mrs. P. must come to understand that she is already in an unconditional love relationship, and that this form of love is the problem rather than the solution. She needs to learn that love is by its very nature conditional and selfish. "Love is the expression of one's values, the greatest reward you can earn for the moral qualities you have achieved in your character and person, the emotional price paid by one man for the joy he receives from the virtues of another."[14]

None of this describes Mrs. P.'s marriage. She must first explicitly identify what her own values are, and determine whether or not they are healthy and achievable. Next, she must allow herself to look at her husband objectively. Where does he meet or fail to meet her rational, healthy standards? Is there evidence to suggest that he will not change? This process might be relatively brief or quite long, depending upon how deeply she holds her wrong convictions about love. In order to change these convictions through therapy, two conditions are critical: (1) She must respect and trust her therapist; and, (2) She must be motivated to accept reality as it is, even if she does not like all of the facts she discovers.

A related problem is, obviously, Mrs. P.'s false alternative between evil and "good" men. This false alternative rests upon an implicit assumption that selflessness is good. Instead of easily recognizing that her husband's pathological cheapness represents a selfless hatred of life, she instead sees it as a moral ideal which simply gets in the way of her having a good time. Unfortunately, she associates having a "good time" with the reckless men of her past who were also selfless and destructive. Mrs. P. must reject the false dichotomy she holds about good and evil, and replace it with an ethic of selfishness.

In theory, couples therapy could be helpful in this situation only if Mr. P. shares his wife's motivation to change the status quo (where necessary). If Mrs. P. agrees, her husband should be invited to one or several sessions so his motivation can be assessed. The therapist needs to be sure that Mrs. P. has told her husband how unhappy she is. If Mr. P. shows a sincere desire to make changes in his own thinking—and not merely expect his wife to do it—then the prognosis for the relationship is somewhat hopeful. If Mr. P. insists that "it's all her problem, not mine," then genuine, long-term progress is unlikely. The essential condition for successful therapeutic outcome is the ability of the participants to understand how their selfless assumptions are destroying their chance to be happy.

THE REAL MEANING OF LOVE AND FRIENDSHIP

Are you a giver or a taker? From childhood, most of us are told that we should be givers, not takers. Such an attitude presents us with a false, undesirable alternative.

In reality, the choice is not between being a giver or a taker. A third alternative exists. It's called *trading*.

Usually, we think of trading in terms of economic exchanges. Trading does, of course, apply to economics. People trade money for goods and services all of the time.

Yet trading does not only apply to the material, economic world. It also applies to the personal, psychological realm. Think about it. You become friends with a person because you like or admire certain things about him. Maybe you like his optimism, or his competence, or the fact that he's funny and entertaining. There are probably many reasons.

Presumably, you also offer the friend something in return. You may or may not know what the "something" is. Maybe he feels that he is too outgoing and he likes quieter people such as yourself. Maybe he's a closet comedian and he likes an audience. Maybe he likes your sincerity and integrity, and he worries that he does not possess these qualities sufficiently.

The same principle applies to a romantic or sexual relationship. We often hear that "opposites attract." This is true because of the trader principle. One member of a relationship is handy around the house while the other is not. One member of a relationship is more emotional, the other more intellectual. One member of a relationship is good at handling responsibility, the other is better at being spontaneous.

Consciously or subconsciously, people "find" each other to balance out what they feel are the missing pieces in their lives. Sometimes this balancing works out quite well, and sometimes it does not. Either way, a psychological trade of some kind is almost always present in a relationship.

Why Love Needs to Know Reason

Most of us are not very aware of the reasons we choose our friends or romantic partners. This does not make a whole lot of sense, if you think about it. We tend to apply thought and reason to the realm of money-making and career building, but not to the realm of friendship and marriage.

Most of us would never dream, for example, of accepting a job or buying a house without analyzing what we want, why we want it, what's the best deal in the market, and so forth. Yet in the realm of friendship and romance, we uncritically assume things like "love knows no reason" or "if it feels good, do it."

Then we wonder why so many of our friendships disappoint us or why so many of our relationships or marriages don't work out. If buying a house purely on the whim of the moment—without thought or reason—makes no sense, then why should choosing a friend or a spouse work this way?

A typical conversation I have with my psychotherapy clients illustrates this point very well:

Therapist: Why are you sad?

Client: I'm sad because my marriage didn't work out. I don't know why. I feel like a failure, and wish I at least knew why the marriage didn't work out.

Therapist: What disappointed you in your marriage? What did you hope would happen that didn't? What expectations were not met?

Client: I don't know. I never thought about expectations. I loved him at first, and then it just faded away. I don't know what I expected.

We have all been taught what this client apparently believes: "Love knows no reason. Love is only about emotion. It's silly and unromantic to analyze the reasons *why* you love somebody, or what you're expecting from the relationship." If you adopt this point-of-view-or, without realizing it, you uncritically accept it—then don't be surprised when you're eventually disappointed. Because love does, in fact, desperately need to become acquainted with reason.

Should thinking and reason be used to *replace* emotion and passion? Of course not! Nothing could be worse than a dry, dull romance devoid of emotion. The whole point of using reason is to make sure that you can guiltlessly enjoy your relationship with wild, emotional abandon.

Love as Trade

Once you accept that reason is a necessary part of romantic love and friendship, then it is easier to see romantic love as a form of psychological trade. You need to ask yourself, "What qualities do I have to offer that somebody else may want? What qualities am I looking for in a friend or a lover?" You need to ask and re-ask these questions over time, because your wants and desires will likely change as you grow, learn, and develop.

Psychological trade means evaluating your potential friend or partner: sensible, benevolent evaluation, not harsh and judgmental evaluation as many think of it. Make sure your evaluations and judgments conform to the facts, not merely your first feelings or prejudices.

If you know you are looking for somebody with a certain set of qualities, then you know how to evaluate a person once you meet him and become familiar with him. If you want someone of high character, then evaluate his character as you learn more about him. If you want someone with a sense of humor, check to see if he has a sense of humor—and if so, what kind. If you want someone with long-range goals as well as short-term ones, ask him about his dreams and aspirations.

You should also expect, and hope, that your potential friend or partner will do the same with you. If your partner does not think about what he wants, then he will tend to feel very passionate towards you in the beginning, but then back away for no apparent reason later on—an all too common experience.

Some people object to the idea of seeing love as trade because it's too "mercenary" or "selfish." It *is* selfish, of course, in the rational sense of taking care of one's own interests and desires and respecting the right of others to do the same. What's wrong with this? And what's the alternative? It's selfish, after all, to make sure you choose the house you want or the career you want. Why not be selfish and choose the kind of friend or spouse you want?

The only alternatives to viewing love as a trade are to either see love as selfless charity or to simply view love as a chemical, physical reaction. In earlier eras, the dominant "ideal" was to view love as selfless charity. Love should be about giving, not taking, we were taught. Consequently, love and marriage became associated with duty, sacrifice, and even misery.

Today the dominant trend is, quite understandably, to rebel against this repressive, hypocritical view. Divorce is now commonplace as people struggle to learn that love should not be about sacrifice and duty.

But many are finding that the modern approach to love and sex is no better. The modern idea is to go with our immediate impulses and urges without regard for reason and facts—often at our own expense and sometimes at the expense of others. "If it feels good, do it," is the closest we have to a guiding principle today. Of course, most people do not act on this "principle" consciously and consistently. Yet the extent to which there is any guiding principle at all, this one is it. It's quite pathetic.

What's the solution? Move away from *both* of these trends. Instead, move towards the idea that love is selfish and personal, but that love also needs the guidance of reason. Move towards the idea that love is a trade.

Should relationships involve give-and-take? Of course. But the whole purpose of give-and-take is that each party benefits. Giving is not an end in itself. Giving only makes sense when you are also *getting* something at the same time. In an economic transaction, you ought to be better off for having spent your money than having kept it. In friendship and romance, you ought to be better off for having spent your emotions, energy, and time rather than having kept them to yourself.

You are not obliged to love others on command, or simply as a duty. Both you and the other individual are supposed to get something out of the love. You should only love—indeed, you *can* only love—when there's reason to do so. This is what love as trade is all about.   ⓣ

14. Ayn Rand, *Atlas Shrugged* (New York: Penguin Books, 1957).

Chapter 14

How to Grow Up Politically & Socially

WHY SOCIAL SECURITY FAILED

Efforts to "reform" the unreformable are for naught. Social Security cannot be reformed. Financially and morally, it is bankrupt.

Think about it. Social Security is not an insurance plan people voluntarily choose from competing plans. It is a monopolistic giant. It coerces people into buying retirement insurance from the government, and on the government's terms. It gives you no other choice.

As a social worker and psychotherapist, I have seen the way Social Security often pays those who fake or manipulate their way into making themselves eligible for benefits.

Let's stop trying to save or "reform" Social Security. Instead, we should phase it out altogether. Current and soon-to-be retirees are entitled to benefits they've paid for, of course. But younger people should have the option (and the responsibility) to invest their benefits as they see fit, in a private and voluntary marketplace.

Let's face the truth that Social Security was a failure and a mistake. Then we can pick up the pieces and move on.

SECURITY WORSHIP—
TODAY'S REAL SOCIAL CRISIS

Job security. *Health* security. *Social* Security. Security, security, security . . . .

Conventional wisdom to the contrary, "security" does not mean the absence of conflict, work or pain. Psychologically, security refers to an emotional state of competence, freedom-worship, and confidence that one has adequate tools to survive and flourish in life. Individuals do not feel secure because others are taking care of them; they feel secure because they are confident in the knowledge they can take care of themselves. The more self-reliant one is, the more secure one will feel.

The sort of security most people yearn for, and too many psychologists and other spiritual-educational-political leaders encourage, represents an illusion. Doing whatever one feels whenever one feels like it will not lead to security. Nor will blindly following the rules of authorities. Neither modern subjectivist permissiveness nor old-fashioned dogmatic authoritarianism represent the antidote to personal insecurity.

The very idea of "security" without effort or initiative, as so many people seek, represents a vicious illusion; an illusion which, in the twentieth century, rationalized every form and degree of government control, from fascism to communism to the dysfunctional American welfare state. Both the National Socialist (Nazi) regime in Germany and the Soviet socialist regime in Russia justified themselves on the idea that the individual has a duty to provide for what politicians see as "the common good," by force if necessary.

In today's American welfare state, operating on the same basic principle, people are forced to support partial income redistribution programs such as Social Security and Medicare not only in the name of altruism, but also in the name of personal security. Only recently, in light of a massive national debt and the threat of fiscal collapse, are an increasing number of Americans starting to recognize that it is impossible to have one's Medicare and eat it too. In other words, it is futile to attempt to ensure security simply by demanding or wishing it into existence through the political process. Moral and fiscal bankruptcy, as events have proven, is the inevitable result of any such attempt. Nevertheless, the popular resistance to cutting such "entitlement" spending shows how far most people have yet to travel on the road to facing reality.

Outside of the political realm, the same false notion of security leads people to inappropriately depend upon relatives for support despite the resulting damage to self-confidence and independence. Family members, armed with clichés about the importance of leaning on one another in times of stress, will often pour emotional and financial resources into relatives who consistently make poor decisions. In the name of compassion and caring, they end up enabling and sanctioning the very behaviors they hope to discourage. Long before the modern welfare state, families were privately subsidizing and enabling alcoholic brothers, unfaithful husbands, and unscrupulous cousins—rationalizing that "but for the grace of God," rather than poor decision making, they might find themselves in the same circumstances.

Genuine security arises from actual, first-hand knowledge that one is both capable and worthy of achieving happiness. In short, an individual must know that he is *able* to achieve happiness (through conscious, responsible action) and, once having attained it, that he *deserves* it. From the earliest stages of childhood, human beings must be taught to think, reason, recognize objective reality, distinguish facts from wishes, and pursue constructive goals to the best of their ability.

Security is an individual matter, not a group matter. It arises within the individual, through the use of his own mind and through his own efforts. Loved ones can support the individual in finding security, but cannot give it to him. External agents—psychotherapists, government programs, self-esteem seminars—cannot possibly substitute for human initiative, conscious thought, and the will to act.

WHY INDIVIDUALS ARE MORE
IMPORTANT THAN VILLAGES OR FAMILIES

Liberals say, "It takes a village" to make a society great and strong.

The conservatives reply, "No, it does not take a village; it takes a family."

Both sides are wrong. It takes an *individual*. It takes an individual to accomplish even modest goals. It takes a special kind of individual to accomplish great things. More often than not, individuals accomplish what they do in spite of the family, or in spite of the village.

It takes an individual to think, conceptualize, plan, and create. It takes an individual to rise above mediocrity, fear, and toward new discoveries.

"Families" do not work, study, and make a living. Individuals do. "Villages" do not discover electricity, or cure terrible diseases. Individuals do. Families and villages are not mystical entities. They are comprised of individuals. It is the brightest, and most creative, of those individuals upon whom the family and village depend.

A society flourishes only to the extent that the individual is respected and valued. A society decays when the individual is denigrated and the "village" or the "family" is held as supreme.

America was once great because the prevailing attitude was in favor of individualism and individual rights. Today, only fading remnants of that earlier idealism remain. Instead, we are left with a choice between a mediocre welfare state and religious dogmatism.

Conservatives and liberals, please note: If you want to save America, you must first champion the cause of the individual. Without the individual, your villages and your families will most certainly perish.

EVADING THE FACTS— IN THE NAME OF "HUMANITY"

The charity organization Habitat for Humanity builds homes for people who cannot afford to buy them. In 1995, organization leaders in Prince William County, Virginia, selected ex-con Donald Dannemiller to move into a house they built. Soon after they selected Dannemiller, they learned that he had been previously convicted of murdering his 13-year-old stepsister.

Dannemiller's prospective neighbors, upon learning of the ex-con's violent history, confronted Habitat for Humanity. They did not want to live down the street from a known murderer. Despite these protests the organization stood by its selection, saying it believed in second chances, even for murderers. In 1996, Dannemiller moved into the house Habitat for Humanity built for him.

In May of 1998, Dannemiller landed back in jail. He was charged with abducting a 12-year-old Manassas, VA, girl from her front doorstep and shooting her in the side with a pellet gun when she escaped (See *The Washington Post* 6/16/98 for further details).

How can an otherwise well-respected charity organization make such a stupid mistake? Was it really a stupid, honest mistake? Or was it much worse than that?

The answer to this question was aptly provided by a Habitat for Humanity official, who made the following statement after the young girl's abduction.

"There is no such thing as a perfect family in which you can predict future behavior," the Habitat for Humanity official said. "We like to believe that it's appropriate to make *rational* judgments about the candidates [for housing] and not to pass *moral* judgments, which is left to a higher authority." [italics added]

The statement says it all. It is much more profound than a casual reading suggests.

Its premise is that there are two realms of reality—two realms which require separate types of judgment: one rational, one moral. The first sphere of reality is the real, physical, material or rational world. The real world consists of cars, computers, houses, clothing, and so forth. It is the responsibility of human reason, science and common sense to figure out this world.

The second sphere of reality is the "spiritual," contemplative or moral realm. It consists of moral dilemmas, character assessments and judgments about who is and is not fit to live among civilized people. It is the responsibility of some mystical Higher Authority—which invariably means, in actual practice, some self-ordained authority here on earth—to make judgments in this realm.

This rational-moral dichotomy implies that reason and common sense are inaccessible to the moral realm. It implies that character judgments cannot be made by careful thought—only by some vague process of which only a select few are capable.

Apparently, it's OK to make judgments about computers, cars, lawnmowers and the weather. But none of us should dare morally judge another *person*. Evidently reason does not apply to this area. It does not matter if the facts—such as having murdered an innocent person—make a judgment inescapable. It does not matter if evading obvious facts—as Habitat for Humanity did in this case—threatens the life of an innocent human being. Individual lives are deemed insignificant when compared to the moral imperative that we never judge anybody, ever. At least, this is how socialistic people such as the Habitat for Humanity spokesman tend to think.

The notion of a breach between morality and physical reality is an ancient idea. It goes back at least as far as Plato. But it is a profoundly wrong idea. It is the mother of all wrong ideas. And if you think that abstract, philosophical ideas don't have consequences for real life, then just ask the 12-year-old Manassas, VA, girl who could have died because of a mistaken idea.

Ideas have consequences. If this particular idea could speak it would say, "Who am I to judge?" No doubt this is what people say to themselves all the time about moral issues. This must be what a student tells himself when he catches another student copying his exam but does not confront him. This must be what a mother tells herself when she suspects her husband is sexually molesting their daughter, but looks the other way. This, no doubt, is what citizens of Nazi Germany told themselves when they became aware of how evil the dictator they voted into office truly was—yet kept applauding him anyway. When otherwise rational individuals abdicate the responsibility of moral judgment, the consequences can be devastating.

For centuries, many religions and philosophies have preached the idea that morality belongs to another realm, and that mere mortals should not make moral judgments. In contemporary culture, liberal-intellectual types feed us the same line in a different form: "Don't be judgmental," they admonish. Facts don't matter. All that matters is being sensitive and compassionate. And what they mean by "sensitive and compassionate" is: look the other way, without ever daring to make moral judgments. "Leave the moral judgments to us—and, by the way, don't even *think* about evaluating what kind of job we're doing."

If mere human beings cannot make objective moral judgments, then none of us can possibly solve moral and practical dilemmas in our lives on earth. If moral judgments are wrong and impossible, then we have no right to put murderers in jail. We have no reason to act and feel indignant if someone robs or steals or rapes us. We certainly cannot bomb buildings known to house international terrorists.

With rare exception, most of us allow some self-important emissary to do the job of moral judgment for us. It may be a self-righteous preacher, a psychologist, or (perish the thought) a politician. In the Dannemiller case, the self-important, self-appointed emissary was Habitat for Humanity. Look how impressive a job this organization did in making a moral judgment for its community! A 12-year-old girl almost lost her life.

Until we all take responsibility for moral judgment, and make it a part of our daily lives without fear and without shame, we can be sure that people like the Habitat for Humanity spokesman will do so for us. It's time to take responsibility for our own moral judgments, and to stop delegating them to people who are no good at it. Otherwise, the body count (literally and figuratively) will continue to grow—and we will have nobody to blame but ourselves.

HOW "BLACK ENGLISH" IS JUST ANOTHER EXAMPLE OF TODAY'S ANTI-MIND MENTALITY

The Oakland, CA, school district has become the first in the nation to recognize black "English" as a language, not slang or a dialect, and is seeking bilingual education aid—tax money—for the black students who speak it. The Oakland school board voted unanimously to force teachers to treat black English (i.e., "axe" instead of "ask", "goo" instead of "good," "I be going to the park" instead of "I am going to the park") as no better or worse—as no more correct or incorrect—than any other language.

It is hard to imagine a more complete form of disrespect for a race of people than this policy dictates. Black "English" is simply a form of street slang. We do not elevate other forms of slang—Southern dialects, working class British "cockney" accents, "hip" slang of the 1960's—to the level of a real language, simply because people are using it. To tell children that they must treat a form of slang as equivalent to the proper form of language upon which the slang depends is tantamount to saying: "You are not capable of learning how to grasp and practice the principles of language. You are, because of your race, fundamentally inferior." Thankfully, many black people such as Jesse Jackson—properly insulted and disgusted by the notion of teaching black "English"—are speaking out against the idea.

It is important to recognize that the teaching of black "English" is not simply a bizarre aberration, or an instance of political correctness run amok. On the contrary, it is part of a wider, and more fundamental, cultural trend: an attack on the very idea of objective reality; on the conceptual integrations, based upon material perceived by the sense organs, which make language possible in the first place. The proponents of such a ludicrous scheme are not so much anti-black or anti-white as they are *anti-mind*. Their hatred of intelligence, of knowledge, and of clarity knows no limits.

In her famous novel *Atlas Shrugged*, Ayn Rand identified the root cause of the irrationality represented by the Oakland school district decision: "Do you think they are taking you back to dark ages? They are taking you back to darker ages than any your history has known. Their goal is not the era of pre-science, but the era of pre-language. Their purpose is to deprive you of the concept on which man's mind, his life and his culture depend: the concept of an *objective* reality."

WHY AFFIRMATIVE ACTION IS UNFAIR

The government has no right to force business owners to hire employees they would not choose of their own free will. If I decide to open a restaurant, no politician has the right to tell me what percentage of my employees must be black, Hispanic, or female, any more than they have a right to tell me how to run my personal life. If I am to be responsible for starting and running my business, on my own property and through my own efforts, then no government has the moral right to tell me whom I may (or may not) hire.

Business owners have no incentive to be racist, sexist, or anything else; their prime incentive is to find the best possible labor at the lowest possible cost. The last thing on a business owner's mind is the race of his employee. If the business owner is rational, he gives the best workers (regardless of race or gender) the chance to advance because it serves his own selfish interest to succeed. If he is not rational, then he will not be in business for very long anyway.

We need to tell our political leaders: "I am not my brother's keeper, and the government has no right to force me to become one—any more than the government had the right to enforce slavery as it did in the 19th century. If *you* want to be your brother's keeper, then you certainly have every right to do so—but on your own time, and on your own budget."

The fact that black people were enslaved in the past, or that women were stereotyped as helpless in the past, does not give today's blacks and women a mortgage on the rights, the lives, and the property of others. My suffering, or the suffering of my ancestors, does not mean my neighbor is obliged to sacrifice for me. Nor does his suffering impose a mortgage on my life, and my freedom.

The same principle applies to any type of private business, organization, or enterprise of any kind. As the American Founders recognized, all individuals possess the natural right to freedom of association. What would a liberal's position be if, say, an ultra-conservative President Patrick Buchanan wished to require a ninety percent white male work force in all companies and organizations? Or to forbid the hiring of legal American immigrants? On what principle would a liberal defend himself, other than the right to associate (professionally or otherwise) with whomever he chooses?

If a private organization wishes to initiate an affirmative action policy for its own employees, then this is certainly its right. The employees are free to resign if they disagree with it. But no government has the moral right to impose such policies on its citizens by force.

We must also reject affirmative action for its more fundamental philosophical premises. The basic premise underlying affirmative action is that of "multicultural diversity:" the idea that objective differences do not exist between individuals or groups, and that diversity must be valued for its own sake.

This idea is sheer nonsense. Diversity is not the essence of a great society; individual excellence is. Individual excellence in pursuing productive work, by one's own free choice and through maximizing one's potential to the fullest extent possible, represents the most moral and the most practical philosophy for human beings to follow. To be born black, or white, or Hispanic is not an accomplishment; to earn a medical degree, to discover a cure for cancer, or to do an honest hard day's work *is*.

Like it or not, objective differences between individuals and groups do exist. Some individuals apply themselves more than others. Some doctors are better than others. Some swimmers are better than others. Some people exhibit more integrity than others. Furthermore, some societies and cultures accomplish more than others.

Can everyone agree that Western civilization, with its almost miraculous medical technology and unprecedented material comforts not even enjoyed by royalty in previous civilizations, is a better place to live and raise children than, say, medieval Europe or Nazi Germany or a starving country in Africa today?

Liberals are correct to condemn, as irrational, the idea that an individual should be negatively judged merely by the color of his skin or his ethnic background. It is equally wrong, however, to *positively* judge an individual merely by the color of his skin or his ethnic background. To be truly color-blind, one must judge an individual objectively, by both the content of his character and the quality of his performance.

What we should all encourage is not diversity, but excellence; not membership in racial or gender categories, but individualism; not government restriction and interference, but freedom. Under today's mentality of affirmative action, we merely replace one form of racism ("You're of no value because you're black") with another form ("Your value lies in the fact you are black"). Most minorities I know are insulted and disgusted by such an approach, and they have every reason to be.

Instead of government-imposed affirmative action, we should all (regardless of race or gender) be equally responsible and free to live our lives to the fullest extent possible.

TV VIOLENCE AND THE FIRST AMENDMENT

Do parents and kids have a right to violent-free television?

No!

Television networks are not public property—nor are they the property of any political pressure group. The networks belong to the owners, who are responsible for making them go on the air each day and without whom there would be no television viewing in the first place. NBC and CBS are private property, no less than one's house, one's car, or one's very life.

Politicians who support government ratings systems refuse to understand that the U.S. Constitution provided for a limited government. A limited government protects individual rights, which can only be violated by the initiation of physical force (or fraud) of one individual against another. Using this definition, it is utterly illogical to claim a "right" to violent-free television.

No right has been violated unless, or until, a broadcaster applies the use of force in making an individual watch a certain television show. On the other hand, government regulation of broadcast material—in the absence of force or fraud by any party—is most certainly a violation of the rights of the broadcaster.

Far more is at stake than the content of a few television shows. Once the door is open to government "management" of program content, the principle is established that the government has the final say in what is shown and not shown on television. Once this principle is accepted, what is to protect us from a dictatorship of a Fascist, Communist or religious variety? The networks have nothing to gain from any compromise, while power-hungry government officials have everything to gain from even a tiny concession.

It is imperative that network officials not budge one inch from the principle of individual rights. To even dignify a politician's summons by agreeing to meet with one is a travesty of justice, unless the sole purpose of the "meeting" is to let the Senator, Congressman, or Administration official know on no uncertain terms that the private property rights of broadcasters cannot and will not be negotiated away.

It is a truly sad commentary on our times that such a debate can even take place without strong objections from every corner of society. The very premise of the "debate" over violence on television suggests that independent broadcasters operate solely with the permission of the government, and that the government has a mortgage on the individual's right to self-expression. If our government shows such little regard for property rights, is it any wonder that crime remains a serious problem?

THE ONLY TRUE CAMPAIGN FINANCE REFORM—STOP LETTING POLITICIANS TAKE EVERYONE'S MONEY

A few years back, the government tried to nationalize health care. Today, politicians are attempting to initiate a government takeover of free speech. The codeword for their plan? Campaign finance reform.

Clearly, as was the case with health care, some type of reform is necessary. With the President, Vice President, and members of Congress openly accepting bribes from foreigners, businesses, and special interest groups, Americans are correct to conclude that something has gone terribly wrong.

The government has no right granting special favors to some members of society at the expense of others, as it routinely does today. Consider the example of corporate welfare. Corporate welfare refers to the billions of tax dollars spent to subsidize industries such as agriculture, manufacturing, corporate advertising, public broadcasting, fishing, and international trade, to name only a few.

People who want to continue receiving this corporate welfare, quite naturally, will pressure elected officials by whatever means necessary to keep the money flowing. In Washington, DC, this pressure takes the form of lobbying: the attempt to convince politicians to pay for enterprises which would not otherwise exist except through the coercion of taxation. Of course, lobbying does not only occur because some people want and demand unearned government handouts. Lobbying can also serve as a means for protecting oneself from the violation of rights by the government. Examples include lobbying for lower taxes, for fewer regulations, and to prevent the socialization of health care or restrictions on freedom of speech.

As government involvement in private enterprise grows, so too does the incentive to bribe politicians and obtain special favors. The fewer activities in which the government involves itself, the fewer incentives there will be for lobbying and outright bribery. This was the simple but profound wisdom behind the Constitutional concept of strictly and severely *limited* government. We should not be surprised that abandoning this wisdom has led to corruption and disaster.

The government should also stop funding political campaigns with tax money. It's clearly not working. Decades of tax-subsidized political campaigns have not resulted in higher quality candidates. Quite the contrary. Consider how dreary and unprincipled our campaigns, especially for President, have become in the last several decades (the period in which public campaign financing has sharply increased). Evidence suggests that public financing leads to the election of "safe," unprincipled candidates who, once elected, become hostages to the demands of the subsidized special interests.

Funding campaigns with tax money is not necessary to keep wealthy candidates from "buying" elections. Steve Forbes and Ross Perot both failed to win the Presidency, despite the fact that each had huge amounts of personal money at his disposal. Forbes and Perot are living proof that money is not by itself a guarantee of success in the political system.

The only proper campaign finance reform is *less* government, which means no more tax-funding of campaigns, no more arbitrary restrictions on spending, and, most of all, a massive downsizing of government (starting with corporate welfare). The incentive for large-scale corruption will disappear.

Regrettably, nearly all of the reform bills being considered under the label "campaign finance reform" rest on exactly opposite principles. They favor more public financing of campaigns in exchange for more government control, including a greatly expanded Federal Election Commission and tight limits on private spending. Proponents of such bills hate private spending, because it is "selfish." They act and speak as if they believe self-interest is inherently evil. If we could only eliminate or outlaw people from acting in their self-interest, they claim, then there would be no problem with bribery and scandal. They ignore the spectacular failures of Communism, the philosophy which tried to outlaw self-interest in Russia and Eastern Europe.

These anti-spenders fail to distinguish between *rational* self-interest, where physical coercion and fraud are ruled out, and conventional "selfishness" in which anything goes. Voluntarily giving money to the candidates whom you support, and who act in your rational interest, is a fundamental right. The real issue is that the government's granting of subsidies and special privileges—along with the resulting special-interest group warfare—destroys the incentive of its citizens to be rational. If the government limited itself to the "basics," such as protection from physical violence and fraud, then what kind of lobbying would be necessary or even desirable? The opportunities for corruption and bribery would be far fewer and the government's ability to control and punish them far greater.

Tragically, the wrong kind of campaign finance reform will restrict freedom of speech, the last individual right protected with any consistency in America. To control the amount an individual or business can spend on speaking is no different from controlling the content of what he is actually saying. The government of a supposedly free country, with a First Amendment guarantee on freedom of speech, cannot in all seriousness tell its citizens: "You are free to speak, but only for 18 hours a day instead of 24, or every day except Wednesdays and Fridays." Free speech, so long as it is exercised with one's own money and on one's own property, is an absolute right. You either have the right, or you don't.

Forcing American citizens, through the coercion of taxation, to subsidize candidates with whom they disagree represents an outrageous violation of individual rights. It defies both the spirit and the letter of the Constitution. All individuals must be left free to support, without limit, the candidates of their choice and not be forced to support candidates with whom they disagree.

Only in a system which allows for freedom of competition will the best candidates, with the best ideas, ultimately win.

THE CRUX OF THE PUBLIC BROADCASTING DEBATE

Public broadcasting is not a proper function of government.

The principle at stake is the right of the individual. If the individual has no right to use his own mind and judgment about how to spend the products of his effort, then he has no rights at all.

A moral government protects its citizens from the threat of physical force. Public broadcasting is immoral because it forces individuals to pay for the promotion of ideas and programs whether they agree with them or not.

People who support individual rights and freedom should put advocates of public broadcasting on the defensive. "*Sesame Street* is supposed to be good for kids," they say. Interesting—but not the point. Make them defend the idea that the producers of *Sesame Street* have a right to make others pay for it. "Barney the dinosaur makes a great profit and is a delight to many kids," they claim. Interesting—but not the point. Make them explain what constitutional right allows Barney's fans to force others to subsidize him.

It does not matter whether public television programs are popular or not. Principles are more powerful than polls. If the shows are "elitist," then let the elite pay for them. If the shows are popular, then let the masses pay for them in the free marketplace. Do not force anyone to pay for them with tax dollars.

THE CULT OF SENSITIVITY

What is wrong with today's society? Why does it seem to be falling apart? Why does nobody seem to have an answer, other than more failed government programs, or a return to puritanical moralism? What is happening to education? Why are crime and drug use on the rise? Why are dishonest, cynical, and unprincipled politicians winning elections, while the better men dare not run? Why, in the midst of so much technological and material progress, are we witnessing an intellectual and cultural collapse?

The answer is contained in two recent examples from our scientific culture and legal system, respectively. You need not be a Ph.D. to grasp the point; in fact, it helps if you are not.

First example: the Mercator Projection. The Mercator Projection is a type of world map that shows areas near the equator as disproportionately small compared to countries closer to the North and South poles. These anomalies occur because distortions in the size and shape of various geographic areas are inevitable when projecting a globe on to a flat surface. Consequently, Greenland appears larger than Australia, even though Australia is actually more than three times the size of Greenland. The map has been in use by scientists and navigators for centuries.

Why would anyone use such a map? To navigators of airplanes and ships, getting to the desired destination is of paramount importance. The Mercator map, because of its construction and its compatibility with scientific navigational systems, enables navigators to accurately do their jobs for the areas in which they travel. They judge the cost of distorting the relative size of certain regions such as Australia and Greenland as worth the increased overall accuracy the map affords. For hundreds of years, the Mercator Projection has demonstrably ensured the safety of countless passengers on ships and airplanes.

Now the Mercator is under attack—*not* for its reliability or effectiveness in navigation, but because it is thought by some to be politically and socially "discriminatory." Because many of the world's poorer nations are located nearer the equator and therefore appear smaller on the map, certain social science "intellectuals" and journalistic commentators think it is racially biased. "In our society," sniffs one such critic, "we unconsciously equate size with importance and even with power, and if the Third World countries are misrepresented, they are likely to be valued less." A map maker in Germany grimly argues that the map is indicative of "European arrogance" and "imperialism" since it makes Europe look relatively larger than Third World countries.

Consider the implications of what these pompous psychologizers are claiming. Airplane and ship navigators who safely help us reach our desired destinations are more concerned with making fun of Third World countries than with doing their job properly and profitably. The cynical intellectuals insist that users and defenders of the Mercator map are not motivated by competence and reason, but rather by racism and insensitivity. Apparently, in the eyes of paranoid social critics, mapmakers are attracted to their professions *not* to produce reliable maps, but to "puff up" the self-esteem of industrialized countries while degrading poorer ones.

Second example: In the late 1980's, a vagrant named Richard Kreimer challenged the Morristown, New Jersey, public library. Kreimer objected to the policy limiting the use of library premises to persons "engaged in normal activities associated with the use of a public library." He also objected to the banning of people with personal hygiene problems. In reality, many of the town's bums had been harassing librarians to the point that some felt compelled to resign rather than put up with it any longer.

Nevertheless, federal Judge H. Lee Sarokin ruled in *favor* of Kreimer. Disregarding the library's complaints against the disruptive presence of vagrants in the facility, the judge claimed that hygiene tests have "a disparate impact on the poor" and that to ban anybody from the library violates the "expressional and associational rights of individuals." Furthermore, the judge moralized, "If we wish to shield our eyes and noses from the homeless, we should revoke their conditions, not their library cards."

The implications of Judge Sarokin's decision are completely irrational. He is saying, in effect, that (1) the central purpose of a library is the expression of "associational" rights, not to provide educational and reading materials in a quiet, clean environment; and, (2) individuals who pay for the library (through taxes, whether they want to or not) have no right to use the library for its intended purposes unless or until they somehow "revoke" the conditions of vagrants and bums. The implication is that clean, self-responsible people have no right to peacefully make use of a library they were forced to pay for, while bums have the right to do whatever they please in the library, precisely because they did not pay for it.

In case you see Judge Sarokin's decision as an unusual, fringe example, consider the fact that he was elevated to the Circuit Court of Appeals by President Clinton in 1994. We can expect many more such decisions in the future.

What kind of irrationality is common to these two examples? How did such obvious assaults on common sense and sanity come to represent the mainstream of opinion, at least among our intellectual and social leaders? And what does this sort of irrationality have to do with the deeper problems nearly everyone senses in today's culture?

Consider the underlying similarities between these two cases. According to one, the primary purpose of maps is not to take people from one location to another safely; the primary purpose of maps is to make sure that people in poor countries *feel* like they are living in wealthier countries. Libraries, according to the other example, are not supposed to provide people with clean, quiet places to read and study; they are supposed to be places where people can do almost anything they please, all in the name of some undefined "expressional and associational rights."

In other words, it's not as important for ships to stay afloat or for airplanes to remain airborne as it is for people in non-Euro-American countries not to have their feelings hurt. Similarly, it's not as important for individuals who pay for public libraries to use them in peace (and free of offensive odors) as it is for bums not to have their feelings hurt. Egged on by pretentious moralizers in the media and the universities, we are becoming a society obsessed with ignoring even the most obvious facts in the name of protecting one another's feelings. According to this mentality, feelings are paramount; facts and logic are either irrelevant or non-existent. The sense organs are unreliable. The human mind is impotent to discover objective truth.

What's true for me is not necessarily true for everyone. There are no absolutes: except, presumably, for the absolute that there are no absolutes.

Preventing hurt feelings of favored groups has become the foremost activity of today's psychotherapists, sociologists, historians, politicians, journalists and even some hard-core scientists. If you prevent hurt feelings (regardless of context, results, intentions) you are good; if you hurt someone's feelings (regardless of context, intentions, results) you are bad. Period. Early 21st Century America has spawned the Cult of Sensitivity.

Ironically, and perversely, the individuals who comprise the victim groups are actually harmed, rather than helped, by their alleged "benefactors." A growing number of them are beginning to recognize this fact. Recently, for example, the Reverend Jesse Jackson visited a Third World country that is home to a Reebok shoe factory. Jackson condemned Reebok for "exploiting" the workers of poor countries by paying them lower wages and "taking advantage" of their poverty. Following Jackson's diatribe, CNN interviewed at least one of these so-called victims who said that she was grateful for the work, and while to an American her salary may not seem very high, it raised her standard of living from the previous squalor she had endured. This woman understands that without the freedom to pay workers less, Reebok will leave her country, her job will be eliminated, and she has no hope of even partially escaping poverty. Reverend Jackson's "compassion" is unwelcome, and with good reason.

Similarly, the plight of homeless persons is worsened, not helped, by their defenders in the churches, the media, and in Washington, DC. Decades of experience have shown that rent control and irrational housing regulations destroy the incentive (and the ability) of housing developers to provide, for a profit, what the government has been unable to do with decades of expensive housing programs. Without the necessary capital drained by taxation, regulation, and rent control, builders do not have the funds to profitably build low-cost housing as they undoubtedly would in an unhampered market. Yet the strongest defenders of rent control and urban housing regulation, and the greatest opponents of the profit motive, are often the very same activists who "advocate" for the homeless.

The lesson from these examples? In today's Age of Sensitivity, don't necessarily blame the individuals to whom you are being sensitized. Don't blame the bums, or the residents of Third World countries, or the homeless. Instead, blame the philosophy, social science, and humanities intellectuals who, apparently having nothing better to do, invent such irrational ideas in the first place. Blame philosophers such as Karl Marx and Immanuel Kant, who popularized these ideas among today's intellectuals. Blame the church leaders who glorify sacrifice and condemn prosperity. Also blame the overtly biased mainstream media, the journalists on CNN, NBC "Dateline," and CBS's "Sixty Minutes," as well as the politicians, who relentlessly seek to pound these mistaken ideas into our minds, ignoring any evidence suggesting conclusions contrary to their wishes.

Substitute the bums in the library or the politically incorrect map with any other such controversy and you will discover the same implications and results. Parents, for example, who place bumperstickers on their cars stating, "My child is an honor roll student at such-and-such high school" have come under attack for hurting the feelings of kids who are not honor roll students. In many schools, advanced placement programs for gifted and talented students are condemned for hurting the feelings of kids who are not gifted and talented. People who earn lots of money, honestly and through their own efforts, are under attack for hurting the feelings of people who do not make as much money. People who choose not to have children or attend church are condemned as "anti-family" and "anti-religion," and are accused of hurting the feelings of people who choose to raise children and attend church.

An ironic but logical observation: as people become more obsessed with not hurting anyone's feelings, people—in general—become less polite and less considerate. Social problems such as crime, prejudice, and violence increase rather than decrease. This is no accident. Human beings do not respond well to guilt, force or intimidation. Thinking is by its very nature both volitional and voluntary. Any attempt to force or intimidate a person into thinking a certain way will usually yield the exact opposite of the intended result. If you try to legislate compassion, you achieve only meanness. If you try to force universal wealth into existence, you achieve poverty and crime. If you place wishes and desires above objective reality, you achieve total disaster.

Sensitivity, a form of emotional expression, can only arise as a consequence of rationally understood conclusions. People do not and cannot feel an emotion outside of the factual context and/or independent process of reasoning which gives rise to an emotion. Emotions and feelings are, by definition, merely automatic (lightning-like) manifestations of value judgments, thoughts, ideas. Emotions represent the result of prior thought. People cannot simply feel "compassion" or "sensitivity" or anything else on cue, or because it's the "right" thing to feel, or because someone suggests, orders, or blackmails them into doing so.

Human beings need *reason*, objective factual context, and logical validation prior to accepting any conclusion—and they must choose to be open to such validation. In order to learn anything, an individual human must first focus his attention and choose to think. This is the basic reason why all thought control programs—whether engineered by Nazis, Communists, or modern-day sensitivity-gurus in our intellectual establishment—are ultimately doomed to failure. Whether such programs have "good" intentions or not is of secondary importance. This fact of human nature transcends race, gender, creed—*and* intentions.

Because human beings are rational animals, who by their very nature must think and reason independently before they can genuinely accept (much less feel) any given conclusion, it is futile and wrong to try to legislate *or* pressure people into taking a certain position. Any attempt to do so represents the height of presumptuousness and pretentiousness.

The examples cited here, including that of the politically incorrect map and the politically incorrect library, point toward an even more fundamental evasion that evidently escapes most of today's cynical status quo: the objectivity of knowledge.

Facts are facts. Bums are bums. If they smell and disrupt the library to the point where staff members are compelled to quit, then they clearly should not be there. Likewise, if a map achieves its purpose of navigating accurately and safely, then it should continue to be used so long as navigators see good reason to do so.

Yet such common sense conclusions only hold weight if one first understands the generalized importance of placing objective facts above wishes and desires. Sadly, at least today, the highly educated seem even less able to grasp this concept than the uneducated masses. This is because our intellectual and political leaders have led us all into accepting wrong ideas: feelings above facts, "sensitivity" above honesty, and politically correct conformity as more important than knowledge, wisdom, and intellectual honesty. Bad philosophical premises, such as these, are the ultimate cause of today's widely recognized social and intellectual collapse.

Only a revitalized culture of independent, reason-oriented individualists who are not intimidated by dogmatic authorities and refuse to follow them blindly can hope to flourish and survive. If you are searching for an absolute truth in today's swamp of wishy-washy mediocrity, try this one: *Think for yourself.* Accept the absolutism of reality, not someone else's self-proclaimed authority, unfounded assertion, or illogical premises. Use your own mind, consciously and intelligently, to form conclusions. Use reason and evidence, not blind emotion, to assess reality. Live guiltlessly by your own judgment, and demand freedom to make your own decisions about your mind, your body, and your property. Do not be afraid to distinguish between the beautiful and the ugly; between a courageous hero and a bum on the street; between truth and falsehood.

Against a society of independent, rational thinkers, today's Cult of Sensitivity establishment will not stand a chance.

COMPULSORY INTERNATIONAL SOCIAL WORK

The United States is wrong to be in any country on purely "humanitarian" grounds.

We are not our brother's keepers. This includes the warring tribes in Eastern Europe. Even if it were possible to settle this age-old dispute, it would not be our moral obligation to sacrifice billions of dollars and even American lives on such an altruistic venture.

The only proper function of government is to protect its own citizens. Let the Bosnian tribes kill each other until they are sick of it. Then, once they are ready to form a civilized society based upon respect of individual rights, we can offer our moral support (and military, if it serves our interest). This day will come much sooner if we leave them alone.

As we enter the twenty-first century, the welfare state is expanding to grotesque proportions. No longer content to redistribute wealth within the country, our politicians now seek to turn the once mighty military into a band of armed social workers. Sooner or later, we will pay a price for this reckless squandering of national defense.

WHY THE U.S. SHOULD BOYCOTT TOTALITARIAN NATIONS

The U.S., through its embargo against Cuba, is simply refusing to participate in that nation's self-destruction. Our embargo tells Cuba, in effect: "We oppose Communism and its crushing of capitalism and individual rights. We will have nothing to do with you. If you want to commit suicide, you will have to do so without our cooperation." By lifting the embargo, the U.S. would help Cuba's government retain its totalitarian grasp—extending its path of starvation and destruction still further.

If the Pope—or anyone else—really wants to build the morale of totalitarian countries such as Cuba, he should tell them to assert, without compromise, the supremacy of individual rights, freedom, and capitalism. He should also explain how evil and dictatorship are morally impotent and can only survive so long as people hold their heads down in humility.

Instead, the Pope grants Castro's Communist government respectability it does not deserve. In exchange for a few crumbs of religious "liberty," which disappear once the television cameras leave the country, the Pope provides the Communists with a cynical public relations opportunity to blame the United States for Communism's failures.

By sanctioning and supporting evil, the Pope gives it strength it would not otherwise have. In the name of humanitarianism, he increases the chance that Cuban dictators will rule the country for many more generations to come.

HOW THE POPE & THE PRESIDENT
SHARE A MISTAKEN MORAL VISION

Pope John Paul II and President Bill Clinton share the same view of morality.

Never mind their well-publicized differences on abortion and sexual behavior. Even when their conclusions differ, they operate under the same moral framework.

That moral framework is self-sacrifice. Self-sacrifice refers to the moral ideal that man's highest virtue is to surrender his mind, his property, his integrity—indeed, his very life—to the need, whim or demand of another.

President Clinton believes that productive Americans must sacrifice their independence and their income so that wealth (or health care) may be redistributed to the masses. The Pope believes that women must sacrifice their happiness and their futures to a theological belief that a fetus is a human life.

Each man understands that physical force—also known as government—is the only means of imposing his philosophical views on an unenlightened population. Each exploits the unchallenged idea that self-sacrifice is a virtue. Both men use guilt as a psychological weapon: President Clinton accuses you of "destroying the Presidency" if you oppose his retroactive tax increase; the Pope accuses you of murder if you question his illogical claim that life begins nine months before the beginning of life. On some issues (such as abortion and gay rights), the two men may disagree; but on many more issues (national health insurance, the welfare state, the injustice of capitalism) the men are in full agreement.

President Clinton justifies self-sacrifice, of course, on the premise that "the uninsured" or "the jobless" or "the poor" must be protected. And Pope John Paul justifies self-sacrifice on the premise that "the unborn" or "the sick" or "the Church" must be protected.

Yet neither is willing to defend the most vulnerable minority of all: *the individual*. I am referring to the thinking, independent, productive individual—the kind of person who assumes full responsibility for his life and asks for nothing in return except to be left alone. Popes, of course, have never understood the virtue of leaving people alone. The Church has been meddling in individuals' lives since the Middle Ages. American presidents used to leave individuals alone—before the advent of glorified busybodies such as FDR, LBJ and now Bill Clinton.

If government is to stay out of our bedrooms, as liberals correctly insist, and stop punishing success and productivity, as conservatives justly demand, there is only one solution: Abandon the morality of self-sacrifice. Reject the idea that sacrificing one's life or one's property is a virtue. Replace it with the idea that independence, pride and self-esteem are virtues and can flourish only in the absence of today's massive government involvement in individuals' lives.

A free society is only a consequence of the morality upon which its government is based. If our government is based on a morality of self-sacrifice, then our leaders will continue to demand sacrifice until there is nothing left to give. If our government is based on a morality of independence and self-interest, then we can expect government to protect us from sacrifice rather than impose it on us.

WHY GROUP RIGHTS ADVOCATES FAN THE FLAMES OF BIAS

Nowhere is the decline of political debate more apparent than in the controversy over "gay rights." The essential political issue is not whether homosexuality is a matter of choice or a biological determinant. This is a scientific question, which only a commitment to the honest and rational pursuit of knowledge can resolve.

The central political issue is one of rights. In the United States—as its political philosophy was originally conceived by Thomas Jefferson and others—the function of the government is to protect individual rights. Since the 1960's, however, the focus has shifted from the protection of individual rights to the protection of group rights. Gay and lesbian activists are simply trying to extend—quite logically—the idea of group rights beyond race and the disabled.

Advocates of group rights claim that the Jeffersonian philosophy of individual rights failed. After all, slavery continued for a full century after the founding of the United States. But the refusal of the Founders to practice their philosophy consistently is not an indictment of their philosophy. It simply means they evaded the principle they claimed to uphold. But the principle remains true nevertheless.

In reality, only individuals have rights. There is no such thing as "group rights." Conservatives must accept that consenting adults are entitled to the sexual partners of their choice, and that laws prohibiting sodomy, for example, are as unconstitutional as they are unenforceable.

Liberals, on the other hand, must accept that the principle of private property—a byproduct of individual rights—requires that employers be entitled to hire whom they please. "Discrimination" (whether rational or not) is a fundamental right, not the violation of rights it is thought to be today. And in a genuine capitalist system, one based on the profit motive, the best and the brightest always triumph, no matter what their race or sexual orientation.

Those who think that only meddling bureaucrats can save oppressed minorities see all humans as helpless, depraved creatures. There is probably more prejudice and hatred in our society today than ever before precisely because of the increasing emphasis on group "rights." The focus must be shifted to individual rights—before the group rights proponents devour us all.

I AM NOT RESPONSIBLE FOR MY NEIGHBOR'S CHILDREN

I reject the idea that it is government's responsibility to provide child care.

To say that the government must take care of "our children" is to transfer responsibility from those who created them to everyone else (or at least the productive ones who pay taxes).

I do not accept this responsibility. I do not have any children. If I did have children, I would consider it my job to care for them—either through staying home with them or hiring a private facility to take care of them. I would not expect my neighbors to drop their interests and responsibilities in order to do it for me. I would be even more horrified by the idea of them being forced, by Big Government, to do it for me.

The government has no right to hold a gun to my neighbor's head to make him take care of my kinds. And forcing people to give up a portion of their earnings to pay for everyone's child care is what this amounts to.

The politicians' idea of nationalized child care—just like their earlier proposals for nationalized health care—rests on the premise of collectivism. Collectivism means that everyone is responsible for everyone else—and by implication, that nobody is responsible for himself. This is nonsense. It makes much more sense for me to be responsible for myself and my neighbor to be responsible for himself.

Even more importantly, no government has the moral right to force me to be responsible for my neighbor. To do so is a violation of my individual rights under the Constitution. Thomas Jefferson and George Washington did not fight for the values of life, liberty, and the pursuit of *other* people's happiness. Individual rights—the rights upon which all other rights depend—refer to the right to pursue one's own happiness.

My message to our government: Please, leave us alone!

Chapter 15

Keep Your Laws
Off My Body

LEAVE US ALONE!

I am a health care provider, and I am worried about my profession. Quality of care is going down. Waiting lists for appointments are growing. Doctors are told to work more and more hours for less and less money.

If you are old and sick, you can no longer obtain treatment without the government's permission. If you need or want the treatment, and Medicare does not cover it, you're sunk. You're not even allowed to pay for it with your own money. Congress and President Clinton passed this law a while ago.

Somehow, these laws are supposed to protect the patient. Yet I don't see many happy patients these days.

Nor do I hear people telling their kids to grow up and be doctors. Medicine is no longer a profession for heroes. Medical school enrollment is down. Doctors don't work for patients anymore. Instead, they are HMO and government employees.

Who's to blame? I know it's tempting to blame the HMOs. But this is like blaming fire for burning down your house. Why not find out who *started* the fire?

The answer is simple. Government—not doctors, patients, or even insurance companies—caused this mess.

Government—not private enterprise—created the bureaucratic monstrosities known as Medicare and Medicaid. If Medicare were a private business competing in a free market, it would have closed its doors long ago. Medicare is bankrupt and inefficient. It survives only because taxpayers are forced to pay for it.

Government—not private enterprise—regulated private health insurance companies to the point where they are no longer truly private. Bureaucrats tell insurance companies whom they may and may not cover, and what the terms of the policies are to be. This is hardly capitalism at work.

Government—not private enterprise—promoted and subsidized the first HMOs, back in the 1970's. Now it blames the "free market" when its HMO idea backfires.

Government—not private enterprise—passed the unfair tax laws whereby employers, but not individual employees, can deduct 100 percent of health insurance expenses from their taxes.

Government wants to completely control the practice of medicine, for our own good. In the process, it's loving us to death. Inch-by-inch, regulation by regulation, socialized medicine was enacted into law over the last four or five decades. And now we've got it. Just look at the results.

What can we do about it?

Expand medical savings accounts (MSAs) to all Americans. MSAs are like IRAs except withdrawals can be made any time for health expenses. Using tax-free dollars from MSAs, people can shop the competitive marketplace to pay for non-catastrophic medical services such as sore throats, eye exams, sprained ankles, and so forth. If more patients spend their own money (rather than the government's or the insurance company's), you can bet that health care costs will decrease.

Make health insurance 100 percent tax-deductible for everybody. This way individuals can buy low-cost/high-deductible health insurance policies which travel from job to job. If health insurance is only used for serious or catastrophic illness, then premiums will be much lower. Car insurance doesn't pay for oil changes or air in your tires. Why must health insurance pay for treating colds and headaches?

Deregulate the medical field. People are not bankrupted by car insurance or life insurance. Why must they go broke paying for health insurance? Prior to the last few decades, Americans did not face such a problem. Government ruined the health insurance industry by demanding that it cover everything—and then wondering why premiums skyrocketed.

Restore the right to private contracts between doctors and patients. Make it legal again for people to purchase health care even when Medicare does not want them to do so. It's outrageous beyond words that government tried to deny us this right. Doctors and patients are adult human beings. We are not children. We are not wards of the state.

Today's third-party payer system is insane. Neither doctors nor patients determine the costs of treatment. Neither doctors nor patients determine what treatment is appropriate. It's totally irrational. Yet nobody can do anything about it without breaking the law. Like former Communist countries, health care in America is on the verge of becoming a black market.

How long can all this go on? How does punishing doctors and destroying the right to private contracts serve anybody's interest?

It's time for the medical equivalent of the Boston Tea Party. Let's throw the government regulators and politicians overboard, and start over. Our very lives depend on it.

WHY HEALTH CARE IS NOT A RIGHT

Health care is not a right. No government can "guarantee" health care for all Americans without sacrificing the individual rights of doctors and patients to freely contract with one another.

A "right" to turn doctors and patients into wards of the government is a contradiction in terms, and should be vigorously attacked as such. The constructive alternative is the restoration of a free market in medicine through deregulation, liability reform, privatizing Medicare and allowing tax-free Medical Savings Accounts for the entire population.

The proper role of government is the protection of individual rights to pursue happiness and to live free of coercion and fraud. It is not the job of government to guarantee the consequences of individual rights, such as health care and other byproducts. If the health care market is deregulated, prices will go down and the great majority of people will be able to afford it. To those who can't, private and voluntary charity will pick up the "slack" just as it always has.

It's time to grow up and get the government out of health care.

LOVED TO DEATH—AMERICA'S
UNRESOLVED HEALTH CARE CRISIS

The Canadian health care system of single-payer, socialized insurance is in trouble. Now, thanks to the ignorance and cowardice of our politicians, the American system is moving in the same direction.

A growing number of Canadian doctors, angry at irrational regulations, are refusing to accept new patients. As the national government slashes spending on medical care in order to reduce the deficit, local provinces are being forced to reduce medical staff. Pregnant women are sent to Detroit because no obstetricians are available. Specialists of all kinds are in short supply. The number of doctors who flee Canada for the United States is doubling.[15]

Does any of this sound like the utopia of "universal coverage" Canadian politicians promised their constituents? Ask the people who have to wait 8 weeks for an MRI; or 4 months for heart bypass surgery; or 10 weeks for referral to any kind of specialist. The hard truth is that socialized medicine is destroying health care in Canada.

Most Americans do not understand that we are headed down a similar path in this country. The same mistaken economic and philosophical ideas that created socialized medicine in Canada are creating semi-socialized medicine in the United States today. The increase in managed care, bureaucracy, waiting lists, and expense of health care is the fault of our government. In its zeal to "compassionately" meet all of our health care needs and demands, our government is loving us to death.

How? To name just one problem, the government allows tax write-offs to businesses for health insurance, but not to individuals. Consequently, the vast majority of people utilize health insurance paid for by their employers. This means that the majority of health care is paid for by a third party. Doctors do not have to worry if they are charging too much; the health insurance company (or the government, in the case of the elderly and poor) will pick up the tab. Patients do not have to shop carefully for doctors and hospitals based on prices; they leave this responsibility to insurance companies and the government—who quite naturally respond by placing controls on the patient's freedom of choice.

Imagine if a third party picked up the tab for any other commodity—such as groceries, rent, television sets, or automobiles. Sooner or later, prices would skyrocket because the consumer would feel no pressure or responsibility for spending carefully. This is precisely what has happened in the health care field over the last several decades. In the 1980's, Medicare officials began to set price controls and regulations ("Diagnostic Related Groups," or DRGs) on the treatment of the elderly. In the 1990's, private health insurance companies followed suit, by developing "health maintenance organizations" (HMOs) and managed care bureaucracies that now drive most doctors and patients crazy with their red tape and arbitrary decisions about who may and may not receive treatment.

Yet if private insurance companies had not taken these cost-saving steps, they would have gone out of business. Why? Because without some kind of controls, the price of medicine—like any other product or service provided for "free"—would have kept rising ever higher and higher, bankrupting the insurance companies who had to pay the bills. Had private insurance companies gone out of business, then the government would have taken over altogether and we would have exactly what the Canadians now have: single-payer, monopolistic, post-office style medical care.

Most Americans do not like the restrictions on choice and flexibility dictated by today's managed care/HMO system. Increasingly, American patients encounter similar versions of what Canadians face: waiting lists for appointments, arbitrary treatment decisions made by bureaucrats rather than by physicians, and the threat of cutbacks in government programs such as Medicare in order to control the deficit. Today, in the absence of rational reforms, the United States teeters on the brink of a Canadian-like system.

A Free Market in Medicine: The Unknown Ideal

How did we get to this point? And, more importantly, how can we reverse course and prevent a plunge into the total disaster Canada now faces? On one level, more people need to educate themselves about basic economics and come to understand that government interference in the medical marketplace has actually increased prices and harmed the doctor-patient relationship, rather than the reverse. Unhampered capitalism—*not* democratic socialism or welfare-state "liberalism"—would actually provide a more benevolent and more affordable health care environment.

A totally free market would allow for the practice of the trader principle, in which doctors and patients (without the interference of third parties) could privately contract and negotiate for services and fees. Operating on the trader principle, doctors and patients could regain both the freedom and responsibility the government should never have taken away from them in the first place. In the marketplace, patients would be free to pursue any treatment they wanted. They would also be responsible for payment, thus making necessary the selection of the best price available among competing medical providers and hospital insurance carriers.

Doctors, likewise, would under capitalism be free to charge what they believed their services were worth; but they would also be responsible for competing in a marketplace where they risked losses if they charged significantly more than their competitors or more than what most people were willing to pay. Patients, shopping as informed consumers in the marketplace, would individually do the work of cost-cutting that the HMOs and government bureaucrats currently do far less efficiently. Doctor and patient, each operating in his or her own rational self-interest, would experience the benevolence and good will that the Marxist-inspired welfare state never could have achieved. Just as capitalism (or, more specifically, the law of supply and demand) succeeds in making food and computers and automobiles and VCRs widely available at prices everyone can afford, so too with medicine and hospitalization insurance—if only the government would get out of the way and let the marketplace work.

It is true that in a free market there would be no price controls on medical professionals. But the law of supply and demand would operate to keep prices from rising beyond the point most people are able and willing to pay. If the cost of health care began to rise, and doctors started to make big profits, then more young men and women would rush to join the medical field. This would increase the number of health providers relative to the number of patients in need of medical services, thereby increasing competition and lowering the costs.

These basic principles of economics would work no differently in the medical marketplace than, for example, in a marketplace for televisions or microwave ovens or automobiles. The fact that medical treatment can be a matter of life or death does not change the basic nature of the economic principles in operation. On the contrary: the life or death nature of medical treatment makes it all the more urgent that the government leave the marketplace alone so it can function rationally.

The only alternative to today's unpopular HMO and managed care bureaucracy, other than a movement towards a Canadian-like government takeover of medicine, is the implementation of aggressive free market reforms. This means allowing all individuals to deduct one-hundred percent of their medical expenses (including health insurance premiums) from their taxes.

This also means privatizing Medicare, as follows: (1) continuing the Medicare program for the current elderly, (2) phasing it out optionally (using tax incentives and medical savings accounts) for the middle-aged, and (3) telling young people that there will be no Medicare program for them and they must start saving for old age medical care on their own, with the help of tax incentives and medical savings accounts.[16] Medical savings accounts function like individual retirement accounts (IRAs), in which the individual saves money for medical care in a tax-free account.

It's time to face facts: Medicare failed, even at achieving its own goals. Health care inflation exploded after the passage of Medicare, at higher rates than even its biggest opponents ever predicted. Accepting that Medicare failed presupposes an acceptance of reality. Young people need not be frightened by the reality of facing a future without Medicare; based on the government's own projections, it's going to be bankrupt in a few years anyway.

Once doctors and hospitals are forced to compete with one another through competitive pricing, and have to answer directly to patients rather than to HMOs or government bureaucrats, then costs will not be inflated like they are now. No, medical care will not be "free" in a free market. But it never truly was free in the first place. Remember that Medicare (like any socialized program) has to be paid for by *somebody*, whether through taxes, government rationing, HMO rationing, or some combination of all three. Nothing, in reality, is ever free.

Why the Ethical Code of Self-Sacrifice
Makes Socialized Medicine Inevitable

A more widespread understanding of how capitalism works will not be enough, however, to end today's gridlock on the subject of health care. If it were, the collapse of communist economies throughout the world, and the failure of welfare-state democracies in Western Europe and Canada (not to mention America's New Deal and Great Society welfare programs), would have resolved the debate once and for all.

Yet the debate is far from over.

In the United States, for example, liberals still insist that more government control over doctors and patients is needed, despite the evidence that government controls have failed. Conservatives, overwhelmed by guilt for their "political incorrectness," likewise proceed, once in power, to expand the role of government in medicine even further.

Obviously, more deep-rooted philosophical and psychological issues must be identified and corrected before the trend toward a Canadian-like debacle can be reversed.

What are these issues? Responses to a Canadian survey on their health care crisis provides a significant clue. In this national survey, the majority of Canadians expressed the view that their socialized system, for all its problems, reflects their collective "generosity and compassion," and that the existence of such a system gives them at least one clear claim to being "morally superior" to the United States.[17]

Imagine! A system which provides—indeed, even mandates—pain, suffering, inefficiency and stagnation can somehow be morally superior to a capitalistic system which (when allowed to function without interference) promotes competition, technological superiority, affordability, and respect for the dignity of the human individual.

In other words, it is supposedly better for *everyone* to have mediocre (or worse) medical care, as is the case in Canada, than it would be for *some* to have excellent care, some to have very good care, and everyone to have at least adequate care (through voluntary charity, if necessary), as would be the case under a system of *laissez-faire* (pure) capitalism.

What kind of moral code could make such an outrageous contradiction possible? By what standard of ethics can one say, "Well, our health care system is a mess, and many people even die needlessly, but at least there's no evil profit or inequality here. We'd rather have people die than have prosperity, because prosperity means inequality and we cannot tolerate one iota of inequality."

The ethical code dominant in Canada, and increasingly dominant in the United States, is the code of altruism, or self-sacrifice: the idea that man's greatest virtue is not productivity and enjoyment of life, but sacrifice, guilt, and the willingness to live solely for the sake of others. In the United States, this ethical code is totally at odds with our constitutional framework of individual rights, which states that each individual has the right to pursue life and happiness to the fullest, without the imposition of force by others.

Tragically, more and more Americans (as evidenced by the continued slide towards socialized medicine as well as other Big Government policies) are choosing the moral code of self-sacrifice over freedom and individual rights, simply because they feel too guilty to do otherwise. The code of altruism, after all, is thoroughly compatible with both the conservative Judeo-Christian ethic, which emphasizes self-sacrifice and minimizes the importance of life on earth (in favor of an afterlife), as well as Big Government liberalism and political correctness, which stresses the replacement of self-interest with sacrifice to the state (for the alleged good of society or some particular group in society). Consequently, both liberals *and* conservatives feel too guilty to reverse the tide of altruism and socialism in the field of medicine, because to do so would mean violating their core ethical beliefs, however mistaken those beliefs prove to be.

How Nationalized Health Care
Requires a War Against Facts and Reality

Even more fundamental issues than ethics add to the perseverance of socialized medicine, despite its notorious inefficiencies. Dr. Ted Rumble, an orthopedic surgeon in Toronto who is cooperating with the doctors' protest movement in Canada, summed up one such issue very well: "The public doesn't want a high quality medical system, it wants a *free* system."[18] [italics added].

My own experience as a health professional suggests that Rumble's statement applies as much to the United States as to Canada. Too many people resent the fact that they cannot have something for nothing, particularly in the case of medical care. In a way, who can blame them? As already pointed out, the government health policies make nearly everyone dependent on a third party—their employer, the insurance company, the government—for paying the medical bills. Like the spoiled teenager who does not have to pay for his car, his gasoline, his clothes, or his education, many American adults feel that their medical care should just be available—*somehow*—and they should not even have to shop for it and compare prices like they feel the responsibility for doing in other areas of life.

To make matters even worse, they are continuously told by the majority of their politicians, their religious leaders, their psychotherapists, their professors, and their media experts that they have a right to health care on demand, as if health care grew on trees.

The strongest proponents of the "right" to health care, and of socialized policies in general, typically possess an underlying metaphysical belief that reality is somehow unfair and unjust. That because health care—or whatever else, for that matter—does not grow on trees, then "there ought to be a law" to make the desired commodity do the equivalent of growing on trees.

Forcing us all to pretend that the nature of reality is other than what it is by having a President sign a feel-good bill is (at best) irrational and dishonest; it also never works, at least beyond the immediate range of the moment. Of course, politicians are always delighted to participate in the charade, if it means advancing their short-term visibility and power. The simple fact remains that we cannot wish—or compel—"free" health care (or "free" anything) into existence.

Wendee Harper, a Canadian citizen angry because the government officials cannot seem to "reform" the socialized system (in other words, to somehow make the impossible "work"), offers a good illustration of this something-for-nothing mentality.[19] What kinds of "reforms" do the Wendee Harpers of the world, outraged by the inadequacies of their socialized system, usually support? Certainly not replacing the socialized system with a free market, which would be both morally and practically superior to the status quo. Instead, they go along with the government's promotion of "utilization review" and "limiting" of "unnecessary" medical visits. In a word: rationing. Then they turn around and whine to the media that the government is rationing, instead of reforming, and wonder why they are distressed and confused.

Among academic and media elites there exists a far less innocent, yet characteristically stubborn, refusal to face the facts. What facts, exactly? The overwhelming evidence that socialism in all of its forms—communism, social democracy, national socialism, welfare state liberalism—has failed by every conceivable economic and moral indicator. Every time socialism is tried, it fails. It fails in exact proportion to the degree it is attempted. It fails both morally *and* economically. By its very nature, socialism has to fail because to accept its basic premises is to ignore the nature of reality.

The childish attachment to the idea of government medicine, in Canada and elsewhere, appears at times almost mystical. A *New York Times* reporter, for example, has described the "sacred place in the shrine of Canadian values" its citizens seem to hold for its disastrous medical system.[20] Former Prime Minister Margaret Thatcher of Great Britain, an unusually determined free market reformer, could not in the 1980's make any real inroads against the English loyalty to their socialized medical system, despite its by then obvious failures.[21] To cite a more recent example in our own country, witness the hysterical rage many American political activists demonstrate if the possibility of cutting the rate of growth of the Medicare program—to say nothing of privatizing it altogether—is even mentioned.

Indeed, religious preachers have good reason to envy the reverence and unreasoned faith given to such bottomless pits as Medicare, Social Security, and Medicaid. While crossing oneself and kneeling at church may be increasingly out of vogue, it is now fashionable to do the equivalent at the feet of Congressmen and Presidents—who are expected to somehow provide for us what we are unwilling to provide for ourselves.

How sad for a society founded on the principles of individualism, freedom, and self-reliance.

Evasion and Denial: The Final Break With Reality

Perhaps the ugliest demonstration of a fundamental idea which enables the dysfunctional and irrational Canadian health system to continue comes once again from the national survey of Canadian citizens.[22] Incredibly, the survey actually found people divided over whether doctors should tell patients that their treatment may not be the best available. Some Canadians responded that they would want to know so they could decide for themselves whether or not to go to the United States for treatment. *But a significant number said they would have more peace of mind simply not knowing.*

If you want to know the essence of psychological disorder, this is it. Psychologists call it "denial." Denial means the false, irrational belief that "if I pretend something is not so, even in the presence of objective facts, it will not be so." Philosophers call it the primacy of consciousness over reality. Ayn Rand, a philosopher who advocated the primacy of reality, referred to the phenomenon of willful evasion as the root of all evil. She defined evasion as "that nameless act which all of you practice, but struggle never to admit: the act of blanking out, the willful suspension of one's consciousness, the refusal to think—not blindness, but the refusal to see; not ignorance, but the refusal to know. It is the act of unfocusing your mind and inducing an inner fog to escape the responsibility of judgment—on the unstated premise that a thing will not exist if only you refuse to identify it, that A will not be A so long as you do not pronounce the verdict 'It *is*.'"[23]

If you want to know the psychological and ethical mechanism which maintains an irrational state of affairs—whether in the case of an alcoholic, abusive father whose problem everyone pretends does not exist, *or* in the case of a child molester, whose activity is suspected within a family but nobody dares say so aloud, *or* in the case of a medical system which leads to inefficiency and death but everyone pretends is "noble"— then evasion is it. Its essence is as follows: "If I shut my eyes and cover my ears, the problem will go away." To the evader, consciousness supersedes reality. What he feels or wishes to be true is put ahead of what is true, and of what the evidence proves.

The ability of a human consciousness to rationally ascertain the facts of an objective reality is cynically dismissed by the evader. With this rejection of the ability to perceive objective reality comes the rationalization of behaviors ranging from lying to child abuse to political dictatorship. After all, if we lowly humans are unable to access reality and to think independently, then by what means do we assert our right to be free? Evasion, and its psychological cousin denial, do indeed represent the root of all evil, at least if the "good" is defined as human survival and happiness.

Doctors Fight Back: Medicine's Last Chance

In the midst of the Canadian health care crisis (and the growing American one) there does exist one hopeful development not seen before, at least not on any organized and public scale: the protest of Canadian doctors against the socialized system. In Canada, more and more doctors are refusing to accept new referrals because of frustration over irrational government policies. They also pressured the government to take only 2.9 percent of their incomes for alleged "administrative costs" rather than the initially mandated 10 percent.[24] Even further, they have fought the government's attempt to force urban Toronto doctors out of their practices into more rural areas farther north.

If Canadian physicians can find the courage to fight irrational and unjust government mandates, then American doctors—who at present still enjoy more freedom than their Canadian counterparts—should be able to muster the same courage. They should assert their moral right to sell their valued services in a free market, with no constraints by the government other than for objectively proven fraud and malpractice. They should give up the illusion of a free lunch offered by the Medicare program, and replace it with the much greater promise offered by the re-implementation of the trader principle into American medicine. They should recognize that patients (consumers), as well as doctors (suppliers), ultimately prosper better in a free market.

Furthermore, in a free society, voluntary generosity and kindness will never be against the law. People, in fact, are more likely to engage in individual acts of voluntary charity when the government does not take forty percent or more of their income to use for welfare state programs.

Too often we all forget that while in a free market there are no limits set on prices, there are also no limits or constraints on excellence, both in medical practice and the development of new technology. We also forget that Canada and other socialized systems only survive because they can lean on the United States both for supplemental care and the development and marketing of ever more sophisticated, life-saving technologies. If we want continued excellence in medicine, we have to be willing to pay for it. The Canadians don't have to pay for it, because they can turn to the United States, which still permits a degree of capitalism in the area of medical technology. But what happens when the remaining remnants of the profit motive and free enterprise are eliminated from American medicine as well?

Capitalism, doctors must not be afraid to point out, delivers the goods—and because of its respect for the rights of the individual, it is the only proper, humane, and moral social system mankind has ever known. If anyone doubts this fact, contrast the results of semi-capitalism in the United States with the results of socialism or semi-socialism in Russia, Nazi Germany, Western Europe and Canada, and draw your own conclusions. There must be some reason why, when the chips are down, everyone comes to America for medical treatment unavailable elsewhere.

Great medical care would never have been possible in a society that did not respect the individual rights of doctors. When told about a patient's refusal to pay for his services, Dr. Aaron Shutt, a fictitious surgeon in the CBS television series *Chicago Hope*, stated, "It's not about money. It is about respect. Surgery is *my* art. It's *my* craft. It's mine to sell; it's mine to give away. People . . . think it's free for the taking. Well it's *not*. And I'm going to do something about it."

It's time for all doctors to do something about it.   ⊕

15. See *The New York Times*, "Doctor, What's the Prognosis? Crisis for Canada" December 15, 1996

16. For more detailed proposals on privatizing the health care field, contact Americans for Free Choice in Medicine, 1525 Superior Ave., Suite 100, Newport Beach, CA 92663 949-645-2622, *e-mail* mail@afcm.org or *website* http://www.afcm.org.

17. *The New York Times*, December 15, 1996.

18. *Ibid.*

19. *Ibid.*

20. *Ibid.*

21. Margaret Thatcher, *The Downing Street Years, 1979-90* (New York: Harper Collins, 1993), pp. 606-617.

22. *The New York Times*, December 15, 1996.

23. Ayn Rand, *Atlas Shrugged* (New York: Dutton, 1957; 1992 edition), p. 1017.

24. *The New York Times*, December 15, 1996.

Chapter 16

Liberating
the Mind

WHY ALL SCHOOLS
SHOULD BE PRIVATE SCHOOLS

In the ongoing education reform debate, one essential question is never raised by the dominant media and intellectual establishment of our culture.

By what right, morally or politically, does the government force individuals to pay for public education? If my next-door neighbor should have no obligation to pay my mortgage or rent, then why should I have any obligation to pay for her child's education?

A free country is supposed to be a free country; this includes making decisions about how to spend one's own money. Money represents a frozen form of man's productive and creative energy; consequently, to forcibly take a man's money is to steal his soul. We cannot let the fact that federal control of education often leads to ridiculous policies (e.g. sexual harassment guidelines for first-graders, black "English" as a second language) distract us from the more basic truth that the government has no business—indeed, no *moral right*—being in the field of education in the first place.

The government should get out of the schools altogether. Total privatization represents the only long-range solution to the education crisis. Privatization may take years to complete, but must be initiated before the meddling, irrational bureaucrats of the world, like perpetually sprouting weeds, take over the education garden entirely.

Tax credits for education and tax-free education savings accounts (similar to retirement IRA's and Medical Savings Accounts) are good beginning steps to privatization. Closing down the federal Department of Education is also a very good idea. Schools should be privately and voluntarily funded *only* by those who choose to attend them. Private and voluntary charities, instead of callous, controlling, and inefficient government bureaucracies, can help poor people as they have done in the past and still do even today. The individuals who pay for the schools—the students, their parents, voluntary benefactors—can privately contract with the school owners and teachers to set appropriate policies and determine specific educational methods, including how to score tests and how much money to spend on facilities.

Needlessly divisive, politicized debates over sex education and prayer in the schools can be left to parents, deciding in the marketplace—*as consumers*—how best to spend their private education dollars. Religious parents will send their kids to religious schools, and secular parents will send their kids to schools who do not teach religion. The same applies to sex education or any other controversial issue. No government authority, "liberal" or "conservative," should have the final say on how all schools resolve these debates.

The intense competition of the marketplace will do for education what it did for other fields free of government intervention: it will keep prices down so that private schools will be accessible to greater numbers of people. Competition will also break the backs of the tyrannical, government-enforced teachers' unions and require educators to do quality work. Privatized schools will require teachers to please consumers—that is, to be *competent*—if they are to stay in business, instead of bribing and blackmailing politicians to do their bidding. In a private market, merit pay represents the *only* kind of pay possible—which is precisely why the nationalized teachers unions are so threatened by even the tiniest hint of competition to the public schools.

Best of all: Once the government stops paying the bills, then it will no longer be able to call the shots. Instead, the proponents of such policies as sexual harassment charges against 6-year-olds and turning street slang into a legitimate language will be off the taxpayer's payroll forever. Rest assured that people with such ideas will never gain much influence in a free market.

Complete privatization of education means that in the marketplace of ideas and teaching methods, the best ones—i.e., the most rational ones, the ones most in conformity with reality, the ones that *work*—will win. Only in such an environment, free of government controls and free of government dogma, can American education finally realize its full potential. We will all be the better for it.

MORAL GUIDANCE & THE SCHOOL CURRICULUM

Many people are shocked by the growing number of school children shooting their teachers, parents and classmates. But if you think about it, it's not so surprising.

Public schools increasingly teach children how to *feel* rather than how to think. They tell children that there is really no such thing as good or bad or right or wrong and that it is bad to make moral judgments.

In a therapy session, I once spoke with a father and his son. I asked the son if his father was correct that the "rap" music the boy enjoyed glorified evil in human beings. Without hesitation the son replied, "Who is my father to judge? There is no such thing as good or bad. So we can't say if the music I like glorifies evil."

I then asked the son, "If you leave this office and a man holds you up with a gun, and takes all your money, would you call this a good thing, a bad thing, or a neutral thing?"

I received no reply. But I knew this boy's teachers had done their job well.

Should we be surprised that some children take what they are taught seriously? If there is no right or wrong, why not shoot your parents, teachers, and classmates when they anger you? If feelings are more important than reason and truth, nobody can (or should) exercise self-restraint.

Private schools do not have these problems. They can teach a code of ethics without fear of losing government financing. Private schools answer to parents who pay the bill rather than to third parties like teachers' unions and bureaucrats.

It is time to totally privatize education and place control over curriculum in the hands of parents (the consumers).

FORCE & INTIMIDATION VS. REASON & PERSUASION—WHY GOVERNMENT EDUCATION CAN *NEVER* WORK

He who pays the bill sets the terms.

Since the U.S. government pays most of the bills for education, in the form of subsidies, grants, and loans, it should come as no surprise that the very same government seeks to set the terms by which the majority of children will learn.

For a concrete illustration of this point, consider the actions of Norma V. Cantu, head of the U.S. Department of Education's Office of Civil Rights (OCR) during the 1990's.

Cantu's Office of Civil Rights, like other similar government agencies, enjoys almost absolute power to impose on schools and colleges throughout the country what its members feel to be "equality" and "justice."

Unlike other Washington regulators, Cantu admits to no pretense at "moderation" or pragmatism. She is a principled, consistent and unapologetic government bureaucrat. In short: she loves her job, and cashes in daily on the mistaken philosophical premises which make it possible.

The nature of those premises can best be illustrated by examining the policies Cantu has imposed since taking office.

Some examples:

- Issued guidelines making it possible for schools to press charges against 6-year-olds for "sexual harassment;"
- Pressured the College Board and Educational Testing Service to make the PSAT (pre-college admission tests) easier for girls so they can score better and win a proportionate share of National Merit Scholarships;
- Accused Ohio schools of racism because a large number of high school students failing an eighth-grade level test were black—even in the face of evidence that the students who failed had high absentee rates and ample opportunity to take remedial courses;
- Reversed earlier Department of Education decisions outlawing government funding of racist (i.e. black only, white only, etc.) scholarships;
- Threatened to withdraw federal funding from schools and colleges who fail to provide identical sports facilities for males and females, regardless of the needs of the individual school.

Cantu's approach to government control of education is best summarized by her own statement: "We don't wait for issues to come to us. We institute our own investigation...I'm not shy about enforcement."

Welcome to the era of entrepreneurial government—or as Cantu calls it, "proactive government." Today, government does not merely enforce laws, once evidence exists for their violation. Now the government actually goes out and looks for opportunities to enforce laws—indeed, as we shall see, to even make new ones on a whim—

at the cost of further violating individual rights. As Cantu herself insists, "The adversarial role [of government] has its place."

In an age of supposed government downsizing and the alleged elimination of federal funds for education, it seems remarkable that Cantu's office not only survives, but expands. On October 1, 1996, an additional branch of the Office of Civil Rights opened in the Washington, DC, area, enabling the OCR to increase its "proactive" caseload. So much for empty political promises that the era of big government is over.

Why Federal Regulation of Schools Makes No Sense

Admittedly, in the cynical, pragmatic atmosphere of today's Washington, it is refreshing to find one government official who subscribes, openly, to a set of principles—and practices them without hesitation. The tragedy lies in the fact that Cantu's principles are profoundly irrational and unjust, and the consequences will be devastating to both an already collapsing public school system and an increasingly statist society.

What are the core, implicit principles to which Cantu subscribes? What are the philosophical premises which make her policies possible—the premises which operate in any era, no matter who happens to be in charge in Washington?

Anti-reality, anti-reason and—only as a consequence of the first two—anti-freedom.

How is Cantu anti-reality? The ideology of the OCR is based upon open hostility to the facts. She consistently disregards the bigger picture—the wider context—in her decision making. In Cantu, we find a government bureaucrat who openly relishes her power and makes no effort to hide her desire to use that power arbitrarily and subjectively.

Consider the case of equal athletic facilities for boys and girls. Cantu feels it is unfair for boys and girls to have sports facilities geared to the specific needs and desires of the male and female students. Consequently, schools must be forced to spend precious money to duplicate boys and girls' sports facilities, whether they need or want these facilities. To the bureaucrats and lawyers at the OCR, no further discussion of the wider context is required.

But, in the real world outside of Washington, DC, the wider contextual questions nevertheless arise. What if more boys than girls want such facilities at a particular school (or vice versa)? No matter—because facts are secondary. What if boys are—as a whole—objectively better than girls at the types of sports in demand at a particular school? What if girls are—as a whole—objectively better than boys at the types of sports desired at a different school? No matter—"fairness" counts, not objective merit. What if a particular school depends heavily on revenue from male athletic competition, and as a consequence chooses to spend more on male sports for its economic survival? Again, such a question need not occur to the OCR staff at the Department of Education in Washington, DC. Economic survival, objective facts, and individual rights are all secondary to what the bureaucrats consider "fair."

Consider another example. Cantu's agency is responsible for the recently publicized "sexual harassment" guidelines for 6-year-olds. According to these policies, first-graders can be disciplined under federal guidelines for sexual harassment. If a boy teases a girl on the playground, the offending student is not simply subject to the criticism and punishment of a teacher or a parent; the offending student is now elevated to the status of a federal criminal.

Once again, the very foundation for such ridiculous regulations presupposes a massive evasion of factual context by those who advocate them. The concept of "sexual harassment," in the proper sense of the term, clearly refers to adult employers who threaten underlings with firing or other negative consequences if those underlings refuse to have sex with them or otherwise respond to their sexual advances. Sexual advances or sexual behavior are completely irrelevant to 6-year-olds. Most 6-year-olds are only starting to grasp the nature of gender differences. Do these facts matter to the OCR? No, because at the OCR, factual context can be ignored in favor of dogmatic, sweeping edicts. Such is the nature of arbitrary, "no-fault" government power.

In both examples, Cantu uses the legitimate concepts of fairness and equality to cover up the fact that objective, rational reasons often exist for discriminating between boys and girls in the field of sports, or between adults and children in the area of sexual harassment. She counts on our willingness—or our fear—to refuse to ask the obvious questions such as, "Isn't there a basic difference between a boy teasing a girl on a playground and an adult employer threatening to fire his employee if she does not have sex with him?" In short, she counts on our refusal to *think*, and on what she hopes is a profound lack of confidence in our ability to form judgments. She can then proceed to issue her arbitrary edicts without question and without opposition.

Like so many other government mini-dictators, Cantu forces the rest of us to pay for her refusal to live in reality. Not only do her policies make no sense; every taxpayer in the country must foot the bill to implement them.

Why Government Educators Must Rely On Physical Coercion

Just as Cantu's policies rest upon the anti-reality methods of context-dropping and intellectual evasion, so too do they rely upon the anti-reason approach of initiating physical force and the assertion of the arbitrary and the emotional over the objective.

Examine the case of the Corpus Christi, Texas, school district. Even though the school district paid for its mostly male sports facilities with primarily private donations, the OCR threatened to withdraw $20 million in federal funds unless they immediately equalized male and female sports facilities. Why? Because Cantu and her colleagues wanted them to do so. Does this sound like a fair, equitable, and just policy? If protection of rights are truly at stake here, what about the parents, students, and benefactors who paid for the sports facilities with their own money? Do they have any rights?

At first, the school district resisted the federal government's control until it recognized that their schools could not survive without the federal money. Remember that the government effectively holds a monopoly on the education of American children. People have no choice about whether or not to pay for public schools. Nobody forces them to buy a certain type of car, or to buy a certain type of car for their neighbor; somehow, in the area of education, such freedom of choice ends. The impotence of the Corpus Christi school district at the hands of the federal government illustrates the truth of Ayn Rand's statement: "If 'the power to tax is the power to destroy,' the power to disburse government funds is the power to rule." Washington, DC is full of petty dictators—little Napoleons, little Hitlers—who understand this principle all too well, and are just dying to rule us.

Imagine the bitterness and hostility which will linger at these schools, long after Cantu's reign at the OCR is history. Does she actually believe that she advances her idea of equal treatment for boys and girls rationally, and peaceably, when she in fact uses brute force and emotional-political blackmail to impose it? Does the fact that she manages to compel parents, teachers, and school administrators to do things her way necessarily mean that she successfully persuades them to her point-of-view?

Of course not. Force and persuasion represent polar opposites. The Cantus of the world rely on coercion and intimidation, not reason; on emotion and context-dropping, not objective facts. In the face of such massive evasion—the sort of evasion required to claim that six-year olds can be guilty of sexual harassment, or that equalizing test scores and baseball fields constitutes "education"—one can only conclude that policies such as the OCR's are motivated by something other than concern for "equality" and "justice." Serious thinkers do not rely on physical force to advance their ideas.

Though the era of big government is supposedly over, the OCR—and countless government agencies like it—continue to ignore the rights of private individuals such as school superintendents, teachers, parents and students. The real meaning behind Cantu's "proactive" law, as its victims most fully understand, is arbitrary, non-objective law. In other words, the OCR can enforce whatever its bureaucrats feel like they want to enforce. Unfortunately, our biased mainstream media and academic establishment do a poor job of informing us of these everyday injustices as they fawn at the altar of an ever-expanding government.

Can Discrimination Ever Be Rational?

A statement Cantu made before a Senate Committee in 1995 reveals the true extent of her opposition to reason, rationality, and the capacity of humans to make objective judgments. She said, "Mr. Chairman, there is no place for discrimination in sports. *Discrimination goes against the very grain of what competition is all about.*" [Italics added].

Nothing could be further from the truth. Discrimination—specifically, *rational* discrimination—is precisely what competition in any endeavor is all about. Discrimination, in the rational sense, is a form of conceptual distinction, a means of separating kinds and degrees of entities from one another. Even using simple common sense, we can all discriminate the difference between an Olympic swimmer and an amateur; the winner of the Wimbleton tennis match versus a beginner; an Academy

Award-winning actor versus a novice. Likewise, a more experienced observer or a professional judge can, using objective standards, discriminate between a good Olympic athlete and the best Olympic athlete in a given category; between a good actor and the best actor, based on a set of observable standards. If objective judgments such as these were not humanly possible, then not even the wisest government bureaucrat would be able to make them for us.

Cantu and the legions of subjectivists in government and academia would have us believe that there exists only one type of discrimination: the irrational kind. The kind of nonsensical discrimination that leads one to treat hasty judgments as truth. The kind of discrimination that leads one to irrationally conclude that a black person has a certain type of character, or a woman a certain type of ability, before knowing anything else factual about the individual person.

While properly condemning these types of discrimination and prejudice, Cantu and other subjectivists try to sneak in the unwarranted conclusion that "since some judgments are irrational, then basic human judgment—by its very nature—is flawed." Since people sometimes use their capacity for reason improperly, the subjectivists want us to believe that reason and objectivity are themselves impossible.

From this foundation that all objective judgment is impossible, and that the very notion of human reason represents a farce, the road to an all-controlling government is not too hard to pave. If individual human beings are incapable of objective judgments, after all, then how can they operate without a big government to do their thinking for them? Or, to put it in more psychological terms: "How can I survive if the government does not take care of me, and tell me what to do?"

Americans Are Addicted to Big Government

Tragically, it is today's voting American citizens who are not only paving the way to bigger government, but also providing the concrete and the bulldozers. Some do not recognize the wide-scale dysfunction they are enabling, because too many politicians (in both major parties) loudly claim they are against big government when closer examination of their actions proves just the opposite to be true.

Ironically enough, the stubborn American addiction to big government politicians and bloated programs contains an internal, if sad, consistency. My experience as a therapist has shown that deep down, too many people feel that they are inadequate to judge anything, even the direction of their own lives. In such a social-psychological climate, the terror many people display at the prospect of making even minuscule cuts in the size and scope of the government should come as no surprise. Their psychologists, teachers, and media gurus, many of whom sneer at objective reality and common sense, have trained them to be "non-judgmental," "sensitive," and "caring"—all at the expense of rationality and intelligence. Feelings, they are told over and over, are ultimately more important than facts and reality. The result? A big government that will not go away, a big government designed to serve as a stand-in for those trained by their newspapers, by their psychotherapists, or by their ministers or preachers, to think, "Who am I to judge?"

Of course, the other side of the question is rarely raised: If human beings are, by their very nature, incapable of objective judgments, then what gives Norma Cantu (or any government authority) the ability, much less the right, to make their judgments for them? Could it be that she, and her many counterparts in Washington, simply want their *own* judgments to rule? In a totalitarian country, you would be jailed, tortured, or perhaps killed for even asking such a question. In today's United States, you may not be jailed, but you will be branded insensitive, a racist or a "hater," and every attempt will be made to discredit you—merely for asking the question.

Even so, the truth remains the truth, reality is what it is, and the question begs for an answer even as it is suppressed. "If man is impotent to think and reason, then by what means do the government authorities—themselves mere human beings—know what I should do? And if man *is* able to think and reason, then by what right do these government authorities chart the course of my life for me? By what right do these authorities tell me how to eat, dress, think, live, have sex, and raise my children?" The absence of this question from today's political and social "debates" merely strengthens its relevance. If its absence continues much longer, the consequences to the mental health and freedom of this country will be devastating.

In the final analysis, Norma Cantu represents nothing more than a parasite on the good will and mistaken assumptions of too many American individuals. Sadly, she is a parasite with the power (at least right now) to pursue her agenda of adversarial, "proactive" government with few restraints other than occasional criticism from an irate Congressman or a once-in-a-blue-moon unfavorable court decision. But, in a democracy, her ability to continue with her agenda is only as powerful as its citizens' willingness to accept her ideas. It is the mistaken *ideas* underlying her policies that must be challenged and defeated.

To subdue Cantu and bureaucrats like her, you cannot simply characterize them as "too extreme" or lacking in "common sense" (even though these points may be true). Instead, you have to check the premises that made it possible for them to rise to power, attack those ideas at their roots, and advance the opposing ideas: reality, reason, and freedom.

You also have to expose their manipulation and deceit and name it for what it is. In Cantu's case, the fraud lies in the equation of her ridiculous policies with the "education" of children. Like all parasites, Cantu exploits a rational concept to advance her own irrational programs. A true robber baron of the intellect, she exploits the rational value of education to justify her preposterous policies which have nothing to do with education.

If you try to oppose her policies of sexual harassment among 6-year-olds as unfair or ridiculous, she will most likely attack by saying, "What? Are you against education? Are you against justice? What kind of hateful person are you?" If you persist in your questioning, however politely, she will wail to the news media that, "The tone of civility has vanished from our public debate." This is precisely the method by which today's big government subjectivists now fight for survival, and manage to win even in an increasingly hostile political and fiscal climate. They don't need to resort to censorship; our irrational, neurotic guilt (so long as we fail to cure it) does the job for them.

If you want justice to triumph, then you must first grasp, and then spread, the idea that reality supersedes wishes. That feelings and objective facts are not necessarily one and the same thing. That human beings are capable of reason, so long as they ground their abstract, generalized conclusions in actual, empirical facts (something the Cantus of the world fail to do). The human mind is not impotent. The individual has both the ability and the right to make decisions about his own life, including his education and his childrens' education, without the imposition of government force.

The alternative to force and intimidation is reason and persuasion. The implementation of reason, practically speaking, is a free market—that is, a totally private sector—of education. Education and the state must be kept separate in the same way and for the same reasons that church and state are separate. "But education is too important!" you might reply. Precisely. It is for this very reason that the government must get out of the education field altogether. The human mind, in its formative stages of development, is too important to leave to people like Norma Cantu. Ms. Cantu's right to spread her ideas must be protected; but everyone else's right *not* to pay for them must be protected as well.

SMOKESCREEN—ADD AND THE PUBLIC SCHOOL SYSTEM

The public school system's obsession with "attention deficit disorder" (ADD) is really a reflection of its own failure to teach kids effectively. The quality of its schools is so poor that large numbers of children simply see no good reason to focus and pay attention. Incredibly, one-hundred percent of ADD-labeled kids referred to my practice attend public—not private—schools.

Replacing the public education system with a private, voluntarily funded one would allow for competition among teaching methods and continuous improvement in quality. Just as computers and automobiles get better and better in the marketplace, so too can education.

Privatized schools would also allow for individual choice. Numerous good educational methods exist. Different methods will work for different children. Public schools, because of their bureaucratic-political nature, have to adopt a "one-size-fits-all" mentality. Their mandate is to be all things to all people. Consequently, they spend far more money per pupil than do private schools, but do not produce good results.

In order to attain excellence, an enterprise or institution must face the risk of going out of business. Public schools, unlike private schools, do not face this risk. They are guaranteed funding no matter what results they produce. In fact, when they fail to produce good results, they usually get *more* funding because the teachers' union monopolies insist that lack of money, rather than lack of competence, is the problem.

This rewarding of mediocrity and failure is a disastrous policy, as well as a raw deal for taxpayers. Parents who want to send their kids to private schools should not have to pay for government schools. Childless taxpayers should not have to pay for *any* schools. To force them to do so is a violation of their individual, Constitutional rights.

The growing endorsement of the ADD label by education officials represents a way to distract attention from the fact that public schools are simply failing at their mission. If politicians and teachers can scream, "We have an outbreak of ADD!" then they need not focus on the fact that more and more kids graduate from public schools unable to read, write, and think.

Sooner or later we must face the real problem. Public schools have failed. They need to be put out of business.   ⊕

Chapter 17

How to Grow Up Morally & Ethically

GUILTY . . . OR NOT GUILTY?

At the root of many negative emotions and psychological problems is unearned guilt. Most of us do not distinguish between "earned" and "unearned" guilt. Earned guilt is taking responsibility for something which you directly caused. Unearned guilt is taking responsibility for something which you did not directly cause.

On the surface, this might sound like common sense. And the distinction between earned and unearned guilt is certainly quite logical. Unfortunately, many of our cultural institutions are not always so logical, and if we fail to think carefully about the issue of guilt we can develop psychological symptoms such as depression and anxiety.

A proper understanding of guilt requires, first of all, an understanding about the issue of responsibility. In my experience, the vast majority of individuals who are psychologically distressed tend to take too much responsibility for things they cannot control, and too little responsibility for things they are able to control.

A man drinks an excessive amount of alcohol, for example, because he worries about whether he will be able to send his infant son to college when he turns eighteen; in the process, his work performance is affected. A woman worries constantly about whether her new boyfriend will cheat on her; in the process, she becomes irritable and obnoxious in his presence even though she cares for him very much. A student obsesses on what his final grade will be; in the process, he is distracted from concentrating on his assignments and term papers.

Once you have a firm grasp of what you are and are not able to control, the issue of responsibility becomes less of a problem. For example, the man who drinks too much will realize that he cannot control future tuition fees; the best he can do is concentrate on his job and save as much money as possible. The woman who worries about her boyfriend cheating on her realizes that she has no evidence of any infidelity; so she resolves to enjoy every moment with him to the fullest. The student who dwells on his final grade will understand that he creates his grade, in part, by the level of concentration he applies to his reading assignment and papers; so he focuses instead on getting his work done.

Now for the issue of guilt. Imagine that you have achieved a college degree, and you are offered a high-paying and prestigious job. One of your close friends, who graduated with you, is having a hard time finding any kind of job. You are both in the same field and have about the same level of intelligence. Your friend says to you: "*It must be nice* to have a good job lined up." You notice that you feel kind of guilty. If you fail to examine this guilt—and determine whether it has any basis in reality—you might be tempted to downplay your achievement, even to yourself. For example, you might think: "I guess I really am just star-crossed. Things always seem to work out for me. I must have a guardian angel watching out for me!" Consequently, you will always feel a little guilty for your accomplishment.

But what about the fact that you may have actually earned the better job—and that it was not merely "luck" or "fate?" If you look at both yourself and your friend objectively, you might discover that you sent out dozens of resumes, while he sent out only three. Or, you might find evidence that you make a better presentation in an interview. The point is that you earned your accomplishment, and you made it happen. While you might feel some compassion for your friend in his struggle to find a job, and you might even choose to give him some suggestions, you will not feel any measure of guilt for your own success.

Unearned guilt often has much more serious consequences. A mother of a teenage boy, for example, reads a book about dysfunctional families. She recognizes characteristics of her own family in the definition of "dysfunctional" offered by the book. The book also says that being dysfunctional is a "disease," and that unless treated by a specific psychological therapy she will continue to be diseased. She begins to feel tremendously guilty because of her failure to seek out such treatment sooner. As a result, she starts to give in to her son's demands to stay out late, even though his grades are poor. He soon is able to convince her to give in to all kinds of unreasonable and unwarranted demands, which in turn leads her to feel even more guilty.

How can you ensure that you will not suffer from unearned guilt? The answer is simple: question your assumptions. If someone says to you, *"It must be nice* to have such a big house," and you feel guilty, then question the basis of the guilt. Did you purchase the house through unethical means, or did you really earn it? Or, if your child says, "You are an abusive mother," then question this before you let yourself feel guilty. Is your child calling you abusive because you physically assault him, or because you will not allow him to use the family car until he stops drinking alcohol? Once again, all of this seems like common sense. But most people do not take the time to question their basic assumptions.

Keep in mind, too, that the idea of unearned guilt has powerful cultural roots. Many religious and political leaders still actively teach children that they are not only responsible for their own errors, but also the errors of those who went before them. Ideas such as these are very powerful, even if you do not think of them very often. It should not be surprising, therefore, that you carry over such invalid assumptions into your everyday life. The good news is that *you* have the choice to think differently, and to enjoy the benefits of a life free from unearned guilt.

THE ROUTE TO HAPPINESS

Most people assume that happiness is a blessing, and not an achievement.

In fact, just the opposite is true. Happiness is a state which must be *achieved* as a consequence of what you do and the way you think. Before one can be happy, one must accept this premise. No amount of psychotherapy, self-esteem workshops or pop-psychology books can help you without an acceptance of the fact that you are responsible for achieving your own happiness.

Once you accept this premise, then you can begin the work of achieving happiness. First of all, you must learn to identify what makes you happy. For some of you, this ability has been so crushed that you might not have a clue as to where to begin. If this is the case, start by taking small steps—such as identifying your preferences. When ordering in a restaurant, for example, stop and ask yourself, "Which item do I really want?" When invited to two separate social affairs, make sure you identify which one (if either) is your genuine preference, and act accordingly. When trying to decide among vacation possibilities, take time to consider which locations you would enjoy the most.

It is necessary to master these small steps before expecting success in the more important arenas of career and romantic relationships. In these more complex areas, you must not only know your preferences, but also the fundamental values which drive your choices. In other words, are you choosing a particular career because it looks easy, and because it is socially acceptable—or because you are aware of the skills it requires, and have both the talent and the motivation to learn them? Are you choosing a particular romantic partner solely because of physical appearance or religious-national origin—or because you know the person well, and have concluded, without ignoring relevant facts, that he or she shares your most fundamental ideals and desires (to enjoy life, raise children, travel the world, be productive and honest, etc.)?

Achieving happiness is no easy task. Even if you accept the idea that it is your own responsibility, you are subject to mistakes and even disasters along the way. But in the long run, and throughout most of your life, happiness will be yours—*if* you first accept responsibility for achieving it.

WHAT'S SO BAD ABOUT BEING SELFISH?

Most of us assume that selfishness is both wrong and unhealthy. But is this true?

Selfishness means acting in one's rational self-interest. Contrary to popular opinion, all healthy individuals *are* selfish. Choosing to pursue the career of your choice is selfish. Choosing to have children—or not to have children—is selfish. Insisting on freedom and individual rights, rather than living under a dictatorship, is selfish. Indeed, even ordinary behaviors such as breathing, eating and avoiding an oncoming car when crossing the street are selfish acts. Without selfishness, none of us would survive the day—much less a lifetime.

Selfishness does not mean self-destructive behavior. In other words, a car thief is not selfish. He has to run from the law constantly, something most car owners never have to do. Even if he escapes the law, he will not experience as much pleasure from possessing the car as would an honest person.

Lying to your spouse, or any loved one, is not selfish. The psychological stress of trying to "live the lie" of an extramarital affair—or any major secret—is enormous. A selfish person understands that honesty is the best policy and the least painful, in the long run.

The opposite of selfishness is self-sacrifice. Self-sacrifice means giving up a greater value for a lesser value. Consider the example of a battered wife, who is married to an alcoholic husband who refuses to seek help. She stays with him for reasons of "security" and "family stability." Yet in the process she sacrifices her self-esteem and physical safety (greater values) to the irrational whims of her husband (lesser values).

Consider the example of the hard-working student who allows a friend to copy his answers on an examination. The student is sacrificing both his integrity and his efforts (greater values) to the laziness and low self-esteem of his "friend" (lesser values).

Or, consider the envious individual who tries to get you to feel guilty for your hard-earned success. "You are lucky to have done so well," the envious person says. "Now you have a duty to share some of your success with others." Certainly, a selfish person wants to share his success with those he genuinely cares about—his family, friends, or children (greater values). But why should he make sacrifices to individuals he does not know or care about (lesser values)?

Selfish individuals give to charity—if and when they choose. A selfish person is not "stingy." He simply values the use of his own judgment in making decisions about how to spend his money, and when to give it away.

Most of us assume that some selfishness is healthy, but "too much" selfishness will lead to loneliness and despair. This idea rests on an incorrect definition of selfishness. Selfishness means acting in one's rational self-interest. By "rational" I mean that one can logically prove that an action is in one's self-interest—in the long run as well as the short run.

For instance, Mr. Jones might think that it is in his self-interest to cheat on his wife, in the short run. But if he considers the long-term, he will understand that he loses her either way by lying to her. If he really loves his wife, he will feel terrible if he lies to her. If he no longer loves his wife, it is senseless to continue living with her and conducting an affair in secret. A selfish individual does not like to lie, because he sees that it does not bring him long-term happiness.

Most of us assume that we cannot be both selfish and kind to others. This is simply not true. If a mother loves her son, it makes her happy to give up some of her money to buy him a bicycle. It is not a sacrifice—it is a supremely selfish act. Both mother and son benefit.

Similarly, the owner of a popular restaurant is not dutifully "serving the public." He provides good food and a nice atmosphere so that he can make a profit and beat the competition. Both owner and diners benefit.

A physician does not provide quality treatment for altruistic reasons. He provides it because he is financially and emotionally rewarded for being competent and caring. Otherwise, he quite appropriately loses his patients. Both patient and doctor benefit from selfishness.

In a rational society, selfishness is encouraged. A rational society is one where individuals are left free to pursue their self-interest. In the process, everyone benefits.

Rational selfishness means acting in your self-interest—and accepting responsibility for determining what truly serves your long-term interest. It is a nice alternative to a life filled with duty, drudgery and disillusionment.

We live in a world which does not even recognize the option of rational selfishness. We are taught, from childhood, that we must be either self-sacrificing or thoughtlessly "selfish."

I maintain that this is a false alternative. Rational selfishness, if practiced consistently, is the means of living both a moral and psychologically healthy life. If you choose to recognize this alternative, such a life can be yours.

ENVY

Envy is the hatred of others' good fortune or success.

Envy is not the same as jealousy. Jealousy is a common—even healthy—emotion which occurs when one recognizes in another a quality or object he wants for himself. A man, for instance, sees his next-door neighbor's new car. At first he feels some resentment that he does not have a new car of his own. But after thinking it over, he realizes that if he really wanted a new car he could afford one; but for now he would rather spend his money on other items. The jealousy disappears.

Or, consider the student who works hard on his term-paper and only receives a "B." His best friend, however, gets an "A." He feels some resentment at first, but then he decides to study every night—like his friend—instead of only on weekends. The jealousy and resentment gradually fade.

As these examples show, jealousy can be a neutral or even positive emotion. It is an inevitable part of human life and should not be ignored. But it is unhealthy to give jealousy too much power. When an individual lets jealousy get out of control, it turns into *envy*.

Unlike jealousy, envy has no positive value. Since envy is a form of hatred, it is a destructive and unhealthy emotion. Like all unhealthy emotions, envy is the result of mistaken assumptions. These mistaken assumptions include: (1) the belief that one man's gain is always another man's loss; (2) the belief that all individuals are equal; and, (3) the belief that a man's destiny is outside of his own hands.

First of all, one man's gain is not always another man's loss. If Mr. Smith opens a hardware store on Main Street and makes a lot of money, Mr. Peters is free to open a better hardware store on 1st Street—and do just as well if he can please enough customers. If Mary graduates from college magna cum laude, there is nothing in her success that prevented Suzie from doing the same. If Mrs. Johnson wins the million-dollar lottery, her first cousin Jane is no poorer than she was the day before.

Nor is it true that all individuals are created equal. Common sense is enough to prove this fact. Some individuals are clearly more intelligent than others. Some individuals are faster runners. Other individuals are better mountain climbers. Some brain surgeons are better than others. A mentally retarded man and Albert Einstein are not equally capable. The list is endless.

It might sound "un-American" or even immoral to claim that all individuals are not equal. But one must not confuse political rights with physical facts. In a free society, all individuals are left free to develop (or not develop) their human potential without the imposition of force by others. But this does not change the fact that each individual is unique, in possession of his own strengths and weaknesses.

Finally, it is not true that a man's (or woman's) destiny is outside of his own hands. While many factors (social, familial, physiological) influence how an individual thinks and behaves, all human beings still have the power to think about and shape the environment in which they live. The greatest proof of this fact lies in the awe-inspiring technological achievements of the past two centuries. No helpless, unthinking animal could have produced a space shuttle or a cure for polio—nor clean water, electricity, and VCRs. In fact, no unthinking animal could even do the job of an ordinary factory worker.

Although envy is a powerful and destructive emotion, it is ignored by most psychologists and psychotherapists. It might be said that envy is the most underdiagnosed of psychological problems. It is also at the root of such problems as depression, anxiety and alcohol abuse. Some therapy patients are even the unwitting victims of psychotherapists who, suffering from envy themselves, simply reinforce the patient's false belief system.

How can envy be prevented? Parents should, first of all, question their own assumptions about envy. If you are a parent, do you hold any of the mistaken assumptions just described? Do you—intentionally or not—convey any of these false beliefs to your children? It is recommended that you seriously question the validity of these beliefs before teaching them to your kids. Teach them to acknowledge jealousy as a natural and normal feeling, but also tell them how they can transform jealousy into positive, productive enterprises.

Normal human jealousy is harmless and, if channeled correctly, can lead to high motivation, self-esteem and success. Envy, however, can only lead to misery and destruction. Healthy assumptions are the only means of preventing—and curing—envy.

THE "M" WORD—A RATIONAL APPROACH TO MORALITY

The old-fashioned approach to morality (selflessness):

- You should think of others, and not yourself.
- You should do for others, without regard for yourself.
- In any dilemma between yourself and others, choose others. Turn the other cheek.
- Underlying premise of the old morality: sacrifice (of yourself to others) is a virtue.

The modern approach to morality (so-called "selfishness"):

- You should think of yourself first. You have a right to be happy.
- You should demand that others do for you, without regard to themselves. You

have a right to health care, a job, housing, a car, schooling, cable television, good dental care, free drug treatment, free abortions, subsidized grants to start a business, etc., etc., etc.

- Make people who believe in the old-fashioned approach to morality feel guilty if they do not want to provide you with your "rights." Remind them of what they profess to believe: that they should always put others before themselves.
- Underlying premise of the new morality: sacrifice (of others to yourself) is a virtue.

Notice that both of these views, while representing the two opposite "extremes" of today's debate over morality, rest on the same basic premise: that *sacrifice is good*. The followers of old-fashioned morality believe that sacrifice is the ideal. The followers of the modern approach believe the same premise. The only difference between the two views involves who is sacrificed to whom. The modern moralists demand the sacrifice of others to themselves. The old-fashioned moralists demand that they sacrifice themselves to others. This pattern is not only observable in the political realm, but in the private realm of family life and personal relationships as well.

The only way out of this mess is a rational approach to ethics. A rational approach to morality does exist. A rational approach to morality rests upon the following:

- Rational self-interest, which means refusal to sacrifice oneself to others or others to oneself.
- Everyone is responsible for his or her own life. There is no free lunch, financially or emotionally. All material products must be earned through one's own efforts. If one must rely on charity, that charity must be voluntary on the part of the giver. Likewise, in personal relationships, one's love and loyalty must be earned. A marriage contract, or blood relationship, are not enough, by themselves, to earn trust, loyalty and compassion from others.
- Productivity, within the range of one's interest and ability, represents the essence of virtue. A truck driver earning an honest living is just as moral as a businessperson earning an honest living. Honesty, productivity, and rationality are the foundation of good character—not giving, helping, and sacrificing. Innovators and producers are heroes; not sacrificers and re-distributors.
- Everyone has the right to be left alone, that is: free from physical force, to pursue happiness as he or she defines it. The only restriction on this right, the only duty to others, is to respect their right to the same. Nobody has a moral or legal right to impose physical force upon or defraud anybody else. You can give, if you want and when you believe the receiver has earned it; but you are not bad if you refuse to make a sacrifice, and you are not guilty for being successful.
- Underlying premise: neither sacrifice of oneself to others (the old-fashioned view), nor sacrifice of others to oneself (the modern approach) represent virtue.   ⊕

Chapter 18

Where Traditional Morality Went Wrong

YOU ARE NOT YOUR BROTHER'S KEEPER

Is responsibility for yourself the essence of morality? Or is responsibility for *others* the essence of morality?

Increasingly, politicians and moralists call upon Americans to take part in "volunteerism" and community service. Their obvious purpose is to call attention to the moral malaise which plagues this country. They glorify the alleged virtues of self-sacrifice and service to others, while they minimize or ignore the qualities of self-responsibility, rational self-interest, and productivity. Americans constantly hear that they must take care of others, rather than take care of themselves.

Nobody ever challenges the ideas of these moralists and politicians. This lack of protest shows how many people accept the idea that responsibility towards others—instead of towards oneself—represents the most important aspect of morality. And, precisely because this is the *wrong* answer, our society is experiencing an unprecedented moral decline.

The Moral "Right" to Pizza: A Case Study

Consider a horrifying example of today's moral inversion. Several years ago, in Pittsburgh, Pennsylvania, a local Pizza Hut refused to deliver to a crime-infested, inner-city neighborhood. The city government's Human Relations Commission (HRC) subsequently charged Pizza Hut with racial discrimination, because the crime-infested neighborhood where it declined to deliver the pizza happened to be all black.

The "right" of a man to have a pizza delivered to his house, according to the HRC's reasoning, comes before all other rights. What about the rights of Pizza Hut? Pizza Hut has every moral right not to be forced to send a driver to any area, especially one where brutal killings are daily events. You and I, as individuals, have the right *not* to enter a dangerous neighborhood if we do not want to do so. Why should we lose this right the moment we become the owner or employee of a company such as Pizza Hut?

The Director of the Human Relations Commission later made matters worse by claiming that a pizza delivery company has the right to avoid bad neighborhoods only if it has a "documented loss history." So an undefined number of its employees must be assaulted or murdered before a company can win back its basic moral right to do business where it pleases!

This is not the end of the story.

One year after the Human Relations Commission ruling, a 34-year-old man was brutally killed while trying to deliver a pizza in another crime-ridden Pittsburgh neighborhood. As the driver lay dying on the street, the boys who killed him sat on a curb and cheerfully ate the pizza.[25]

Upon hearing of such a horrible crime, most of us ask, "Why? What is happening to a society where young men gleefully kill, for nothing more than a pizza? Into what kind of moral abyss have we allowed ourselves to be hurled?"

Then, most of us shake our heads and conclude, "There are no simple answers. Mine is not to reason why. Who am *I* to judge, after all?" We go about our business, until we hear about the next ghastly murder. And the cycle repeats itself.

In fact, there is a simple answer to the question of why such crimes take place. The answer is that a large number of people, including the overwhelming majority of officials who run our legal and educational institutions, have accepted the idea that responsibility towards others—instead of responsibility towards oneself—represents the essential feature of morality.

The boys who killed that pizza delivery man grew up in a society where everyone is taught that he is morally obligated to be his brother's keeper. They grew up in a world where they were told that they have a right to free health care, a right to welfare benefits, a right to free education, a right to family leave from work—in fact, a right to almost everything imaginable.

So what's wrong with this?

Remember: to claim a "right" to something produced by someone else implies a corresponding right to physically force, if necessary, someone else to pay for it or provide it to you. In short, these violent young men grew up being told that everyone in society has an obligation to be their keepers, and to give them whatever they feel they need. The youths simply decided that *they* will be the kept, and the rest of us will be their keepers. Sacrifice—of others to themselves, in this case—is the ethical code they relied upon in rationalizing away their guilt for murdering an innocent man. If sacrifice is a virtue, as we are all taught, does it not make sense that the pizza man had a moral obligation to give the boys the pizza when they demanded it?

These murderous youths and the Director of the Pittsburgh Human Relations Commission operated on the same basic moral premise. The Director of the HRC told Pizza Hut they must sacrifice their workers' well-being and lives, if necessary, to deliver pizza to a man who wanted it. The youths told the delivery man he had to sacrifice his life, if necessary, to give them the pizza for free because they were hungry and wanted it. What real difference does it make, morally, if the Director issues his edict from a comfortable government office or the hoodlum issues his edict on a dark street?

If this comparison seems unreasonable to you, then consider another question: How do you teach troubled, potentially violent young men to respect property rights and individual rights if they are also taught, in contradiction, that others owe them a living? After all, if somebody owes you a living—whether this means child care, health care, schooling, flood insurance, computers, or whatever—then it seems reasonable to conclude that they also owe you a pizza. If we are all obliged to sacrifice for each other, as most of our moral and political leaders repeatedly tell us, *then somebody has to collect the sacrifices.*

Self-Responsibility vs. Responsibility for Others

Were these young killers ever taught that moral people should be their *own* keepers, not their brothers' keepers? Of course not. This would mean teaching them individualism and self-reliance. Such ideas are "insensitive, heartless, and cruel," claim the great majority of today's leaders and teachers, right-wing and left-wing, religious and secular. Yet notice how the decline of individualism and self-responsibility has coincided with a proliferation of violent crimes which seem to defy all rational explanation. Witness how today's obsession with "sensitivity" and "compassion" has not prevented the most grotesque instances of their opposites from taking place.

Today, the notion of taking responsibility for oneself has all but vanished from our legal and educational institutions. Politically correct (and politically subsidized) teachers and professors, with rare and heroic exceptions, continue to teach the stale, rotten 1960's idea that "what's right for you and what's right for me may be different," and that therefore there are no moral absolutes. (Notice how they are *absolutely* sure that moral absolutes do not exist).

Attorneys argue with gleeful cynicism that their violent clients were not responsible for their actions because they were under the influence of drugs, alcohol, hormones, or emotions: the modern, secularized version of "The Devil made me do it." Psychotherapists, psychiatrists, and clergymen—rejecting reason in favor of subjective whim or faith—teach clients to not be "judgmental," thereby leaving them morally impotent against armed thugs and others who deserve harsh judgment. Human Relations Commissions and judges literally force business owners to serve clients at the risk of death—sending pizza delivery men to neighborhoods where they, themselves, would never venture.

Happily, not everyone thinks like these attorneys and human relations commissioners. In some intellectual circles, the idea of self-responsibility survives like a lonely patch of beautiful flowers, blooming in the midst of a field of weeds. To the great majority of people outside of the political-media-therapeutic establishment, self-responsibility and rational self-interest still represent virtues. If many people did not think this way, society would long ago have reached a state of total collapse.

American society still enjoys an unrivaled degree of economic productivity and growth in technological development. Morally, however, more and more Americans—under the influence of rotten ideas from academia, politicians, and the media—seem to be moving in the opposite direction. For the most part, today's media and academic establishment sneer at the idea of self-responsibility as old-fashioned and "simplistic." Indeed, they do not even permit the use of the term "morality" in polite discussion. Many of today's intellectual leaders fear that reintroducing the concept of morality will lead to religious dogmatism and even dictatorship. They do not understand, or do not want to understand, that a rational approach to morality is possible and, in fact, necessary.

The Courage to Judge:
A New Moral Code of Responsibility and Reason

An individual needs a moral code to guide his life.[26] A moral code should not merely be some remote abstraction designed to make somebody feel good while talking about it. A proper moral code should also be of practical day-to-day use in helping a person achieve both happiness and survival. A moral code needs to be clear and concrete enough for everyone to understand, but also broad and abstract enough to apply equally to all members of the human race.

What should be the essence, or core, of this moral code? Self-responsibility, based upon adherence to reason over emotions, and respect for reality over wishful thinking. True morality consists of acting in your rational, objective self-interest. If you want to be ethical, then you should act on your intelligence, not on your emotions. You should be honest and strive for integrity, for consistency between thought and action. You should also value independence and pride above humility and dependence. Above all, living a productive life, in legitimate work of your own choosing, should be the measurement of a moral life.

Easier said than done? Yes. Is this an excuse for not striving to achieve it? No. Will there be consequences to your overall happiness and functioning if you ignore the need for morality? Simply look around you, at today's world, and answer this question for yourself. Listen to any psychologist call-in radio show or watch any television talk show and judge for yourself if people are happier and healthier without the aid of moral principles to guide their lives. Without rational moral principles, nothing remains to guide life decisions except subjective whim-worship or blind obedience to authority: to do whatever you feel like, or to do whatever some guru or dictator tells you to do.

Productivity and achievement, rooted in objective thinking, goal-setting, and the will to act, represent the core of a rational morality. People who consistently practice such virtues need not be at the mercy of their feelings or at the mercy of a dictator. The good life is by necessity a productive one. In judging a person at the end of his life or after his death, you should not ask: "What did he *give?*" or: "How many weekends did he spend in the soup kitchen feeding the homeless?" or: "How much money did he give to charity?" Instead, you should ask: "What did he create? What did he produce? What did he accomplish?" or: "How well did he use his talents? What were his successes?" or: "How well did he focus, and use his mind?" and: "Did he enjoy life?"

The willingness to make objective, fact-based moral judgments is crucial to developing into both a virtuous *and* efficacious person. The words "good" and "bad," "should" and "ought," once again need to become acceptable in polite company.

You ought to make careful moral judgments—and make them proudly.

Example: A man who works hard to keep a roof over his head and takes responsibility for the children he created is a good man. A man who walks away from his kids is a bad man.

Example: A woman who believes she should be judged strictly by her objective merits is a good woman. She values productivity and individuality above all else; the fact that she does so in a world sometimes biased against women only makes her all the more heroic. A woman who believes she should be advanced in a career strictly for reasons of her gender, regardless of merit, is an immoral woman. She places her desire for power (or, more precisely, the illusion of achievement) above the virtues of honest accomplishment.

Example: The criminal who wastes his potential and seizes the property or lives of others is, without question, immoral and evil. The lawyers, social scientists, and philosophers who claim that the convicted criminal cannot be held responsible for his actions are, arguably, even more immoral. Their vicious, false arguments not only set the criminal free to harm more victims, but also give budding offenders the "courage" to embark on such a career when they might otherwise have felt pressure to be responsible and productive.

Example: The scientist who labors day and night to find a cure for cancer is a great, highly moral man because he is productive, focused, and rational. As a consequence of his productivity and rationality, countless members of society will also benefit from the cure he eventually discovers. But these benefits are merely side-effects, however important, of the scientist's more primary and fundamental virtues.

Without his choice of the rational values of productivity and achievement, there would be no cure in the first place. If he is truly moral, it is not the desire to serve humanity that motivates him to continue his research; it is his desire to do excellent work, and to take pride in it, and even to be recognized for it through financial or other reward. Yes, he may also take satisfaction in the fact that humanity benefits from his efforts. But the true achievers of civilization value, above all else, their ability to attain excellence. Their personal love of their *work* and its rewards—not their love of the abstraction "humanity"—motivates them to get up in the morning.

Giving Is Not an Obligation, But a Choice

Charity begins at home. If you want to give away some of what you earn once you have earned it, this is your choice and your right. But your only obligation is to your own well being and the well being of those closest to you: any children you create, a spouse to whom you make a commitment, or business associates/partners to whom you make legal or ethical commitments.

Charity is fine and benevolent when voluntary, and when not treated as a selfless, sacrificial duty. It is widely recognized, for example, that Americans have always been the most generous people even though (until recent decades) they have historically been taxed and regulated less than any other society in history. But the moment charity becomes a "right," or a duty coercively imposed upon others, the spirit of benevolence and true generosity disappears; the demand that others must pay your way whether they want to or not creates the ugliness, violence and general mean-spiritedness we see around us today.

In the realm of ethics, charity is only a side issue. To act charitably does not represent the essence of goodness and morality. Charity does not begin to compare to the advantages, personal or social, brought about by productive work and the rational pursuit of self-interest.

Computer genius Bill Gates, whose productive and business ability almost single-handedly inaugurated the Information Revolution, has done infinitely more to advance the progress of the human race, rich and poor alike, than Mother Teresa or any selfless server of humanity ever will. A century earlier, entrepreneurs such as

Andrew Carnegie and Henry Ford helped lift America to new heights. Without their efforts, today's unprecedented technological prosperity and material comfort would not have been possible. Likewise, the inventors of life-saving medical technology, the productive business geniuses who made possible the abundant supermarkets most of us take for granted, and the financial wizards on Wall Street who take risks and invest in new products that would never otherwise come into existence, deserve all the financial and personal profit they attain.

Productive work, along with the rationality and self-responsibility which makes it possible, represents the essence of morality. This concept is not limited to business and science. It also applies to the arts and the humanities. Great dancers, actors, musicians, and playwrights provide hope and inspiration—the emotional fuel necessary for the entrepreneurs and scientists to continue achieving in their own work. Yet great artists, like great technological innovators, are not (nor should they be) motivated by the colorless abstraction of "serving humanity." Genuinely great artists are motivated by their unwavering dedication to and passion for their work, along with the desire to be compensated with money and applause. The motive which makes them so good at what they do is inherently selfish; and they should feel no shame for this fact.

If you still find these arguments unpersuasive, then consider one last question. Without the selfish producers and achievers whom you may consider immoral or, at best, amoral, and without all the benefits of the supposedly evil capitalist society, then how are you supposed to feed and care for the world? Remember that when Mother Teresa developed health problems, she did not turn to third-world missionaries for medical treatment. She turned to the technology created by the productive, by the rational; by the capitalists. Without the hated achievers of a capitalist society, the humanitarians would not last for five minutes.

Being Your Brother's Keeper is the Problem, Not the Solution

Any society where the great majority attempt to practice the ethical code of being their brothers' keepers will ultimately develop into two dysfunctional groups: One, a group of people so busy taking care of others that they neglect their own lives and loved ones; second, a group of people eager to capitalize on others' sacrifices by attaining something for nothing. In short: those who make the sacrifices, and those who collect them.

Wherever sacrifice is widely accepted as the ideal, individuals increasingly become either *self*-sacrificers or *other*-sacrificers. The self-sacrificers act as if virtue applies to them but not to others. Hence, they have no difficulty letting criminals go free, surrendering half of their income to bureaucratic welfare regimes, and allowing all the other monstrous injustices we see today. Self-sacrificers are very hard on themselves, and too easy on others.

The other-sacrificers are represented by the moochers who seek, and increasingly attain, something-for-nothing. They demand free housing, free health care, free flood insurance, and even free pizza. A few, such as the pizza delivery man killers, resort to physical violence; the majority rely on physical coercion through political pressure-groups in Washington, DC and state capitals. In such a sociopolitical context, society increasingly becomes comprised of so-called "saints" and "sinners" who play the role of givers and takers. This false dichotomy leaves little room for the rational individual who neither wants to sacrifice nor be sacrificed, but just to live his own life productively, to peacefully trade with others, and be left alone by the government.

As we enter the twenty-first century, the decline of self-responsibility and its inevitable consequences are increasingly apparent for all to see: random violence, theft, illiteracy, declining test scores, record numbers of unwanted pregnancies, unprincipled political and business leaders, and all the other well-documented modern ills. A generation ago, these consequences of the something-for-nothing, sacrificial morality were barely visible. In another generation or less, on our present moral course, these consequences will be much more visible than today. Either we continue the destructive cycle of being each others' keepers; or we reject this impractical, immoral philosophy and replace it with the ethics of rationality, productivity, and self-responsibility.

It's time to change moral course. Without a decisive U-turn in the realm of morality, today's technological and material progress will gradually enslave us rather than liberate us. Only with a new moral code will the twenty-first century be a happy and prosperous time in which to live. Rationality, productivity, and self-interest—*not* ever increasing doses of sacrifice and selflessness—represent the true solutions to today's moral crisis.

TURN THE OTHER CHEEK?

Eliette Ramos' 19-year-old son was murdered in 1997. His body was found in an Aspen Hill, Maryland, garage—burned, sawed into pieces and dumped in a garbage bag.

The accused murderer of Ramos' son, a young man named Samuel Sheinbein, fled the United States for Israel shortly after the murder. Conveniently claiming Israeli citizenship, he sought and was granted immunity from extradition by Israel. This means that he will not have to be tried in the United States for the murder.

How does Ms. Ramos feel about all of this? Does she believe that she should "turn the other cheek" and forgive her son's murderer? That she should love her enemy more than herself and her late son? According to what most of us are taught, she *should* feel this way. She ought to forgive and forget. She should leave the judgment to God, and not dare pass a moral judgment on her son's murderer.

Instead, she showed the courage to speak her thoughts and feelings publicly. Ms. Ramos said she wants other Americans to feel "outrage" over the fact that Sheinbein avoided extradition to the United States. Refusing to deny the truth, she asked, "How can anyone understand this ridiculous decision not to return Sam Sheinbein back to Maryland to face his crime? This is a person who brutally murdered and dismembered my only child."

Any loving parent would feel this way, of course. But Ms. Ramos had the courage to say so out loud. Most would be afraid to appear vengeful or unforgiving. Anger and vengeance, even when obviously rational, contradict the underlying ethic of our society: to forgive, to be non-judgmental, to absolve even the unrepentant of their sins.

David Gelernter, the survivor of a 1993 Unabomber attack and the author of *Drawing Life*, puts it eloquently: "A society too squeamish to call evil by its right name has destroyed its first, best defense against cutthroats. Our best line of defense against crime is to hate it."

Grow Up America!

THE CASE OF THE SICK SISTERS—HOW TRADITIONAL MORALITY IS DESTROYING PSYCHIATRY

Compassion is not a duty. You are not obliged to love others, causelessly and self-lessly. You are not obliged to feel emotional simply because someone else feels emotional.

Nor does it even help others when you attempt to "feel their pain."

Imagine that your friend Joe is experiencing a strong emotion. Joe's feelings may or may not be based on logic or facts. If not, it is sad that he has this internal conflict and inconsistency. It is regrettable that he has to some extent lost touch with reality. You might want to help him see how his emotions make no sense. You could even suggest he see a professional. However, you do him no favors by pretending to empathize with Joe's feelings when, in truth, you have no rational idea why he feels like he does.

Empathic phoniness is never the answer.

For an illustration of empathic phoniness at its most condescending, think about a typical television journalist, such as Diane Sawyer or Katie Couric. The next time you see one of them talking to a victim of some real or alleged injustice, look at the expression on the interviewer's face. Look at the fawning, phony look of compassion she displays. Watch for the deliberately furrowed eyebrows, the self-congratulatory look of pitiful remorse. It *has* to be phony, because the interviewer could not possibly have developed a deep enough relationship with her subject to experience such a strong emotional response.

One wonders if such a television journalist enjoys the fact that she has the opportunity to look compassionate in a society so hooked on the feeling of others' pain. In a perverse sense, she might even relish the fact the other person is suffering—precisely because it gives her a chance to look humane and concerned. *Looking* and *appearing* humane and concerned are the cardinal virtues, at least by the standards of today's cultural and media establishment. As *Washington Post* columnist Robert J. Samuelson correctly points out, "Pursuing conspicuous compassion has become a form of status-seeking to see who's the most 'caring.'"

Compassion Obsession and Its Effect on Mental Health Treatment

For an example of the same underlying principle applied to a different field—psychiatry—consider the case of Darlene and Nora. Darlene and Nora are sisters. Nora is severely depressed and has moved in with Darlene. Darlene feels imposed upon but is afraid to send Nora back home. "My sister is depressed and I can't abandon her," she insists. "Because of her emotional state, she is incapable of doing anything." She has tried twice to take Nora to the airport to send her back home. Both times, Nora experiences a panic attack before getting on the plane and Darlene rushes her to the hospital, losing the money spent for the flight tickets.

Darlene is insistent that somebody, somehow, immediately "fix" her sister. She tells psychiatrists they must "chart a new course" for her sister's life. She insists, "You have to *make* her feel better," as if someone could externally control her sister's mind. She approaches mental health professionals like a religious person approaches God: *not* a "God" who helps people help themselves; but rather one who takes over altogether and makes everything perfect without any effort on the believer's part.

Here are some of the factors Darlene fails to consider. She does not recognize that Nora is trying to convince everyone, including herself, that she is helpless so that she does not have to face reality. This way, she will not have to take responsibility for herself. *Saying* that she's unable to do anything for herself will make it true, Nora feels. Convincing significant others—such as her sister Darlene—to agree with and "feel" her feelings will somehow make her feelings even more true. Nora operates on the basic, core premise of most mentally troubled people: "If I feel it—and if I wish it—and if I convince others of it, even falsely—then it will *be* true."

Darlene fails to see beneath her sister's "illness" of depression and anxiety to understand what irrational motive the symptoms may be serving. In other words, she fails to see that her sister is depressed for a purpose—the purpose of not having to return to reality: a purpose which is, of course, irrational and not even in Nora's own objective self-interest.

Nora cannot, of course, merely snap her fingers and instantly "get over" her depression. But, by acting as if her sister is totally helpless, Darlene is ensuring that Nora get sicker and sicker. In telling Nora, "You are diseased and need to be taken care of by psychiatrists and hospitals who want you to depend on them," Darlene is harming rather than helping her sister. By participating in Nora's self-delusion, she gives Nora incentive to further engage in it. She is hastening the day when Nora's neurotic depression turns into something much more serious: a complete break with reality. A psychosis. Total and possibly irreversible insanity.

At this juncture, what Nora needs most desperately are lessons in regaining independence—not lessons in fostering ever more dependence. She needs a plan for returning home, to face her problems head-on rather than mooching off of her sister indefinitely and growing worse and worse. Nora needs lots and lots of rational ideas to counter the irrational ideas rapidly taking hold of her consciousness. Rational ideas include telling her that she still can think, she can reason, she can set goals, she can distinguish objective reality from internal feelings, and she can move beyond this unfortunate but temporary depression. All the family members and mental health professionals she sees must consistently "pound" her mind with these rational ideas. Is there an absolute guarantee that these methods will work? Of course not. But there is an absolute guarantee that trying to "feel" and agree with Nora's emotions will send her over the psychological cliff.

Will Nora need psychiatric medication? Perhaps—but only as a supplement, not a substitute. Medication and hospitalization, when absolutely necessary, are means to an end—not ends in themselves, as many suppose. They help some people more than others. Usually, medicine is only a temporary benefit at most. It cannot replace the need to learn healthy, reality-oriented thinking. No pill can replace the act of thought.

Instead of telling her sister to "get help" from people who have a financial and/or ideological motive to keep her permanently dependent on them, Darlene should instead encourage Nora to help herself. She should also look for professionals who share the same goal and philosophy: to help Nora help herself. A good therapist will assist Nora with trying to focus on reality, to see the advantages of facing reality, and to set small goals ("baby steps") to help her move forward. The competent therapist will also help Darlene not attribute more power to Nora's irrational emotions than they merit.

Sadly, Darlene and Nora are not likely to find genuine help in today's mental health field. The overwhelming majority of therapists and psychiatrists—whether for financial or ideological reasons, or both—will seek to foster dependence as a means of "cure." Even among those therapists who sincerely do not want to foster a dependence, there will be a tendency to ascribe more power to the "sick" woman's emotions than the emotions really deserve. In other words, they will likely panic when they see how strong Nora's emotions are. They will automatically assume, just like Darlene, "I need to feel her pain." They will not aggressively challenge the irrationality of Nora's thoughts. "No," they think, "that would be heartless and cruel." Even clinicians trained in cognitive therapy—who supposedly believe that only reason can be used to battle irrational thoughts—will often go wobbly and fall prey to the depressed woman's false belief that she is completely helpless and hopeless.

Legal Issues

To make matters even worse, these mental health professionals practice in a larger cultural context where it is remarkably easy to sue. In many people's minds, God is dead—and they now look to mental health professionals to solve problems they would never have expected even a supernatural entity to fix. When God let their parents and grandparents down, they had to live with it and get over it. If a mental health professional lets them down today, by not magically making their lives perfect, they can call their attorney.

In all fairness to many of today's psychiatrists, their tendency to fall into the "feel-your-pain" dysfunction often represents a simple act of self-protection. So long as they are perceived as being "compassionate," then they can escape a lawsuit—even if the alleged compassion helped nobody.

Consequently, too many psychiatric "helpers" become part of the problem rather than part of the solution. The more wobbly and weak the mental health professionals and Darlene act, the more upset Nora becomes. Why? Because when you are in a state of profound panic, it does not help to be surrounded by people who merely feel your panic along with you. Nora needs calmness and strength, not more panic. She needs facts, logic, and reason—not only warmth and hand-holding.

Nevertheless, the more upset Nora becomes, the weaker and more hysterical Darlene and many of the mental health professionals become. Nora, in response to the growing panic she sees around her, experiences still more anxiety and depression. "My God," she'll think. "These people can't help me!" Eventually the vicious cycle reaches a dead-end. Poor Nora collapses into complete psychosis, at which time some form of dependence or hospitalization is probably unavoidable.

Such is the state of the mental health and psychiatric profession today. Not all cases are as extreme as Nora's, of course. But most of them unfold, to one degree or another, on the same basic principles and themes.

Ethical Issues

One little understood but crucial factor underlying this state of affairs is the ethics of self-sacrifice. Self-sacrifice, the ethical code universally accepted by traditional religions and secular humanist intellectuals alike, says that when we see someone in pain we must always feel their pain. Even if the emotional pain is the consequence of ideas which make no sense. Even if hyper-compassion ultimately leads to hurting, rather than helping, the person in pain. Even if the suffering individual needs "tough love" rather than blind, reality-faking, unconditional love.

Under the moral code of self-sacrifice, hand-holding becomes more important than mind-mending.

Compassion—which means, quite literally, "to suffer with another"[27]—represents an end and a goal in and of itself, according to the Judeo-Christian-modernist ethics implicit in contemporary psychiatric treatment. This irrational ethical code also implies that it is cruel to challenge the mistaken thoughts and ideas of the person who feels depressed or otherwise neurotic. In fact, we are told, it is judgmental and politically incorrect and un-Christian to even label someone "neurotic." If someone feels badly, they can't help it. We need to *feel* for them, *feel* with them, indulge their pain and show everyone else how "compassionate" we are. So what if the troubled person ultimately is harmed by it? So what if we sacrifice our own rational judgment and common sense in the process? So long as we are—or at least *look* to others like we are—compassionate, then all is fine.

As long as self-sacrifice remains the dominant ethical code, there is no way for a rational psychotherapeutic culture to ever take hold. The wider American society, if it is to survive and flourish, first needs a new moral code to replace the sickening, ineffective, and degrading ethics of self-sacrifice. Mental health professionals are no less influenced by this mistaken, senseless approach to ethics than anyone else; if anything, they practice it even more consistently than the layman.

The dominance of self-sacrifice-as-the-ideal is one of the fundamental reasons why mental health treatment is so ineffective yet so popular at the same time. It is ineffective because it is based upon the totally irrational code of self-sacrifice, which cannot work and will never work at achieving mental health and happiness. Yet mental health treatment remains remarkably popular, because the code of self-sacrifice is so deeply entrenched in everyone's subconscious minds that they feel comfortable and at-home when they recognize it in the actions of their therapists, social workers, and psychiatrists.

Perhaps even more compelling, the guilt-ridden relatives of psychiatric patients (such as Darlene) can shift responsibility for their depressed or depraved loved ones onto the mental health professionals. "I don't have to feel their pain any more," they can tell themselves. "The doctor can." Notice the hypocrisy implicit in a code of ethics nobody wants to follow or can follow but still feels he *should* follow.

Heaven help the occasional therapist or psychiatrist who dares to take a tough-love, non-Christian, non-politically correct approach. He or she will experience the wrath not only of the family members still caught up in the ethics of self-sacrifice; he will experience the disapproval and censure of the mental health establishment as well. Until a dominant majority of mental health professionals have rejected the traditional approach to ethics, and replaced it with reason and personal responsibility, psychiatry will continue to be ineffective—yet popular.

Conclusion

Do the sick get better in such an ethical-psychological context? Of course not. As the example of Nora illustrates, they actually get sicker. Nora would have been better off without *any* mental health treatment than what passes for "treatment" today. The well get worse too. Everybody loses, because they are caught up in a way of thinking about ethics which leads to nothing but suffering, despair, and disaster.

Indeed, it is a tribute to the human spirit that it has survived two thousand years or more of living under the guilt of self-sacrifice and compassion-worship as the alleged ideals. But even the human spirit, resilient as it is, will not survive too much more of this ongoing ethical onslaught. It is time to change. It is time for young men and women, interested in reforming the mental health fields along with the other humanities fields such as philosophy, to sweep aside the ethics of self-sacrifice and persuade the masses of what many of them already suspect: that it is moral, healthy, and efficacious to live for themselves, to live by reason, and to never sacrifice their health or well-being to the alleged good of others—particularly in the name of "compassion." ⚛

25. Like the Pittsburgh Human Relations Commission, the San Francisco Board of Supervisors also decided to make it illegal for Domino's (or any fast-food deliverer) to refuse to provide services in dangerous neighborhoods. A San Francisco pizza delivery man was also murdered.

26. For a more detailed philosophical analysis refer to, "The Objectivist Ethics," in *The Virtue of Selfishness*, by Ayn Rand (Signet, 1961).

27. See *Webster's New Universal Unabridged Dictionary, 2nd Edition* (New York: Simon & Schuster, 1983).

Chapter 19

Voluntary Servitude

WHY VOLUNTEERISM IS NOT THE ANSWER

What's so great about volunteerism?

Volunteerism rests upon a terrible, anti-American idea. It teaches young people to feel guilty for success and achievement. "Look how those poor people suffer!" advocates of volunteerism say. "And look how comfortable *you* are." Such statements falsely imply that *your* comfort and success somehow cause pain and suffering in others. How can we expect young people to accomplish anything while feeling guilty for success and achievement?

Volunteerism also undermines personal responsibility. It tells people, "You are responsible for the poor, the weak, the homeless, and the drug-addicted." It altogether ignores the need to be *self*-responsible.

Ironically, if more people were self-responsible there would not be much need for charity. Personal responsibility is actually quite selfish. It takes a profound level of self-respect and self-love to pay one's bills on time, to honor one's business commitments, and to tell the truth.

Those who obsess on service to others invariably neglect their own needs and obligations. In the name of supposedly saving the world, self-sacrificers end up harming themselves and the ones who matter most to them.

Worst of all, preaching and imposing selfless service on young people destroys youthful innocence and excitement. It crushes the wide-eyed awe and passion for life which all children initially exhibit.

Imagine a young person who wants to be an astronaut, a scientist, or a successful business owner. He needs encouragement and inspiration. He wants to hear from adults that achievement of these goals is possible. What does he hear instead, from today's so-called moral leaders? "Off to a soup kitchen with you!" No wonder so many high school students turn to drugs.

Instead of teaching kids volunteerism, we should challenge them to find productive careers they can love.

It is much easier to tell kids to volunteer their lives away than to teach them how to think, produce, create, and enjoy. If you want young people to be socially responsible, then teach them to love themselves first. Teach them how to think critically, objectively, and independently so they can survive and flourish. Send them to the library or the laboratory—*not* the local homeless shelter.

Any society worth living in requires strong, ambitious individualists, not selfless apostles of humility and service. We should drop the pretense that charity workers are saints of civilization. The true saints of civilization are the self-interested, creative geniuses who make our lives happier, safer, and prosperous.

Consider the magnificent feats of today's world. Watch a jet take off or land at an airport. Look at the lights of your city at night. Walk through your house and marvel at the clean water, the cable television, the fax machine, the cellular phone, and the microwave oven. Then ask yourself who made all this possible. Millions pursuing self-fulfillment and happiness—or millions volunteering at charity work? Who created these wonders? Henry Ford, Thomas Edison, Bill Gates—or Mother Teresa's nuns?

Volunteers do not discover computer microchips, cures for disease or the many life-saving values we all take for granted. America, the most productive and wealthy society in history, did not rise to greatness on the shoulders of social workers.

Self-interested, profit-seeking people make the world a better place. We can all learn from their examples.

VOLUNTEER... OR SLAVE?

Greg is a busy high school student. He never skips class. He works three evenings per week to pay for his car. He spends the rest of the time studying or with his girl-friend. His goal is to become a physician. He is intelligent, purposeful, and well on his way to success.

Yet Greg is a target.

A target of what? Drug dealers? Drugs would never tempt him. Terrorists? Not physical ones. Greg is actually the target of an *idea*—an idea held by most as a self-evident truth. A "truth" promoted by as universally beloved a figure as Colin Powell.

The idea? "Volunteerism." Volunteerism means that the essence of goodness is ser-vice and sacrifice for others. If you give a bum a dollar, you are a good person. If you give up a few hours of your week, then you are a really good person. If you give away all of your possessions, and move to the poorest country you can find to wallow in dirt, poverty and disease with the victims of some dictatorial government, then you represent the moral ideal.

Greg is confused. He sincerely feels he *is* a good person. Yet he does not want to sacrifice time from study, work, and his girlfriend to toil at the local soup kitchen, as his school's "volunteerism" policy requires. Greg believes that his time is his proper-ty. Just as nobody has a moral right to take his car or his books, nobody has a moral right to steal his time and make him serve somebody else.

Greg decides to call his family's minister about his dilemma. The minister tells him that he should pray to God for guidance. This is no help. Greg then resolves to talk to his school counselor. The school counselor tells him that whatever Greg *feels* is right is, in fact, right. This, too, is worthless advice.

Next, Greg goes to his uncle. His uncle is a professor of history at a local, highly respected university. His uncle tells Greg that the moral ideal is indeed to serve oth-ers. He believes, in fact, that the United States is an immoral country because it allows "too much" selfishness. Volunteerism, he insists, will correct this problem. "After all," he asks Greg, "you're going into medicine. Don't you *want* to serve people?"

Greg is shocked and angered by his uncle's question. He never planned to go into medicine just to serve others. Of course he wants to cure patients. But his real passion is for knowledge and competence. Besides, without knowledge and competence, treatment of patients is impossible. And he wants to earn a good living for his work—whatever the market will pay him.

"Why can't you give up a few hours of your week to think of someone else besides yourself?" Greg's peers ask. "You don't need to be a saint. Just be a good person once in awhile." Greg begins to grasp the true meaning of sacrifice as the so-called moral ideal. The more he gives up, the better a person he is. Only if he gives up everything— his career goals, his girlfriend—can he be a fully moral person. Yet nobody expects him to follow the moral ideal consistently. Under the ethical code of sacrifice, the only way to practice it is to violate it. No wonder people are so cynical!

For the first time in his life, Greg becomes depressed. He feels that he must choose between being a good person or a happy person—or, even worse, some murky compromise between the two. Unlike the compromisers, he wants to resolve the contradiction—but he does not know how. He begins to procrastinate. He snaps at his girlfriend. He acts resentful, for no apparent reason. His grades start to slide. Ever so slowly, something starts to die inside of him.

Greg does not yet realize that it is his commitment to excellence, his passion for competence and knowledge, that is starting to fade. He *can* resolve his conflict—but only if he challenges the opinions of others. He *can* start to feel motivated again, but only if he adopts the idea—without reservation or contradiction—that his life belongs to himself and nobody else.

Greg's dilemma is now the nation's. The ideas of Greg's uncle enjoy increasing acceptance by many Americans. Increasingly, the best and the brightest of America's young men and women are to be sacrificed on the politically correct altar of "volunteerism."

"But what's wrong with charity?" you might ask. Nothing—so long as the charity is voluntary, and does not impose sacrifice on the giver. The beneficiary of the charity should also be genuinely unresponsible for his plight. To give money to the widow of a murder victim is one thing; to give money to a drug abuser is another.

Charity is not, however, the essence of morality. Productive achievement in the career of one's choice, along with the pursuit of rational happiness, is the true essence of morality. This is true on the social as well as the individual level. Think about it. If everyone followed an ethics of charity and self-sacrifice, society would become an impoverished wasteland where everyone gives and serves but nobody produces or achieves. (For a real-life example, look at the former Communist countries). If—on the other hand—everyone followed an ethics of productive and responsible self-interest, there would hardly be any need for charity in the first place.

Americans should not be told to take care of each other. They should instead be told to start taking care of *themselves*. The solution to today's moral crisis is not more and more self-sacrifice, "community service," and volunteerism. The answer is love of life, self-responsibility, and the pursuit of excellence and achievement.   ☯

Chapter 20

Personal

Responsibility

"IT'S NOT MY FAULT!"
THE PSYCHOLOGY OF VICTIMIZATION THEORY

A data processor for the Philadelphia School District was fired in 1980 for arriving late to work virtually every day. He sued his employer under the Pennsylvania Human Relations Act, claiming that his "neurotic compulsion for lateness" qualified as a disability. In court, psychiatrists testified that the man suffered from a "behavioral aberration that is deeply rooted in his personality and almost certainly had its origins in conflictual interaction with his parents in early life."[28]

In Michigan, a former brewery worker convinced the state's Court of Appeals that he was entitled to worker's compensation benefits because he had become an alcoholic while working for Stroh's Brewery Company. Although the company did not force him to drink beer, he successfully argued that the presence of free beer to all employees (a benefit demanded and won by the man's union) created his alcoholism and Stroh's was therefore responsible.[29]

Jeffrey Dahmer, the infamous serial killer convicted in 1991, was originally found guilty of sex-abuse charges in 1989. Instead of jailing Dahmer, a Milwaukee judge put him on probation, permitting him to serve a one-year sentence on a work-release plan. His main concern, the judge told Dahmer, "was therapy, and I'm really concerned that we don't have a program in place right now...But if there is an opportunity to salvage you, I want to make use of that opportunity."[30]

Two years later, Dahmer was arrested for murdering and dismembering more than a dozen young men, including the older brother of the boy Dahmer had been charged with molesting in 1989.

What psychological concept unites these three rulings? What makes such obvious assaults on any rational notion of justice possible?

The Theory of Victimization

Victimization theory refers to the view that human beings are not responsible for their actions and must therefore seek excuses for their behaviors in external or psychological sources (childhood, "society," Western culture, white masculine oppression, "social attitudes," the "unconscious," etc.) The victim view takes its cue from the resentful cry of the child: "Don't blame me. It's not my fault!"

Despite the growing outrage many Americans feel over the obvious injustice of treating criminals like victims, the theory of victimization retains remarkable popularity. Television talk shows and news programs shower attention on both real and imagined victims, competing to interview them and treating them like honored celebrities. Ratings soar. Pretentious "self-help" authors preach the victimology of everything from "inner-child syndrome" to the so-called disease of shopping addiction. Their books sell by the millions. A psychic sued a physician for "interfering" with her seance, claiming that her powers were blotted out by a CAT scan. Although the judge in the case ordered the jury to ignore the claim of psychic damage, the jurors took only forty-five minutes to award the psychic $986,000.[31]

In some cases, such as the psychology professor who complained that she was the victim of sexual harassment because of the presence of mistletoe at a Christmas party, victimization theory inspires more laughter than anger. In other cases, such as the Milwaukee judge's notion that therapy was somehow an adequate substitute to holding Jeffrey Dahmer responsible for his actions, the victimization view can lead to tragic, unthinkable consequences.

Victimization Theory Is The Product of Bad Psychology

Most people do not understand that the root cause of victimization theory is intellectual, not political or legal. Victimization theory, first and foremost, is the psychological and legal step-child of determinism. Determinism refers to the philosophical view of man as the helpless pawn of forces outside of his control. Largely taken for granted among social scientists and other humanities scholars, determinism serves as the foundation for the most influential psychological, social and economic theories of our day.

Mental health professionals, terrified of appearing "judgmental," encourage their patients to altogether replace the concept of morality with eloquently psychologized excuses. As one critic writes, "In place of evil, therapeutic society has substituted 'illness;' in place of consequence, it urges therapy and understanding; in place of responsibility, it argues for a personality driven by impulses."[32]

In order to eradicate victimization theory from American society, professional intellectuals, psychotherapists and other concerned individuals must first attack its mistaken premises and identify the correct alternatives.

Psychologically, victimization theory rests upon an erroneous view of human emotions. Instead of seeing emotions as the by-product of thoughts and conclusions which a person may change, victimization proponents see people as completely helpless over their emotions and impulses. They assume that merely because someone feels something, he cannot accept responsibility for what he does while experiencing the feeling. Victimization theory enables people to arbitrarily invent "diseases" of behavior and psychology while conveniently ignoring human free will.

In reality, human beings are capable of changing their emotions through rational introspection and other methods. Introspection, the basis for most cognitive methods of psychotherapy, helps the individual learn to apply reason to his emotions as opposed to repressing them or blindly acting upon them. While it may be difficult to change troubling emotions, a person can still accept responsibility for not acting on them.

For example, a mother might feel like brutally striking her screaming, ungrateful three-year-old child. This emotion conflicts with her intellectual view that hitting children is wrong. Yet she cannot simply snap her fingers and make her desire to hit the child go away. She can, however, choose either to act on this feeling or restrain it in one of two basic ways.

She may, out of ignorance, restrain the feeling with a psychologically unhealthy method such as repression, telling herself, "This is an evil feeling. I must not think about it anymore. I must shut it out."

Or, she might use a more introspective or common sense approach such as attempting to identify more rational methods for disciplining her child.

Either way, whether repressing or using reason and common sense, the mother makes a moral choice to ignore the impulse to physically abuse her child. She could have hit her child, but she chose not to do so.

Emotions and Behavior Are Not One and The Same

Joe might envy his best friend's new car. While the envy might be based on a mistaken assumption (such as the idea that Joe can never purchase a similar car for himself), Joe is still capable of identifying this mistaken assumption and consciously changing it.

Even if Joe continues to feel envious, he does not have to act on this emotion. Feeling envy, as many people do at one time or another, is not the same as acting on the envy.

Emotions and actions are two separate entities. While the truth of this statement may seem obvious, victimization theorists often ignore it. They exaggerate the importance of the emotional state of the "victim" while downplaying (if not denying) the importance of individual choice and behavior.

This distortion has the effect of blurring, or even eliminating, the distinction between emotions and behaviors. Consequently, the man who suffers from "neurotic compulsion for lateness" cannot accept responsibility for his lateness; after all, his feelings of not wanting to get up at 6 AM to get ready for work make it impossible for him to do so. The employee, who drank the free beer at the Stroh's brewery cannot accept responsibility for his actions; after all, his feelings of wanting to drink the beer are indistinguishable from the behavior. Jeffrey Dahmer should not have to suffer the legal consequences of molesting minors; after all, his feelings of desiring to have sex with children are inseparable from his actions.

Defenders of the victimization view will counter that individuals cannot choose their feelings. Such counter-arguments miss the point. Of course people do not consciously choose to feel a certain way; feelings and emotions are the by-product of many factors—intellectual, psychological and even physiological. Emotions, by definition, refer to automatic, subconscious and unintentional responses. Emotions represent the conscious by-products of ideas, ideas which one can change through rational, conscious discussion with oneself, a friend, or a psychotherapist.

People can refrain from acting on their emotions, furthermore, through either repressing them or attempting to think them out logically. Thinking them out logically is always the preferred approach, of course, because the individual can actually solve problems created by mistaken emotions and prevent them from interfering with future functioning. But even repression, while psychologically undesirable, is morally preferable to acting blindly on one's emotions, especially in serious cases where such actions can have dire consequences for oneself and/or others.

The Role of Psychotherapy

While therapy can certainly foster the development of psychological health (and, perhaps indirectly, morality) in an individual, it cannot force morality or psychological health on anyone. The client must be willing and honestly motivated to engage in psychotherapy if he is to benefit from it.

Therapy is not a passive form of "treatment," such as surgery and most other forms of medical intervention. This distinction is crucial. It is poorly understood or simply ignored by the legal professionals and media gurus who promote psychotherapy as the panacea for all social and moral problems.

The Alternative To Victimization Theory

The alternative to victimization theory starts with a recognition of several crucial concepts:

1. Emotions are simply automatic versions of thoughts and ideas.
   Example: John feels very anxious. He learns from introspection that he's thinking, "I'm in danger when I go to work because I might make a mistake." The emotion of anxiety is the automatic response to this underlying thought.

2. Through thinking, one can apply reason to one's emotions, learn the thoughts underlying the emotions and decide upon the appropriate course of action.
   Example: Suzanne feels angry. Stopping to think about her feeling, she discovers that she feels angry at her sister who did not give her a more expensive birthday gift. At first she remains angry, but then she remembers that last year her sister gave her a very expensive gift. She decides to let go of the feeling and not bring it up to her sister since she sees no good reason for doing so.

3. Emotions are distinct from actions. Simply because someone feels something does not mean he must act upon it.
   Example: Bill feels that his business partner is lying. For a moment, he wants to accuse him outright. He quickly decides not to do this, since he sees no basis whatsoever for his feeling. He later discovers there was an honest, and easily corrected, misunderstanding between them. He feels relief that he did not blurt out his suspicion earlier.

4. The healthy method for restraining irrational behaviors is the insertion of thought and reason prior to action. Healthy people follow the principle, "Think before you act." The unhealthy method involves repressing one's emotions as a means of restraining behavior.
   Example: Jerry sees an opportunity to steal $500 from his employer. He immediately admonishes himself for having such a feeling, reminding himself, "Thou shalt not steal" and forcing himself to think about something else. (Repression)
   Example: Marcia sees an opportunity to steal $500 from her employer. She

acknowledges the feeling without condemning herself. She decides that the price and the inconvenience of having to always cover up the lie, never knowing when it might come back to haunt her, is not worth it. She also recognizes the evil of allowing herself to violate the individual rights of another person to his property. She does not take the money. (Insertion of thought prior to action)

5. Everyone has the choice to think before he acts or, at the very least, to repress a desire prior to acting on an emotional impulse. The availability of these options means that people are responsible for their actions even when overcome by emotions or psychological problems. In short, psychological factors cannot explain away moral responsibility.

Conclusion

Jeffrey Dahmer clearly had psychological problems. He experienced emotions of wanting to molest, kill and dismember other human beings. Yet the emotions themselves did not actually cause Dahmer to act on them. In the end, Dahmer chose to act on his emotions rather than repress them or attempt to resolve them in psychotherapy.

No number of psychological factors can ever change the fact that an individual either allows himself to act on his feelings or elects not to do so. Victimization theory seduces reasonable people into ignoring this crucial point and accepting the idea that violent criminals are not really responsible for their actions.

Few, if any, victimologists are consistent enough to consider Jeffrey Dahmer a helpless victim. But in a world where over-drinking, overeating, and even arriving late for work are all considered "diseases," how far can we be from one where killing and dismembering are also seen as tissue-driven rather than choice-driven? If the alcoholic and the oversleeper can sue for damages, then why not the ax-murderer as well?

Victimization theory will remain an influential factor in American society until more psychologists familiarize themselves with accurate theories of human emotions. When more people come to understand that ideas cause emotions, then more will want to hold criminals and other "victims" of their feelings responsible for their actions.

THE PSYCHOLOGY OF RESPONSIBILITY

Psychologically, responsibility represents the dominant emotional state of a human being who enthusiastically and realistically seeks control over his own life and happiness.

Why should one be responsible?

Three schools of thinkers eagerly compete to answer this question.

The first are the Puritans. Puritans believe one should be responsible because it is "the right thing to do." Some Puritans contend that God has commanded men to be responsible. Others claim that the requirement of self-responsibility is an intrinsic fact of nature, both irreducible and outside the realm of human reason. Still other Puritans assert that responsibility arises from a moral duty to society, or one's fellow men, without any reference to the self. If people stop acting responsibly, such Puritans insist, then society will collapse and individuals will have failed at their central purpose of keeping the social order intact.

The second school consists of the modernists. Modernists, unlike the Puritans, do not treat responsibility as a moral ideal. Instead, they resentfully accept it as a necessary evil. Life would be better, modernists sigh, if only human beings did not need to take responsibility for their actions. If only life could be like the mythical Garden of Eden, where men and women did not need to work and think, all would be well. Because of man's tragic, "fallen" nature, modernists believe outside forces—especially the government—must regularly intervene to save human beings from themselves.

The third group of thinkers, the smallest of the three, favor the rational approach to responsibility. Unlike the modernists, proponents of reason extol responsibility as a moral ideal and do not lament the need to be responsible as a tragedy of the human condition. They encourage responsibility not because it benefits society or God, but because of its practical, concrete benefits for those who practice the virtue consistently. People who consistently act responsibly feel better and are more efficient at living, they argue. Advocates of reason see responsibility as both psychologically practical and morally necessary for all human beings.

The Failure to Integrate Morality With Practical Self-Interest

While Puritans sometimes reach reasonable conclusions, they travel an entirely different intellectual route from the rational thinker. A Puritan, for example, will oppose sexual promiscuity because he believes that the individual has an obligation to society to follow certain norms of behavior and prevent the spread of disease. The proponent of reason, in contrast, will oppose sexual promiscuity because the individual has an obligation to *himself* to seek genuine intimacy and avoid harmful consequences such as disease.

In this example, as many others, the rational thinker forms his moral convictions based upon the observations of his own senses and complex integrations known as concepts. The Puritan, in contrast, simply accepts a principle of morality dogmatically, whether on faith or on the word of a moral authority in whom he effectively places blind trust.

Unfortunately for the human race, any traces of a rational approach to the issue of self-responsibility which may have appeared throughout history (e.g. the Renaissance, the time of the founding of the United States) soon extinguished themselves due to a lack of serious philosophical foundation. In our own culture today, we witness a clash between an angry resurgence of the moral Puritans, on the one side, and the intellectually (and fiscally) bankrupt modernists on the other. Today's Puritans assert that we must return to moral commandments of responsibility in order to preserve the social order. Modernists, on the other hand, insist that responsibility is impossible to achieve without external assistance, and that everyone has to be forced to rely upon everyone else through "Social Security" and other coercive government institutions.

Puritans offer the ideal of self-responsibility without a proper motivation (i.e., one's own life). Modernists reject the ideal of self-responsibility as impractical, and attempt to persuade people (sometimes with great success) that a government-run welfare state serves their interests much better. Neither side succeeds in merging the idealism of the Puritans with the practical, self-interest motive of the modernists. Until morality and practicality are integrated in the minds of most people, today's social and political problems will remain unresolved.

The Psychology of Responsibility

The mentally healthy, rational individual experiences responsibility on an emotional level. As psychiatrist Tom Rusk writes, "Responsibility is ... a feeling about ourselves and our existence ... In fact, loving responsibility is the natural feeling state of a healthy human being."[33]

How one views responsibility determines how one will feel about it. If one accepts either the Puritan or modern view of responsibility, then one's psychological state will likely be characterized by feelings of envy, resentment and self-pity. Resentment, according to Rusk, is a festering bitterness about the way things are, an angry feeling state that assumes something or someone else is to blame for one's predicament in life. Chronic, unwarranted resentment amounts to a refusal to accept the facts of reality. Minor resentments, of course, come and go in the happiest of people, but when this feeling becomes a frequent or perpetual response to life problems, one's ability to function psychologically is endangered.

Consider the man, for example, who works in a highly dysfunctional work environment. His two supervisors often give him contradictory orders. He is frequently given responsibility without appropriate authority for carrying out various tasks. He has tried every conceivable method to correct the problem and none has worked.

Instead of accepting the fact that circumstances will not change and that he should seek another job, he attempts to sue his employers for job harassment and to seek disability payments from the government for mental stress. He soon discovers that the legal and bureaucratic agencies designed to protect him from his job are even more dysfunctional than the job itself. He develops a sense of anger, despair and resentment, and starts to focus on how evil "the system" is rather than developing a plan for finding a new career for himself. He blames his employers, his physician, and his attorney, but fails to see that even under difficult circumstances he still can choose a different set of goals for himself.

People with a rational sense of responsibility do not suffer from chronic states of resentment, anger or despair. They certainly experience such emotions, but these emotions do not dominate their mental lives. If they are in a difficult situation, they do everything possible to get out of it.

Chronically resentful people, on the other hand, hold the basic premise that life events are somehow conspiring against them. They seem unable to simply accept facts as given. They are unwilling to concentrate on what they actually can control, instead raging over what they cannot hope to control.

Why Irrational Views of Responsibility Inevitably Lead to Resentment

The Puritan philosophy inevitably leads to resentment because it tells the individual, in effect, "Be responsible because I say so. You owe it to God and society; that's all the reason you need." This irrational demand treats responsibility as a selfless duty, a demand against which any sensible person will eventually feel a need to rebel.

The modernist view likewise leads to a chronic emotional state of resentment. Modernists tell the individual, in effect, "You are not capable of being responsible. Consequently, you cannot be free either. You must serve others and force them, in turn, to serve you, if you are to survive." Social Security and other dysfunctional wealth-transfer programs illustrate the modernist view perfectly. Instead of planning their own retirements responsibly, younger people are forced to pay money to older people on the premise that they will receive the same treatment when, and if, they reach old age. In the welfare state, everyone is responsible for everyone else, and nobody is responsible for himself.

Once this philosophy is exposed for the dishonest and patronizing appeal to fear and low self-esteem it represents, independent-minded people will eventually rebel against it as well. Unfortunately, without better intellectual and moral guidance than what the Puritans and modernists have to offer, such rebellions will not go very far. Only a rational approach to responsibility will set the stage for real change.

Integration Between Conscious and Subconscious

Conscious adherence to a rational definition of responsibility does not automatically guarantee a healthy psychological state. As a psychotherapist, I encounter many otherwise rational people who have internalized, on an emotional level, a sense that reality is somehow against them, almost as if reality had a will and consciousness of its own.

A woman, for example, who does not think that reality has a will and consciousness of its own might nevertheless believe that, "It's just my rotten luck to plan my vacation in a rainy week. Why does this only happen to me?" Or a man, for example, who certainly thinks that one should have sufficient evidence before drawing conclusions, will nevertheless feel, despite evidence to the contrary, that his boss was out to get him from day one. Such contradictions between actual knowledge and emotional response represent the essence of psychological conflict in an otherwise rational human being.

The psychological advantage of holding rational intellectual views is that one can more persuasively talk oneself out of the invalid feeling until, eventually, new feelings combined with functional behaviors are learned. Good psychotherapy can certainly assist in this regard, although nothing, not even therapy, can replace a person's 24-hour-a-day commitment to challenging and resolving contradictions between his intellectual and emotional perspectives.

Responsibility In Action

Responsibility, in the context of an individual's everyday life, consists of a never-ending commitment to keeping his actions consistent with his ideas, observations and intentions.

Consider some practical applications of this assertion.

Keeping commitments. Responsible people keep big commitments as well as small ones. They do not make promises indiscriminately, particularly promises they are not prepared to keep. If they say they are going to call you back, they call you back. If they agree to wash your car for thirty dollars, they wash your car for thirty dollars. If they agree to stay faithful to a romantic partner, they stay faithful.

Self-sacrificers and other dysfunctional people feel guilty for failing to do their "duty" to another when they break a promise. Sometimes they feel so guilty, in fact, that they will repress or evade the motives for their actions, thus creating the appearance that they are inconsiderate or "selfish." Instead of acknowledging their responsibility for always arriving late for dinner engagements, they become defensive and hostile when confronted with the fact. Instead of accepting responsibility for a botched job, and trying to discover the causes of their errors, they try to blame someone else.

In reality, such people are not selfish at all, at least not if "selfish" means a commitment to acting in one's objective self-interest. They suffer from a *lack* of self-esteem, including a failure to recognize that keeping a commitment serves their own interests even more than those with whom they associate. They fail to understand that it feels better to bring closure to events, to bring things "full circle" rather than to leave them "hanging."

Taking care of one's physical requirements. Responsible people are responsible, above all, to themselves—their bodies as well as their minds. They exercise. They eat well. They obtain regular medical consultations, as appropriate. They drive carefully. They keep their physical environments clean and safe. After intense mental activity, they go outdoors and allow some oxygen into the brain. They never forget that the mind does not function outside the context of a healthy body.

Thinking benevolently. Responsible individuals assume that others are trustworthy and well-intentioned unless they see factual evidence to the contrary. They always allow room for the possibility that a conflict with another person might be due to an honest misunderstanding. They recognize that it serves their rational self-interests to practice benevolence, particularly since honest misunderstandings happen frequently. Instead of turning their lives into adversarial nightmares, at war with everybody and suspecting the worst in everyone, they assume the best unless or until the facts require them to think and act otherwise.

Allowing feelings into consciousness. Feelings are not necessarily facts, but they are nevertheless an important aspect of human nature. Responsible people are willing to identify feelings and, when those feelings are based upon facts or rationally defensible arguments, guiltlessly allow themselves to feel passionate about their conclusions. They do not disown their emotions, across the board, in the name of "rationality." Instead, they treat their emotions with respect while recognizing the need to distinguish between fact and feeling. Because they think carefully, they have earned the right to feel passionately.

Staying true to rational judgment. Many people misinterpret the notion of rational judgment as simply a variation of Puritanism. In other words, to choose objective judgment over emotional impulse amounts, in the eyes of many, to simply another way of repressing feelings and being inappropriately harsh with oneself. In reality, just the opposite is true. It actually feels better to stay true to one's rational judgment because of the resulting sense of independence, freedom and serenity one experiences from doing so consistently. Staying with rational judgment and observation also makes mistakes more tolerable, allowing oneself to say with conviction, "I did the best I could."

Adopting a day-to-day philosophy of optimistic realism. Optimistic realism presupposes a commitment to identify facts of reality, but to also view facts from a positive perspective. A man dislikes his unchallenging job yet sees no realistic alternative at the present; however, he also sees an opportunity to buy a second home at the beach where he can spend weekends and pursue other interests. He does not disregard the reality that his job is unchallenging; at the same time, he finds a more positive way to view the situation and creates a new goal for himself.

Optimistic realism doe not mean evasion of negative facts, nor a denial of the fact that genuine tragedy does occur in life. Instead, optimistic realists approach life with the consistent view that most negative facts can be turned into positive opportunities with mental and physical effort. The optimistic realist is a psychological entrepreneur, always looking for personal opportunities to exploit even in the midst of his own occasional pain, discomfort, or confusion.

Of course, optimistic realism will not flourish in a society where economic or intellectual freedom is stifled. Instead, negativism and cynicism will gradually come to dominate the minds and hearts of most people. American psychologists have named the last several decades the "Age of Anxiety," a label suited to the fact that freedom has become increasingly restricted in the United States. Pessimism leads people to think that government authorities must take both responsibility and freedom away from them. This loss of freedom and responsibility, in turn, leads to decaying social conditions (e.g., soaring health care costs, mediocre education, acts of terrorism such as Oklahoma City) which seem to justify the imposition of ever more government controls.

Conclusion

A rational approach to responsibility is essential to a healthy psychology as well as to good character. It eliminates needless confusion over what one *should* do versus what one *wants* to do.

A psychologically healthy person has internalized the rational approach to responsibility into every corner of his life. Emotionally as well as intellectually, he approaches life with neither guilt-ridden Puritanism nor helpless modernism. Instead, he understands the most important motivation for acting responsibly: himself.

STOP FEELING LIKE A VICTIM

Are you resentful, angry, and fed up with the world?

Do you feel like you are constantly putting more into relationships, personal and professional, than you are getting out of them?

Do you feel like everyone else around you is cold-hearted and "selfish," and that you are the only one trying to live by the standards of selflessness, "compassion," and give-give-give?

Are you mentally and spiritually exhausted?

Do you sometimes wonder what the whole point of living is?

If the answer to all or most of these questions is "yes," then may I make a suggestion?

Change your moral code. Change your *modus operandi*. Change the way you approach the world.

Stop telling yourself that in order to be a good person you must sacrifice. Stop acting like a martyr, and then rationalizing that this is the essence of moral virtue, of good character, and that it will eventually get you what you want. None of these myths are true.

Stop telling yourself that the more selfless you are, the better person you are.

Stop postponing life for "someday," whether "someday" means retirement, when your ship comes in, when your luck starts to change, when you win the lottery, or when you enter a mystical afterlife.

Stop talking on the phone to, making dates with, or otherwise spending time with people who are not good uses of your time. It is not only unfair to yourself; it is dishonest. You are letting this person think you really value him or her when you do not, or you are misleading them into thinking you value them more than you really do.

Start making your actions 100 percent consistent with what you think, and what you know. Start practicing justice, not only towards others but towards yourself—especially towards yourself.

Tell the truth—not just to others, but to yourself. Do not only tell the truth, but practice the truth as well. Living according to truth—defined, objectively, as the facts of reality—is the opposite of faking life, or living a lie as so many people do to one degree or another. Life is not a dress rehearsal, a "test," or an experiment. Life, in the real world, is the only place where you can or will experience happiness; happiness outside of real life is a contradiction in terms.

Unmask the myth that rejecting self-sacrifice means the end of morality and the end of good will among men. Nothing could be further from the truth. In fact, just the opposite is true. Think of how resentful you feel when you are *obliged* to do something, as a duty that somebody else imposed upon you. Think of how you would resent your spouse, for example, if someone had coerced you into marrying him. Think of how you would feel differently about your children were you forced to conceive and give birth to them by a party other than yourself. Ask yourself which is better: loving as a duty, or loving by choice? Is there really any contest?

Nobody, at least nobody half-way honest and healthy, likes to be forced to do things. Why? Force is at odds with human nature. Human beings are rational animals. This means they need to think about, understand, and comprehend a certain course of action before embarking upon it. The natural, appropriate response to "Do this because I tell you to do it" should be: "Why? Why should I?" An individual with high self-regard does, in fact, respond this way, and feels no shame about this fact. An individual with average self-regard will want to know why, but feels at least a little guilty about it. He will ask the question "why," but only to a point; after all, he has been taught, it is not good to be extreme about things (even correct or good things). The person with the lowest self-regard of all will respond: "OK. I will do what you say. I should just do what I'm told. Who am *I* to demand reasons?" But even this kind of person may resent such commandments over time, sensing but not fully understanding what is wrong about them. He may eventually rebel. If not, his subconscious will rebel for him, in the form of depression or countless other psychological problems.

To fight psychological problems, accept your true nature as a human being. The Freudian psychotherapists would like you to think that your true nature is that of a depraved animal with instincts you cannot control. Many religions preach that your true nature is that of a depraved sinner who is beyond salvation in this lifetime.

Your true nature is to be a happy, self-fulfilled and self-responsible human individual. This does not mean that happiness is automatic, nor that it is guaranteed. It does mean that happiness is possible, *if* you choose happiness as your central goal and *if* you use rational judgment in finding things to make you happy.

Rational judgment will keep you from falling into the trap of thinking that range-of-the-moment activities, such as drug abuse or sexual promiscuity, can really bring you happiness. Practicing realistic thinking, geared towards reality and not solely your momentary wishes, will lead you to set goals and ultimately achieve them. Thinking long-range, even as you live in the here-and-now, will help you integrate goals and process, and keep you from becoming either a drifter who never accomplishes anything or an obsessive-compulsive control-freak who never stops to enjoy life's everyday pleasures and joys.

Most fundamentally, you must accept that you should pursue happiness as well as accept responsibility for determining what your course of action will be. Learn the value of both freedom and responsibility for your own life. *This* is the way to overcome your depression, anxiety, or whatever label you attach to your psychological problems. Do not worry about the fact that these ideas contradict what you were taught: to go with your feelings instead of your head, or to live for others rather than for yourself. The ideas you were taught do not work very well, do they? Try a different approach, and judge for yourself which way is superior.

WHO SAYS YOU HAVE A "RIGHT" TO YOUR FEELINGS?

Many psychologists claim that you have a "right" to your feelings. Rather than a political right, they are referring to a psychological "right" to unconditional acceptance of your feelings by others.

Is this claim correct?

No—at least not if a "right" means you are allowed to assert your feelings without giving any explanation for them.

Feelings, first of all, are nothing more than automatized thoughts: thoughts which happen instantaneously, outside of your immediate conscious control. Because feelings happen outside of conscious control, they may be either rational or irrational, logical or illogical, fact-based or fantasy-based (or a mixture of each). Facts and feelings are not necessarily the same thing.

If you feel, for example, that someone is watching you behind your back, you have no way of knowing whether this feeling is fact-based or not until you turn around to see if anyone is there. It is not appropriate to scream for help, or call the police, merely because you *feel* that someone is behind you.

If you feel angry that a co-worker did not remember your birthday, whether your feeling is valid or not depends upon the facts of the situation. If you both had agreed months earlier to exchange gifts, and you even gave this very co-worker a gift on his birthday three weeks ago, then you certainly have a right to feel angry. On the other hand, if you never discussed giving gifts and you only mentioned your birthday once in casual conversation, then you do not have a right to feel angry.

If you feel betrayed because your husband says he does not want to have children, after telling you prior to your marriage that he did want to have children in the near future, then your feeling is based upon logic and facts. If you allow yourself to get pregnant, secretly going off birth control without even raising the subject of whether to have kids with your husband, then you have no right to feel betrayed. He never gave his consent to becoming a father; *he* is the one who should feel betrayed.

Whether or not you have a "right" to feel something depends upon whether the feeling conforms to the facts of reality. Sometimes, the facts are obvious and easy to discover. Sometimes, the issues are more complex and require much thought and analysis. Either way, facts must be the ultimate basis for determining whether feelings are valid or not.

None of this means that feelings are intrinsically "bad" or always irrational. Sometimes a feeling can be right on target. But there is no way to objectively validate the feeling as being accurate without first trying to match it against the facts.

What does all of this mean for your mental health? It means, first of all, that feelings are part of human nature and you have to pay attention to them. Ignoring them will not make them go away. Nor will ignoring feelings ensure that you never are affected by them. Festering, unexamined feelings eventually have ways of asserting themselves in inappropriate, even embarrassing ways. If you refuse to acknowledge anger, for example, then you will eventually blow up at somebody for a small injustice because you can no longer tolerate ignoring this important and often rationally justified emotion. Feelings exist, and they must be acknowledged.

So how do you acknowledge feelings to yourself? By developing habits of introspection. Pay attention to what your feelings are and then try to discover their causes. For example: "I feel angry right now. Why do I feel angry? What is causing this feeling? What was going on just before I started to feel it? What facts, if any, make this feeling justified? What facts, if any, do not make this feeling justified?"

The essence of mental health, then, is learning to monitor your feelings rationally. To rationally monitor feelings means honestly and objectively matching them against observable facts of reality, with the use of logic. The greater your mental health, the more harmony will exist between your reasoning mind and your emotional state. In the mentally unhealthy individual, thoughts and feelings are in a continuous state of war. In the mentally healthy individual, thoughts and feelings are generally at peace.

What happens if you discover a feeling that conflicts with the facts, but you continue to feel it anyway? First of all, remember that you are not a robot. Simply because you correctly identify a feeling that conflicts with facts does not guarantee it will go away immediately. In some cases it will, and in some cases it will not. If you are afraid that somebody is behind you, for instance, and you turn around to find nobody there, the feeling of fear will go away almost immediately. However, in other cases it may not be quite so simple. Sometimes you might need to repeatedly remind yourself of the facts, and let the irrational thoughts fade out gradually. Sometimes you might need to talk the issue over with a friend or psychotherapist, to help accelerate the process of phasing out the illogical feeling response.

Remember that feelings are powerful, automatic habits that do not always die easily. You can continue to feel an illogical emotion even after you have determined for yourself, intellectually, that it is indeed illogical. The important thing is that you do not *act* on the emotion once your own logical, fact-based judgment has told you not to do so. For instance, if you learn that standing on an unstable ladder caused you to fall, then you should not stand on that ladder again, even though you feel like doing so because you are in a hurry. Similarly, if you learn that a former girlfriend is dishonest and cheats on you, you do not reconcile with her simply because she begs you to come back and she makes every effort to be nice to you. Feelings eventually pass, but objective facts of reality always have a way of reasserting themselves if you choose to ignore them.

Many self-help writers and psychologists assert that feelings and emotions, not thinking and reason, form the core of what makes us human. This is not true. Although human beings experience complex emotions that other animals do not, all human emotions are ultimately caused by thoughts, ideas, and reason. To feel angry, for instance, you must have some concept of what constitutes fairness and unfairness. To feel happy, you must have some concept of what is good and what makes life worthwhile. Because human beings can reason and form concepts, they experience complex emotions as a consequence of what they think. To claim that feelings represent the essence of being human is to ignore what made feelings possible in the first place: the conscious, thinking mind.

To reason is not the same as to perceive. Both non-rational animals and humans can perceive two pieces of meat in front of them. But humans can also abstract the concept "two." Humans can also ask themselves: Where did this meat come from?

Who produced it? Who has a right to it? Why? How much of this meat should I eat to maintain a balanced diet? Do I even want to eat it? What spices should I use? Such questions do not concern an ape, a giraffe, a rhinoceros, or a dog.

Feelings, then, are mere consequences of what truly makes us human: our ability to form concepts; to abstract, not merely to perceive; to form judgments and make complex choices, not merely act on instinct. If you allow yourself to believe that feelings have no causes and form the essence of what makes us human, then you are putting yourself on the level of an animal. Animals can be enjoyable or useful, but they simply do not operate at the same level of sophistication as humans, the conceptual animals.

Since feelings are only the result of thoughts and ideas, it clearly makes no sense to claim you have an unconditional, blind "right" to your feelings. You owe it to yourself, more than anybody, to identify the extent to which your feelings match (or do not match) the facts of reality, and then to act accordingly. You owe it to yourself because this is how mental health is achieved, and this is how you can survive and flourish in life as a happy person. As a consequence, you will also develop self-discipline and be able to live in a civilized manner with other human beings. But your primary obligation is to yourself: if you want to be happy, you have to live not by feelings, but by facts and reason.   Ⓣ

28. *School District of Philadelphia v. Friedman.*

29. "Trouble Brewing," BNA's *Employee Relations Weekly*, 26 November 1990.

30. "Earlier Prosecutor Urged Prison for Dahmer," *Milwaukee Sentinel*, 26 July 1991.

31. Walter Olson, *The Litigation Explosion* (New York: Dutton, 1991), p. 152-53.

32. Charles J. Sykes, *A Nation of Victims* (New York: St. Martin's Press, 1992), p. 13.

33. Tom Rusk, *Instead of Therapy: Help Yourself Change & Change the Help You're Getting* (Carson, CA: Hay House, 1991), p. 23.

Chapter 21

How to Say "No" and Mean it

HOW TO SAY "NO" AND MEAN IT

The single best illustration of low self-esteem is the inability to say, "no."

Saying "no" represents a crucially important life skill. Saying "no" is a way of recognizing, and showing, that a dividing line exists between you and the rest of the world.

The act of saying "no" implies that your possessions, your mind, your very life and soul, belong to you alone. Nobody has a right to your life, your mind, or your possessions except for you.

Saying "no" does not mean dismissing responsibility. You are still responsible for keeping promises and honoring commitments; but which promises to make, and to whom, or whether to even make any promises at all, is entirely up to you.

Saying "no" does not mean you will lose friends, or that you are anti-social. On the contrary: If you continually say "yes" when you mean "no," you will either break promises you were never prepared to keep, thereby alienating others, or you will carry out the promises half-heartedly, even resentfully. Dishonesty is not the way to win friends and keep them.

To say "no" convincingly, you must first believe that your life belongs to you.

Mistaken, irrational ideas about ethics, self-sacrifice, and responsibility represent the most likely explanation for why you cannot say *the n word*. Most of us have internalized the idea that self-sacrifice is virtuous. Ideas have consequences, and the idea of self-sacrifice is an old one. Sadly, some of today's psychologists are attempting to lend scientific credibility to the notion that self-sacrifice and selflessness are the ideal, as well as the key to psychological health. This article will demonstrate that nothing could be further from the truth.

I will illustrate some mistaken, self-sacrificial assumptions which typically create anxiety over saying "no" to others. You might accept some of these erroneous assumptions. You might consciously disagree with them, but on a subconscious level they could still influence you, particularly since you hear them preached everywhere: from religious leaders; from psychologists; from politicians, left-wing and right-wing; from mothers, fathers, grandparents; from military heroes and anarchist groups; from Nazis and Communists; from television commentators and newspaper journalists; from uncommitted, pragmatic middle-of-the-roaders. They all believe in self-sacrifice—or at least, they *claim* to believe in it.

Not surprisingly, then, difficulty saying "no" stems from deep-rooted and profoundly fundamental origins. To figure out why it's hard for you to say "no," you have to challenge some ideas you may never have questioned before this point. As a reward for such a difficult task, you will finally be able to take charge of your own life and set it on a more satisfying course.

As you read about these mistaken assumptions, try to consider if any of them influence your own behaviors and emotions.

1. **Feelings:** "I owe my life to others. It is wrong to be selfish. I must always put others above myself. Granted, not everybody can be a saint all of the time; but the ideal is to serve others. The more I give up, and the more I serve others, the better person I am." **Rational response:** You do *not* owe your life to others. Your life belongs to yourself, and nobody else. Your neighbor's life belongs to himself, and nobody else. The only obligation or duty you have towards others is to respect this fact. You are not your brother's keeper; nor is your brother *your* keeper.

The proper, true definition of "selfish" is to act in your objective, actual self-interest. Behaviors mistakenly labeled "selfish" do not in fact serve your self-interest. For instance, it does not serve your interest to lie to your spouse, a person you supposedly care about more than anyone on earth. It does not serve your interest to indulge a drug or alcohol addiction, when that addiction inhibits your ability to think, produce, and make a living. It does not serve your interest to alienate your friends by treating them badly. Yet all of these behaviors are inappropriately considered "selfish."

The more you seek to enjoy life, to gain new knowledge, and to act in your genuine self-interest, the better person you will be. Competence and productivity—not selflessness and sacrifice—represent the essence of goodness. Others have a right to say "no" if you request their time, their labor, or their property. You have an equal right to say "no," to keep your property or time, no matter who makes a claim on them. If you value yourself and respect the need for others to value themselves, then you are a good, just and fair person. Only when you expect either yourself or others to give up this need and right are you unfair or unjust.

Example: You have a choice between either spending a Sunday afternoon relaxing in your back yard or going to your cousin's daughter's graduation. You really don't know or care for your cousin very much. You want and need the time to relax. The right thing to do? Stay home and relax. You do not owe your time to a cousin you barely know. You are not obliged to go to the graduation unless it offers some actual benefit, pleasure, or value to you.

Example: An acquaintance from college asks if he can "crash" on your living room floor when he is in town. You normally don't like having guests because it disrupts your work schedule. You don't even know this person very well. The right thing to do? Tell him it's not convenient for you to have guests, but you can suggest a few good hotels. You do not owe the privacy of your home to an unwelcome guest.

2. **Feelings:** "Nice people do not hurt others' feelings. Nice people try to make everything smooth and calm. Mean people are ruthless, sarcastic, and even take pleasure in hurting others' feelings. I would rather be a nice person than a mean person. Treating others kindly, even if you dislike them or dislike something they did, represents a virtue." **Rational response:** This distinction between "nice" and "mean" people represents a false alternative. No rational reason exists to deliberately hurt someone else's feelings; only sadists get "pleasure" out of such activity. Just because you are not a

sadist does not mean that you are obliged to sacrifice your opinions, your time, or your property to others, all in the name of "not hurting their feelings."

Phony, patronizing "niceness" is dishonest. Isn't honesty more important than kindness for kindness' sake? In reality, you have no means of showing kindness towards others except by being honest with them. Honesty and kindness cannot be separated. Would you want people to lie to *you*, just to make you feel better? If not, then how could you claim such a right for yourself?

Honesty precedes kindness. Genuine kindness, as opposed to phony platitudes, must be earned. Do not give away your kindness promiscuously.

You need not choose between being either a pit-bull or a doormat. Communicate calmly, assertively, and honestly, and expect those with whom you deal to do the same.

Example: Your friend asks you for your opinion about his career plan. You think it's a mistake for him to go to journalism school instead of finding work for a newspaper. Yet you do not want to hurt his feelings. What is the appropriate thing to do, if he's truly your friend? Tell him your honest opinion, and the reason for it. If you really care for him, you will place honest judgment above feelings. You can tell him politely and respectfully—but still honestly.

Example: Your daughter asks for your feedback on a paper she wrote for school. You think that it's generally well written, but it makes several points poorly. The nice, right thing to do? Praise her good points, and criticize the weak spots, telling her why. She needs, and hopefully even wants, your honesty and objectivity more than she needs your "strokes."

Example: You find out that your best friend is cheating on his wife. You know for a fact he is lying to her about where he's spending his evenings, and she believes him. You believe his behaviors are wrong. Since you also consider his wife a friend, you are concerned for her well-being. He repeatedly puts you in situations where you have to help him maintain his deceit, such as letting his wife (your friend) believe his lies. Is it virtuous, or healthy, to withhold your view? No. Should you give your opinion and the reasons for it? Absolutely. You cannot use false kindness to fake a friendship. The two are mutually exclusive.

3. **Feelings:** "If I give, then I will eventually get in return."
   Rational response: Sometimes people will return your favors; sometimes they will not. If you give to a friend, family member, or professional associate—or anyone of objective value to you—then you are not necessarily sacrificing; on the contrary, the very act of giving in such contexts often involves personal pleasure. But if you subscribe to the belief that saying "yes" indiscriminately—to anybody, for any reason—will necessarily lead to rewards over the long run, then you are sure to be disappointed.

It is fine to be generous to certain individuals because you have objective reason to expect they will (or already do) make the relationship a two-way street. But do not keep throwing yourself into relationships or situations which hold no real, observable benefit to you. Life is too short to waste on selfless endeavors.

Example: You repeatedly agree to work the night shift for a co-worker when he asks you to do so as a favor. You do so selflessly, asking nothing in return. After a few months of helping him out, you ask a similar favor of the same co-worker. He refuses. You are enraged. "I didn't want to do his night shifts!" you fume. "So he should do me a favor now, even if he doesn't want to." Wrong. If you never wanted to do the night shifts, you never should have agreed. You could have said "no." You also could have made your agreement to help him conditional upon his returning the favor at a later time. Like it or not, you have only yourself to blame.

4. **Feelings:** "I was always taught that true goodness consists of giving, without expecting to receive."

   Rational response: What you were taught was dead wrong. Selfless giving is *not* the way to become a virtuous person, at least not if virtue consists of being benevolent, productive, peaceful, and happy. Just the opposite is true. Living for yourself, while respecting this same right in others, will help you develop into a happy and competent person. Selflessly denying yourself everything, all in the name of "virtue," will eventually lead you to bitterness, resentment, and possibly despair.

Do not misunderstand. There is nothing inherently wrong with giving. But there is a big difference between giving out of selfless duty and giving because you see evidence of an equal or greater return on your personal investment. Just as it would be foolish to invest money in a worthless used car, so too is it foolish to invest your time and energy in a personal relationship where the other individual has nothing to offer you—such as a good sense of humor, a keen intellect, companionship—in return. Human relationships should involve an exchange of values—whether those values are financial and material, or intellectual and emotional. The exchange of such values ought to be mutually beneficial, rather than sacrificial or one-sided.

Most importantly, never give of yourself when another expects your offering as a "right" to which he is entitled. Nobody has a mortgage on your life. If somebody demands even a single penny of you, not as a non-sacrificial favor but as a moral right, then you should absolutely not give him anything. To do so would be an abdication of your self-esteem, the ultimate surrender of the principle that your life belongs to yourself.

Nobody owns your life except for *you*. Neither your possessions nor your soul represent community property. Anyone who demands your time, money, or emotional support as a duty is a parasite and a moocher.

Example: You give a friend Christmas gifts for two years in a row. For the same two years in a row, he does not give you any gifts in return. He nevertheless graciously accepts and keeps your gifts. He does not even offer an excuse for not giving you a gift. Should you give him a gift in year three? No. Participating in a one-way street is neither virtuous nor healthy. You are not obliged to give without receiving.

Example: A relative for whom you have mixed feelings calls you and bends your ear about her personal problems. She makes little or no effort to ask anything about your life, or your problems. She acts as if she has a right to your time, and when you try to set a limit on her demands she becomes angry and calls you selfish. What should you do? Tell her politely, "You're right. I *am* selfish. I respect my right to my own time, and I respect this same right in others. I never try to steal someone's time any more than I would steal their money. Maybe if you thought this way, you wouldn't have so many problems."

5. **Feelings:** "I can't be a happy person unless I am also a giving person."
   Rational response: Why you give—and whether or not such giving objectively represents a sacrifice to you—will determine whether your giving is healthy or neurotic, proper or improper. Voluntary, non-sacrificial giving is honest, benevolent, and healthy. Selfless, sacrificial giving, or giving brought about by coercion or emotional intimidation, is dishonest, cynical, and ultimately self-defeating to both the giver and the recipient.

Selfishness, in the rational sense of the term, does not rule out the option of giving. It simply means that you should only give to those whom you value, when it is not a sacrifice—and when you are sure your generosity will be used productively.

Examples: To give healthily means to give freely, consciously, and non-sacrificially. You give your kids time and love because you value them, you freely accept the responsibility of raising them, and they represent a very important part of your life. You treat your employees well because you want them to work harder and remain loyal to you. You give your spouse time and love because you value her character and her beauty, because you chose to be with her, and because you selfishly enjoy the experience of being in a committed relationship. You might voluntarily give to medical research because you want to keep yourself or a loved one from getting a horrible disease, or to honor the memory of someone who died from a disease.

To give neurotically, or sacrificially, means to give either because you allowed yourself to be coerced into doing so, or because you allowed yourself to be emotionally intimidated into doing so. In neurotic giving, you give up an objectively greater value to an objectively lesser value (again, where the standard of "value" is your happiness). For example, you "loan" money to a dysfunctional or distant relative because, you rationalize, "blood is thicker than water." You give lavishly to charity because you feel compelled to "give something back to the community," as if you somehow *stole* something from others by making an honest living. You give your employees everything they demand because you fear they will not like you or they will chastise you as "greedy." You let friends, or even people you do not know very well, impose on you because you fear they will not like you. You dutifully support "Big Government," and surrender 30 or 40 percent of your income to pay for programs which (in most cases) will never benefit you personally. Why? Because you allow politicians, preaching the philosophy of self-sacrifice, to intimidate you into accepting as a moral duty the financial support of your countrymen (or even the entire planet). In the context of self-sacrifice, the notion of "all for one and one for all" represents a sucker bet.

6. **Feelings:** "Saying *no* makes me a bad person; saying *yes*, especially when I don't want to, makes me a good person. How can I possibly be a good and healthy person if I am not a giving person?"
Rational Response: Giving does not represent the essence of goodness. Productivity, honesty, being reality-oriented, and vigorously pursuing happiness in life *do* represent the essence of goodness. If you want to be a good person, then strive first to be productive, goal-oriented, and happy. Giving is a peripheral issue when compared to the more fundamental issues of basic survival, productivity, and psychological happiness.

What about others? Will society fall apart if you place your own needs ahead of those of the larger group? Of course not. Think about it. If literally everyone worked at being productive and happy, and followed a philosophy of rational self-interest, there would not be anyone for whom to sacrifice. The only people in need would be the occasional genuine victims of natural disaster or biological illness. Charity, in such cases, would be voluntary, temporary, and certainly not sacrificial. Remember that voluntary charity existed long before the welfare state, and will continue long after its demise.

On the other hand, if everyone valued dutiful service above productivity and competence, as the advocates of self-sacrifice want us to do, then what kind of world would it be? For a concrete example in our own times, look at the former Communist countries in Russia and Eastern Europe. These countries formed governments based on the "ideals" of sacrifice and selflessness. Profits and private property were outlawed. In most cases, individuals could not choose their own careers. In many cases, they could not plan the size of their families. The pursuit of public welfare was everything; the pursuit of private welfare was considered evil and therefore outlawed. As it turned out, only the political rulers and dictators were allowed to have everything they wanted—not through their own effort, of course, but at the expense of millions.

What did these countries produce, compared to the relatively selfish countries of Western Europe and the United States? Did the inventors of the automobile, the airplane, and the computer emerge under sacrificial Communism, or under freedom? Where would you rather live, and raise your children? In a country committed to sacrifice and dictatorship? Or in a country which (more or less) respects the rights of individuals to control their own lives, such as the United States?

If you define happiness rationally, there need be no conflict between pursuing happiness and the good of society.

Example: A scientist who pursues a cure for cancer or Alzheimer's Disease, for personal reasons of winning a Nobel prize and for a genuine love of his work, is a good person. His pursuit of these private goals will, as a secondary consequence, potentially lead to good for the human race as a whole.

Example: A business person who makes a lot of money, because of a desire to be rich and to dominate a particular market, benefits others even though this is not his specific intention. He creates jobs, opportunities, and new products, perhaps even at a lower cost than would otherwise be the case if his competitor remained unchallenged.

Example: A productive, hard-working person who selfishly cares about his property and his family is not a threat to society. On the contrary, his desire to acquire and sustain his values—family, property, and so forth—makes him willing to cooperate in forming and supporting a police force, a military, and a court system designed to protect the rights of all individuals, himself included.

7. **Feelings:** "I should turn the other cheek when someone commits an injustice against me, at least if it's a small injustice."

   Rational response: If something is in fact an injustice, even a small one, you should *not* turn the other cheek. You should, at a minimum, comment on the injustice or, in more severe cases, take some form of action to retaliate against the injustice. A consistent policy of turning the other cheek inevitably destroys self-esteem, encourages moral cowardice, and leads to greater injustices throughout the world.

In issues great and small, turning the other cheek is damaging to your self-esteem as well as unjust to everyone involved. It harms yourself and, in the long run, harms those individuals toward whom you claim to feel benevolence. By enabling, participating in, or sanctioning others' unhealthy behaviors, you help them continue on their self-destructive path as well as sacrificing yourself in the process. You jump onto their sinking ship—and you go down with them.

Example: Consider a small injustice. Your friend agrees to meet you at 8:00. He arrives at 9:20. He offers no apology or excuse; he acts as if his lateness is appropriate behavior and you should accept it. To say nothing, or to do nothing, merely compounds the injustice. You are acting unjustly against yourself; you are also participating in, and even enabling, the friend's ethical or psychological problem. If you don't say or do anything, he will keep on treating you, and others, in the same disrespectful way. As the friendship deteriorates because of unexpressed resentment, both parties lose.

The identical principle applies to large injustices as well: prejudice, dishonesty, fraud, theft, and the initiation of physical violence. Why on earth is it "moral" to turn the other cheek against a rapist, a murderer, or a con-artist? It should be easy to see why it is senseless to turn the other cheek when others lie to you, emotionally blackmail you, or physically threaten you. Unless you are suicidal, to equate turning the other cheek with "morality" represents a mockery of morality.

8. **Feelings:** "Saying *no* risks having somebody dislike me, or reject me."

   Rational response: First, you cannot read someone else's mind. What you interpret as rejection by the other person, after you tell him "no," may simply be disappointment; not disappointment in *you*, personally, but merely disappointment that his desire remains unfulfilled. Assume he is simply disappointed, not angry, unless or until you see solid evidence to the contrary.

Second, no reasonable or healthy person will respect you any less for saying "no." Quite the opposite is true. A healthy person will respect you more for saying no, especially if you say no in a mature, calm, non-defensive way. Any disappointment or irritation on his part is temporary; the increased respect for you will be permanent. The increased respect you have for yourself will be lasting as well.

Finally, the opinions and views of others do not determine reality. Reality is made up of facts, not others' opinions. Someone's opinion or judgment of you may or may not be reasonable; it may or may not be based upon facts and logic. So do not hastily conclude, merely because someone feels a certain way, that his feeling is fair, reasonable, or accurate. Just as you can be mistaken, another person can be mistaken as well. Go by your own rational judgments, and hold your ground. Dare to act and think like an adult.

Example: A friend asks you to take off work for half a day and drive her to a routine doctor's appointment. Although your friend had no way of knowing, the favor would represent a sacrifice to you because you are currently spending your time on a very consuming work project. The deadline for the work project is approaching. You explain this fact to your friend and, because she is important to you, you offer to take her to a Saturday appointment if one is available. Your friend declines your offer of a compromise, and thereafter begins to act in a distant, "pouty" manner towards you. Should you reverse your decision? Absolutely not. Sadly, you have to accept a troubling discovery about your friend. She is, in fact, not truly a friend. She expects you to sacrifice for her—that is, to do something for her even though you would have to harm your job performance to do so. Friends don't ask friends to sacrifice. What she wants is a parent or a caretaker, not a friend.

Example: A client in your business asks you to finish the job a week earlier than called for in the contract. You respond that you will work longer hours, but you are still not willing to compromise on the quality of your work by rushing it. You explain that you take pride in what you do and you want to do it well. You also remind the client that you are sure he does not want a second-rate product. At first, he seems disappointed but nevertheless agrees. When the job is finished, he is delighted with the result. He remains a loyal customer and sends you new business. You discover that holding your ground, and temporarily disappointing someone important to you, need not result in disaster. More often than not, quite the opposite proves true.

The inability to say "no" is the emotional symptom of holding a mistaken, irrational ethical code. Your psychological state and personality is determined, ultimately, by your more fundamental philosophical ideas, including your ideas (however implicit) about what is ethically proper. You are free to change these ideas if you discover them to be mistaken.

Tragically, the "ideal" of self-sacrifice is widely preached, particularly by people who seek to manipulate you and make you feel guilty. Such manipulators sanctimoniously lecture on the "virtue" of sacrifice, but notice that they usually demand sacrifices of *you*, not of themselves.

Why should you give up your happiness, or even a portion of it, simply because someone says so? Remember that living according to your self-interest does not rule out the possibility of giving. Try to distinguish between benevolent, non-sacrificial giving and actual sacrifice. To give money to a charity you believe in, and in an amount you can afford, is non-sacrificial and benevolent; to give money to a charity you know little about, or disagree with, is sacrificial. To take over some of your co-worker's responsibilities when her husband dies of cancer, a co-worker whom you know would do the same for you, is benevolent and non-sacrificial; to protectively take over a co-worker's responsibilities when she is repeatedly caught in lies and shows evidence of a drug problem, is sacrificial and foolish. To work a second job to put your son through college, a son who shows the aptitude and motivation to achieve, does not represent a sacrifice; to work a second job to put a stranger's son through college, or even your own ungrateful son who shows no aptitude or motivation, represents a sacrifice. What actually constitutes a sacrifice depends upon the context.

Both the traditional and modern moralists count on your failing to recognize the difference between objectively rational, non-sacrificial giving and actual sacrifice. They want you to drop the context. They want you to think: "If I don't give, regardless of the circumstances, then I must be a bad person." Having to choose between being a miserable martyr, or, conversely, someone who does whatever he feels like whenever he feels like it, represents the very false alternative these moralists want you to accept. The traditionalists will tell you to be a martyr; the modernists will tell you to do whatever feels right, and to forget about morality. In other words, you can be "moral" (that is, a martyr) and not achieve happiness, *or* you can pursue happiness, but forget completely about morality. What a lousy choice!

You actually have a third alternative: to pursue happiness, but to do so rationally and honestly; to be selfish, but not in the sense of sacrificing others; to be moral, but not in the sense of sacrificing yourself.

The ability of the traditional moralists to continue manipulating you with *the s word* ("selfish"), and with their false alternative, is only as strong as your willingness to let them. Stop letting them! Their psychological hold over you is only as powerful as you allow it to be. Your choice of ethical code determines whether you will feel chronically guilty or consistently happy to be alive.

If you really want self-esteem and psychological health, you must first examine your underlying moral premises about the issues of giving, sacrificing, and self-interest. Don't let others do this thinking for you. Your ethical principles—the means by which you will survive and attain happiness—are too important to delegate to others.

Adopt the philosophy of rational self-interest, whereby you make no sacrifices to others and demand no sacrifices of them. Instead of living by the creed, "You sacrifice for me and I will sacrifice for you," you can now live by the creed, "Neither you nor I shall sacrifice for each other." It's fair. It's rational. It works. It allows you—and others—an equal opportunity to live happily without guilt.

We are entering the twenty-first century. We live in an era of unprecedented technological and material progress. More and more societies, East and West, are moving (however slowly and with frequent contradictions) in the direction of science, technology, and freedom. Yet the prevailing ethical code, and approach to human psychology, is still medieval.

It's time to move beyond the *modus operandi* of the Middle Ages. Martyrdom and self-sacrifice are neither heroic nor healthy.   ⌾

Chapter 22

Not to *Return* to Morality—But to Discover it

GUILT AND EMOTIONS

It is a fact that guilt represents a crippling psychological problem.

It is also true that guilt represents the foundation for a healthy and ethical approach to life.

How can both of these statements be correct?

In order to answer this question, we must first define guilt.

Guilt refers to the evaluation, in the form of an emotion, that you are responsible for a particular event or set of circumstances which are negative or harmful in nature; in other words, the sense that you have acted against your values.

You might feel guilty because you believe you are responsible for being late to a meeting. Or you might feel guilty because you feel responsible for failing your computer science class. Or you might feel guilty because you assume responsibility for hurting the feelings of your child when you yelled at him. Each of these cases involves an evaluation of self-responsibility for an event which is harmful either to yourself or someone/something important to you.

In each of these cases, assuming the basic facts are correct, guilt represents an appropriate, healthy, and entirely rational emotion. If being on time for a meeting is important to you, then without guilt you will not feel motivated to be on time in the future. If passing your class or getting your college degree represents a value to you, then guilt over failing (or the prospect of failing) is an important tool in helping you study and focus your mind on the subject. If you want your child to grow up in a fair and rational environment, then your emotion of guilt over yelling will help you remember to try reasoning with him in the future.

Notice as well that rational, appropriate guilt presupposes a commitment to values. You cannot feel guilty for acting against your values unless you actually value something or someone in the first place. Unless you love and value your child, you will not feel guilty for yelling at him or hitting him. Unless you value your home, you will not feel guilty for leaving the stove turned on when you go to work. Unless you value the prospect of a long and fully focused life, you will not feel guilty for smoking, abusing drugs, or overeating.

How, then, can guilt become a crippling psychological problem?

Guilt becomes a problem when people hold themselves responsible for events over which they have no control, or circumstances for which they have no responsibility.

Many people, for example, feel guilty for their feelings. They assign the same metaphysical status to their feelings as they do to actions. Thinking about having an extramarital affair, to such people, represents the same thing as actually having an extramarital affair. Wanting to tell a lie is no different from actually telling a lie. Desiring to hit your child is a sin, just like actually hitting your child is a sin. Many religions still teach that sins of "omission" (thinking about doing something wrong) are, in their own way, just as bad as sins of "commission" (actually doing something wrong).

According to common sense and logic, an enormous difference exists between wanting, thinking, or wishing versus actually doing something. Unfortunately, as children we are not always taught the most rational ideas. When we are taught irrational ideas, those ideas become internalized and automatized in the form of adult psychological problems. Let us consider the root of some of those problems.

Traditionally, many well-meaning parents and religious authorities have taught children to avoid "bad thoughts" or not to think about doing "bad things," since thinking about them can increase the temptation to do them. In some respects this argument contains merit, in that it encourages self-discipline and the productive use of one's mind. It also contains some very large mistakes because it teaches children to repress and condemn their emotions rather than acknowledge and rationally deal with them. It teaches them that if they pretend not to have a desire to do something wrong, then that desire somehow disappears from existence. In short, it teaches them to evade reality at a time when they need to be learning how to cope with and live in reality. In teaches them psychological denial instead of self-awareness and introspection.

What is the alternative to this psychological denial? Certainly not what we see being taught today. For the last three decades or so, we have seen the rebellion against the traditional approach to guilt and morality. We have witnessed the attempt to replace repression and moralism with subjectivism and permissiveness. Alas, the rebellion is little better than the state of affairs which preceded it; and in some respects, it is much worse.

Today, we are told by liberal psychologists, teachers, and modern spiritual authorities that moral concepts of "right" and "wrong" are meaningless and damaging. We are taught not to judge, because moral judgments are *judged*—by these experts (note the inconsistency)—to be wrong. We are told to adopt a policy of anti-principle—on principle. Kids are not merely taught, as they should be, that feelings have a different metaphysical status than actions; they are also taught to do whatever they feel like and not worry about right and wrong. To even concern yourself with moral questions, about right and wrong in any context, means that you are "judgmental" and too hard on yourself. Any infringement on whims and desires is feared to be a death-blow to a child's fragile self-esteem. If feelings and desires collide with reality, then feelings must always win.

Is it any wonder that so many of these kids enter their teenage years confused, angry, and poised to escape reality through the use of drugs and alcohol? In such a context, drug and alcohol abuse actually makes a lot of sense. If you are taught throughout your most formative years that your mind is impotent to make judgments, that you cannot even trust the conclusions of common sense observation, and that it is somehow *bad* to make distinctions between good and bad, then what is the point of having a mind in the first place? You might as well do drugs and try to find some pleasure that way, since rational pursuits of pleasure remain meaningless if your mind is incapable of rationality in the first place.

For many kids, drugs and alcohol offer a tantalizing escape from the Pollyanaish dictatorship of today's "feel good" educational programs. Unfortunately, the politically correct, nationalized public school system teaches Johnny not how to read but how to be "sensitive," not the virtues of freedom and independence but the "ideal" of welfare state dependence (and obedience). Mind altering substances also offer reassurance that what they were taught is true: that feelings and desires are supreme over objective reality. It is hard to argue with such reasoning if you are in a perpetually stoned or drunk state, as any recovering addict will tell you.

Conservatives, whose influence is growing, understandably look at today's approach to guilt and morality and speak out against it. Even honest liberals are starting to speak out against today's outrageously ineffective and expensive school system. Unfortunately, what do most of them offer us as an alternative? A return to the very situation that created the current mess. A return to traditional morality. To the old idea that you should repress your feelings, ignore your desires, immediately rejecting them as self-indulgent and focus instead just on following commandments set forth by religious authorities. Yet how is this old approach any fundamentally different from today's idea that you should repress your judgment, ignore your common sense and your abstract reasoning?

The conservatives tell us to give up our minds to religious authorities. The liberals tell us to give up our minds to secular authorities. In the area of guilt and morality, the conservative and the liberal visions, while superficially in opposition, actually represent two varieties of the same fundamental argument: anti-self and anti-reason.

The conservatives tell you (and your children) to ignore your feelings, rather than reaching rational judgments on your own through reason and introspection. They encourage you to feel guilty if you even pay attention to your feelings, much less for trying to examine them rationally. The liberals teach you (and your children) to pay attention to your feelings, and to act on them, but not to apply reason and logic to them because this is "mean" and unfeeling towards others with different feelings.

The conservatives tell you to blindly trust in religious edicts (rational or otherwise), in place of your own rational judgment. The liberals tell you to blindly trust in your feelings, relying on secular authorities (usually government schools and welfare state programs), in place of your own rational judgment. Notice that both sides are trying to repress (if not eliminate) independence, self-reliance, and objective assessments of reality.

What is the specific rational alternative to this false dichotomy? To place rational, independent, and objective judgment over and above emotional repression and subjective feeling-worship. Children (and, when possible and necessary, adults) need to be taught rational ideas, such as the following:

1. Objective reality exists separately from your feelings.
2. Feelings can either be an accurate reflection of objective facts, or a total distortion of objective facts. Facts are primary.
3. Reason and critical thinking, at one's level of ability and development, are the means to assessing the difference between what's going on inside (consciousness) and outside (out there, in reality). The purpose of childhood education is not to

put kids "in touch" with their feelings, but to teach them how to think critically about the world in which they live.

4. Reason and critical thinking represent the alternative to blind following of commandments or religious doctrines, on the one hand, and blind worship of or indulgence in one's feelings, on the other. This does not mean that all religious principles are wrong, or that all feelings are wrong; it simply means that the final arbiter in such disputes needs to be one's independent, thinking, judging mind, a mind in pursuit of objective truth based upon actual facts.

5. Never feel guilty for your emotions. Feelings have no moral status. Feelings simply happen, or come up, as a result of certain ideas, subconsciously stored in your mind. Analyze your feelings to see if they are mistaken, or to see if they are consistent with the facts of objective reality which you see, know, and understand. But never feel guilty for them.

6. *Do* allow yourself to feel guilty in either of the following two situations: when you refuse to think, or, when faced with a conflict between rational judgment and your emotions, you act on your emotions.

7. Acting on emotions is not wrong because it is self-indulgent or because it is harmful to society; acting on emotions is wrong because it harms your life, and it is not in your long-term, objective self-interest. You owe it to yourself, more than anyone or anything, to think and act according to your reasoning mind.

Guilt can either be a tremendous problem or a liberating influence. It poses a problem when you blame yourself for things over which you have no control: such as the fact that you have emotions, including at times mistaken or distorted emotions. Guilt represents a liberating influence, however, once you recognize that while you cannot directly control your emotions, you *can* control the use of your conscious, thinking mind as well as your actions. If you use your mind consciously with an orientation to reality, you can use guilt as a tool, instead of as a weapon of self-destruction.

TO JUDGE OR NOT TO JUDGE?

Legitimate, rational judgment is the exercise of forming and holding opinions about individuals and situations based upon objective observation of the facts of reality.

The extent to which you allow emotions (detached from facts) to contaminate your objective judgment is the extent to which you are being judgmental. Emotions are fine as consequences of rational, fact-based judgments; emotions should not, however, serve as the basis for judgments.

If you know a young man who uses drugs every day, misses half of his college classes and shows no evidence of ambition or goals, you are right to judge him as a troubled, aimless individual who is going nowhere fast. On the other hand, if you conclude that another young man is a drug user merely by the school he attends or his choice of major, you are being judgmental.

If you determine that a businessman is sleazy and dishonest because he lies to his clients and shows a consistent record of selling shoddy products, then you are making a rational judgment. If you conclude that a businessman is sleazy merely because he is a businessman, then you are being judgmental.

If you meet a black woman with a young child and immediately conclude that she is a welfare mother, you are being judgmental and arguably racist. If you meet *any* woman, of any race, and discover that she collects welfare checks, makes no effort to work, and repeatedly becomes pregnant, lying to her sexual partner that she is using birth control, then you have reason to judge her as a freeloading parasite.

Once you judge someone using rational standards, then you have earned the liberty of expressing an emotional reaction about him. If the *facts* tell you the individual has integrity and intelligence, you allow yourself to feel warmth and admiration. If the *facts* tell you the individual has no integrity and does not use his talents well, you allow yourself to feel dislike and disgust. To the rational person, emotions are the result—not the cause—of objective observation and analysis.

If you experience emotions without a factual base, this fact does not by itself mean you are irrational; you are irrational only if you let the emotion affect your conscious evaluation of the situation one way or the other. If you meet someone for the first time and notice a sense of like or dislike, you are not irrational. You are irrational only if you claim to know something about his intelligence, worth or moral character based solely on this initial "gut" feeling. It is not the presence of feelings that makes you judgmental; it is what you *do* with these feelings, consciously and through action, that counts.

In today's subjectivist-mystical cultural climate, psychologists and educators discourage rational judgment altogether. They inappropriately lump judgmentalism into a package deal which includes legitimate judgment as well as irrational judgmentalism. Not a week goes by in my practice, for example, where a client does not say to me, "I hate to sound judgmental, but..." I often interrupt the client and ask him to define "judgmental;" almost invariably, the definition is dangerously vague and shows traces of the false package deal. Consequently, the individual feels guilt-ridden not because he acts on irrational judgments, but because he seeks to make judgments at all.

Failure to distinguish between legitimate, rational judgment based upon observation of the facts of reality versus judgmentalism detached from reality can lead to unhealthy false alternatives. You will come to feel that you must choose between (1) Pollyana-like political correctness, in which even obvious facts must be ignored so as to be "sensitive" to others, or (2) hostile, hateful rejection of facts in favor of whatever prejudice or whim suits one's fancy of the moment.

As an illustration of this false alternative on a society-wide level, witness the growing polarization between hysterical do-gooders who favor censorship to enforce their opinions, on the one side, and cynical, hateful nationalist-racists who seek, without evidence, to blame economic and social problems on entire groups such as foreign corporations, immigrants, and particular racial groups. The do-gooders want to inhibit all forms of dissent in the name of "non-judgmentalism;" the haters want to "judge," but without the responsibility of having to prove their judgments are true. Neither side realizes, or chooses to recognize, that human reason represents the only viable alternative.

It is not judgment itself that you should avoid, but judgment detached from objective facts and logical arguments. Rational, fact-based judgment is a necessary component of human survival and happiness. Choosing the right marital or business partner requires judgment. Buying the right car involves judgment. Even deciding how to cross a busy highway at the appropriate time entails a judgment. Rational judgment is good and necessary, and is not the same as judgmentalism.

THE ADVERSARIAL VERSUS THE REALISTIC APPROACH TO LIFE

Two approaches to life, especially in the business or professional environment, characterize most human interactions. The first is the adversarial mentality; the second is the realistic mentality.

The adversarial mentality rests upon a series of illogical but (to some people) emotionally appealing ideas about how human beings can most effectively get along with one another. Here are a few of the mistaken assumptions an adversarial person typically holds:

People are unworthy of trust until proven otherwise; they are guilty until proven innocent. To some, this might sound like a realistic although not ideal view. But is it even realistic? No. First of all, trustworthy people do exist in most settings. Yet if you start with the premise that nobody is trustworthy, then you will tend to treat them in a manner consistent with your expectation. You will be abrupt with them, you will act suspicious towards them, you will not maintain eye contact or show that you have any regard for them at all. Thus, your expectation becomes a self-fulfilling prophecy. Because you expect everyone to be untrustworthy, you treat them as such; because you treat them as such, then they do in fact become your enemies rather than your friends.

Everyone else is dishonest, so I might as well be dishonest too. Since dishonesty is usually exposed over the long run, how practical is it? Once you develop a reputation for dishonesty, people will not be comfortable doing financial or emotional business with you. Even more fundamentally, dishonesty creates a breach between yourself and reality, between yourself and the facts, that is not only stressful to maintain but also harmful to your self-esteem and self-worth. Because true happiness depends upon accepting reality, you compromise that happiness by establishing a gap between your mind and the real world. Consequently, the basic "dilemma" about lying should not be: "Will I get caught or not?" but rather, "Do I want to live in reality or not?" To a rational, healthy, life-valuing individual, the answer is obvious.

Conflicts of interest are inevitable and unavoidable. Whether or not this is true depends upon how one defines "self-interest." If one defines self-interest as doing whatever you feel like for any reason whatsoever, then conflicts of interest certainly are inevitable. If I feel like stealing your car, and you do not want me to take your car, then there exists a conflict between your interest and my interest. If, however, one defines "self-interest" in rational and objective terms, then no such conflicts exist among sensible, honest people who respect others' psychological boundaries and property rights. A rational person wants to pursue his goals and obtain happiness, but he also expects (indeed, wants) to pay for it and does not want to impose force or fraud on anyone else. So, if a rational person covets your car, he'll figure out a way to purchase his own. Likewise, if you can find a work environment where people are expected to respect each other and are appropriately punished for failing to do so, then conflicts of interest need not be inevitable.

Resources are limited; life is a "zero-sum" game. Quite the opposite is true. Given the nature of reality, good side-effects often result from otherwise negative events. Losing a job can be a terrible experience; but it can also afford you the opportunity to try something different. Living in the city has the advantage of convenience and access to more cultural resources; even so, being transferred to the country allows the advantage of less crime and often friendlier people. One type of job offers one set of opportunities; another job offers another set. Tradeoffs are everywhere. Even in tragic circumstances, such as death of a loved one, individuals have reported (after the grief subsides) discovering opportunities to pursue new types of relationships and activities they previously had not attempted.

Life is not a zero-sum game where one person's gain is always another person's loss. If your neighbor makes a million dollars honestly, he has not stolen something from you; he has simply made a million dollars because he worked hard at selling something that is highly valued by others. Similarly, if your neighbor or coworker is happy, you should not resent and envy him for taking more than his "fair" share of the "happiness pie;" instead, try to figure out what principles he followed and apply those principles to your own life.

Realistic, rational assumptions contradict the ideas of the adversarial mindset.

It is realistic to assume people are trustworthy until or unless objective reasons exist to think otherwise. Evil does exist, and irrationality does exist. But most people are not evil and irrational, at least not in a society where freedom and rationality are respected. If you assume everyone is irrational, you place yourself in a lose-lose situation: when you meet people who are in fact irrational, you have no way of distinguishing them from those who are healthy; and when you meet people who are decent and healthy, you are unable to recognize them and benefit from knowing them.

It is realistic and most certainly in your self-interest to be honest—if you define honesty as adherence to the facts of reality, and self-interest as being in touch with reality. In order to understand honesty as a moral virtue, you must simultaneously understand the psychological benefits of staying in touch with reality and being honest with yourself at all times. You should be honest because you owe it to yourself to cope with and remain aware of the facts of existence. Honesty towards others is made possible by honesty towards yourself.

Perhaps the single greatest cause of psychological dysfunction is dishonesty with oneself. People deny, evade, and rationalize all kinds of problems until those problems become too obvious to ignore. Psychological denial, one form of self-deceit, allows individuals to excuse their loved one's alcohol abuse, sexual abuse, or other forms of self-destructive behavior. Individuals who learn, at an early age, to introspect and be honest with themselves are much less likely to develop psychological and behavioral problems as adults. Awareness of your feelings and motives makes it harder for you to hurt yourself or hurt others.

Most people think of honesty as a selfless commandment, something good in theory but not workable in practice; something which requires self-sacrifice and selfless "nobility." Nothing could be further from the truth. Honesty is selfish, a necessary and practical principle for both survival and happiness. Superficially, honesty sometimes seems impractical in a world where the majority presume it to be a moralistic commandment rather than a practical principle of life; but aren't the majority also now in therapy, on Prozac, or experiencing "mid-life" crises and adversarial divorces? They have gained nothing from their cynical beliefs about honesty.

It is realistic to assume that there are no inherent conflicts of interest among rational people. Disagreements, perhaps; but not conflicts of interest. In a rational society, as opposed to the semi-rational one in which we now live, everyone would leave everyone else alone. The childless atheist would not have to pay for the schooling of the Christian fundamentalist's kids; nor would the Christian fundamentalist have to pay for the childless atheist's health care. Instead of everyone being responsible for everyone else, everyone would be responsible for himself. Nobody would be allowed to impose force or fraud on anyone else, either through common criminal behavior or the political process of forced redistribution; everyone would have a right not only to the privacy of his bedroom, but also to the sanctity of his wallet. Responsibility for others would be a voluntary choice. Responsibility for oneself would merely be accepted as a fact of reality.

A conflict of interest certainly exists between a person who minds his own business and an irrational person who wants to impose force on him. This is why a limited government is necessary to protect us from those who would impose physical force upon us. Unfortunately, because we live in the era of activist government, many of us have no choice but to join political pressure groups to keep our interests from being sacrificed to those who want something we have (usually our money). But this is the fault of our political system and the dysfunctional ideas which made that system possible; it does not mean that the world, by its very nature, *has* to be an adversarial place.

It is realistic, as well, to approach life from an opportunity viewpoint as opposed to a zero-sum viewpoint. Those who look at the world from a zero-sum viewpoint are chronically angry, resentful, envious, and even hateful. They do not accept responsibility for their lives; they expect, and often demand, that others assume total or partial responsibility for them. They are often dishonest, evasive or manipulative, but have no difficulty rationalizing such behaviors since they see themselves as victims of reality while conveniently filtering out all evidence suggesting the contrary. They see everyone else's gain as their own personal loss. They do not hold themselves at all responsible for their own failures, but they are quick and ready to pronounce a happy, successful person guilty as charged for taking more than his "fair share" of happiness. Psychologists typically encounter extreme examples of such individuals, and refer to them as "borderline personalities." Whatever one chooses to label them, they are not representative of an orientation toward reality.

The opportunity-oriented person is the opposite of the adversarial borderline personality. The opportunity personality is reality-oriented, self-responsible, and, as a consequence, capable of achieving some degree of happiness, both fiscally and emotionally. He understands that optimism, grounded in reality, represents the best means to success in life. He does not waste time on cynical, adversarial, zero-sum victimology; he grasps that the *real* victims are the naïve souls who accept such ideas.

Even if you agree with the realistic outlook and strongly favor it over the adversarial view, keep in mind that from time to time you might experience emotions which conflict with your conscious beliefs. If this is the case, do not condemn yourself for experiencing the contradictory emotions. Simply accept the fact you felt them, consciously correct and challenge them, and resolve not to act on them in future situations. With honest and consistent effort, you will gradually improve over time. A good therapist can help you in this task if you find it difficult. Repeated "reprogramming" measures such as these can help you integrate and internalize the rational approach to life that, on the intellectual and conscious level, you have already accepted as your own.

WHAT, EXACTLY, IS WRONG WITH "EXTREMISM?"

At first, this might sound like a shocking statement. But think about it. What does "extremism" really mean?

Most of us associate the idea "extremism" with excess, irrationality and evil. Adolph Hitler was evil not because he was a dictator who massacred millions of innocent people and turned others into slaves of the state, according to this popular definition, but rather because he was an "extremist." Think of the enormous logical error here. This idea implies that Hitler was evil not because of what he did, but because he did too much of it!

The proper way to condemn a person such as Hitler is to identify his evil ideas, along with his evil actions, and then explain why those actions are evil. Such an approach presumes that one has a definition of "good" and "evil," is prepared to apply it to a particular situation and stand by it. For example: "Hitler subscribed to the evil idea that the individual owes his life to the state and to whatever dictator happens to seize power. He used this idea to justify the brutal extermination of millions of innocent people, and also to justify the establishment of a totalitarian dictatorship."

Notice how this analysis does not ignore the responsibility of defining what is "right" and "wrong," "good" or "evil." One does not say, "What Hitler did was right for Hitler, but not necessarily for you or me."

Now think of how people misuse the concept "extremist" in a more day-to-day context. "There's nothing wrong with developing an interest in science," a father might tell his son. "Just don't take it to extremes, that's all." Now what should the boy conclude from this statement? That the study of science is good, but that it's wrong to value something—even a good thing—too much? How does this make any sense? If something is good, how can you do too much of it? Granted, one needs to take breaks, stop to eat and sleep, and pursue other values in life (such as friendship, romance, etc.), but is this what the father is really implying here? Or is he perhaps sending his son the message that he should not do too much of a good thing, precisely because it is good? That to value something "too much," even something objectively good, is somehow wrong?

In today's "feel-good-at-any-price" culture, where the predominant view is that there is no such thing as "good" or "bad," right or wrong and—even worse—that there is no objective, human method (such as reason, or even common sense) for distinguishing good from bad, the issue becomes especially confusing for kids. Without an objective definition of "right" or "wrong," a child might vaguely feel that Hitler is evil without knowing why. In the absence of a good reason, he is left with the fuzzy conclusion that Hitler was evil because he was extreme. But doesn't this mean that anyone who pursues a value with consistency, even a rational and good value, is also evil (or at least dysfunctional)? If extremism is always a vice, no matter what the situation, then how many *good* things are wiped out along with the bad? Because so many well-meaning parents and teachers spread such mistaken ideas, is it any wonder so many kids feel compelled to turn to drugs, alcohol abuse or some other form of mediocrity?

To criticize "extremism" really amounts to criticizing consistency and integrity in human beings. Anyone who holds a strong position, consistently and with integrity, is cynically dismissed as "extremist" regardless of what position he happens to uphold. Under such a world view, hard-working, creative, innovative geniuses, such as Albert Einstein, Thomas Edison, or contemporary computer wizard Bill Gates, are inadvertently "lumped" into the same category as an Adolph Hitler, an Ayatollah Khomeini, or a Stalin. After all, both Hitler and Einstein share one trait in common: an extreme, unyielding commitment to their goals.

In any life dilemma (global or individual), the choice should not be between "extremism" and mushy, wishy-washy compromise of a "good" and "evil" that nobody is willing to identify explicitly. Instead, the choice should be between consistent adherence to rational, life-serving values (such as science, genuine art, technology, skill) or adherence to self-destructive, anti-life values (such as violence, theft, and fraud). "Extremism" in the pursuit of a good and happy life is a virtue, not a vice.

WHY RAISING KIDS IS SELFISH AND OTHER SHOCKING TRUTHS

Q: In your argument for promoting rational selfishness against self-sacrifice, your comments like "choosing to have children or not to have children is selfish" indicate to me that you have missed a major ingredient in your thoughts.

Your concept of self-sacrifice doesn't seem accurate with what I've experienced. Your comments indicate that anything "self-sacrificing" which people do is really done with their own interests at heart.

I find it hard to agree. I know many people who sacrifice money, time and energy in the name of serving their fellow man, with no aim for reward or pleasure from it. It seems that your view would step in at this point, and state that they would do it because they know they will feel good about it in the end, and because of that, they are selfish. Am I reading you right here?

A: Let me make sure you understand exactly what I mean by "selfish." What I mean by the term is just this: acting in your own objective, rational interest. I maintain that it is a *good* thing for people to act in their self-interest; it's good to be selfish, in this rational sense, when making life decisions.

If a person is financially and emotionally prepared to have children, for example, and he very much wants to do so—then he's acting in his self-interest by having a child. This is a good, proper thing to do. It is wrong and unhealthy to have children if you don't want to, if you're not prepared to do so, or if doing so would undermine other goals that you judge as more important to your life and well-being.

I'm sure you'd agree that many people have children for the wrong reasons, or before they are ready. I believe the world would be a much more benevolent place if people approached having children (or other responsibilities) with a thoughtful, self-interested standard instead of the usual platitudes such as, "It's just what one does" or, "It's your duty whether you like it or not." Duty breeds resentment; and resentment causes parents to be less than nurturing, or even abusive, towards their children.

There should be no unchosen obligations, other than those imposed upon us by reality. It should be an individual's conscious, deliberate choice and absolute moral right to judge what is or is not in his own self-interest—so long as he does not impose physical force or fraud on somebody else.

No, I don't believe that people who sacrifice themselves are necessarily doing so with their own interests at heart. Some, no doubt, really do mean to sacrifice. They think it's proper to sacrifice and they do so proudly, no matter how much pain and misery it causes them and their loved ones. They live the lives of martyrs, thinking martyrdom to be the ideal instead of the miserable neurosis it actually represents. My psychotherapy practice includes many people caught in the martyrdom trap.

Still others, no doubt, merely pretend to sacrifice because they've been taught it's the "right thing to do"—but then behind closed doors they do whatever they feel like, regardless of the consequences to themselves or to those about whom they allegedly care. Such people have, correctly, rejected the idea of self-sacrifice. But they don't possess the honesty or the courage to identify a new moral code. Instead they collapse into a nihilistic, impulsive life of acting on their whims. This is the modern understanding of "selfishness," but there's nothing self-interested about it.

Sooner or later, the sacrificer feels compelled to reward himself with pleasure. What kind of pleasure? Usually mindless, impulsive, self-destructive pleasure of one sort or another. Drug and alcohol abuse, compulsive shopping, compulsive sex, or gambling addictions represent only a few examples.

As the consequences of the self-destruction build, a tension to return to "the good old days" of self-sacrifice grows. Like the pendulum in a grandfather clock, prevailing moral codes (within either an individual or a society) swing back and forth. Yet our presumed choice—between nihilistic impulse-worship *or* self-sacrifice—represents a completely false alternative.

You mentioned that you know people who "sacrifice money, time and energy in the name of serving their fellow man." If they are truly acting against their own interests, I would not canonize them. On the contrary: I would condemn them for wrecking their lives and any chance at earthly happiness. If they marry someone they don't love purely out of pity; or if they choose a career they know they don't want merely to please a parent; or if they deliberately suppress their intelligence so as to appease the envy or low self-esteem of others—all of these selfless, sacrificial acts are dead wrong.

Selflessness is not a virtue. It's a vice. Otherwise suicide—the ultimate act of self-sacrifice—would be the highest virtue of all.

Some people *claim* to be sacrificing when, in reality, they are not. A young woman might give birth to a child, for instance, and then resent the child for all the unanticipated responsibilities it causes. Another woman might choose a difficult career, and then resent the business world for all the burdens it imposes upon her.

If she had the child, or chose the career, out of selfless duty—not because she wanted to but because she felt she had to—then she did indeed make a sacrifice. All she can do is acknowledge that she acted on the wrong moral premise, and switch as best she can to a self-interested course of action in the future.

If, on the other hand, she consciously and voluntarily chose to have the child (or the difficult career) because she really *wanted* the pleasures or rewards associated with the added responsibilities—then she needs to work on reminding herself that her responsibility was a chosen, self-interested one. "I made my bed," she can tell herself. "So why don't I try to enjoy it?"

In the realm of ethics, human beings have really botched things up. We have it all backwards. There should be no unchosen obligations. If you allow unchosen obligations into your life, you had better make some changes—and fast! Otherwise you will end up, as so many people do, feeling like you are a victim of others—when, in reality, you victimized *yourself* because of the senseless code of sacrifice you allowed yourself to accept.

As for people selflessly "serving their fellow man"—you seem to take it as a self-evident truth that this is a good way to be. I totally disagree, even from my own selfish perspective.

Personally, I would much rather go to a doctor or a surgeon who passionately loves his work, as opposed to one who chose it solely as a sacrifice to please his mother, "society," or the government. Wouldn't you?

If I were a child, I would much rather be raised by parents who wanted and freely chose the responsibility of parenting—a responsibility they treat as a rewarding challenge rather than a selfless duty to be despised and resented.

Likewise, I sure hope that the architect and the elevator inspector upon whose talents I depend to safely lift me to the thirty-second floor were motivated by rational self-interest—and not hateful, resentful self-sacrifice. The same goes for the airline pilot who flies me across the continent, the captain of the cruise ship who takes me through shark-infested waters, and the car mechanic who fixes the brakes on my Honda. Don't you agree?

I know we are all trained to think that selflessness represents the ideal, while self-interest is intrinsically evil. Yet if you carefully study the facts of reality, including the particulars of your everyday life, then you will find that precisely the opposite is true. Self-interest is not only best for the individual; it is best for society as well.

The "morality" of self-sacrifice is the greatest and most vicious lie ever propagated. The only end it serves is the motive of those who want to control and dominate you. After all, *somebody* has to collect the sacrifices. It is an ethical code for slaves and masters—encouraged by those who are more than happy to be your masters.

Ten minutes of clear, honest thinking wipes out centuries of falsehoods. I reject the great lie that sacrifice is "virtue"—and, if you value the quality of your life, so should you.   ⏏

Chapter 23

Excellence— the Road Less Traveled

EXCELLENCE—THE ROAD LESS TRAVELED

"It's not *what* you know, it's *who* you know." So claim the apostles of mediocrity.

This statement summarizes the dominant idea underlying many of today's widely acknowledged social and psychological problems.

To place an emphasis on who you know instead of what you know is irrational for two major reasons.

First, it sets up an unjustified false alternative. You do not have to choose between knowledge and people. Why live either in an ivory tower, detached from the real world of human relationships, *or* compromise all intellectual integrity and dispense with independent thought altogether? Intelligent, independent individuals can choose to interact with other intelligent individuals. You need not choose between ideas divorced from reality, on the one hand, and reality divorced from ideas, on the other.

Secondly, and even more fundamentally, this statement implies a dreadfully anti-human, anti-life idea: that there is no such thing as knowledge, so you might as well just get through life by being popular.

Just imagine if Albert Einstein had thought this way. Or Galileo. Or Aristotle. Or Jonas Salk. Or Henry Ford. Or Bill Gates. Or Thomas Jefferson. Imagine if any creative genius or innovator in human history had stopped his work and decided, "It's not *what* you know, it's *who* you know. Forget about knowledge; it's not possible anyway. Besides, being an innovator makes you unpopular. I had better check my opinion polls and see where I stand today. I cannot tolerate being disliked."

Perhaps more frightening: what if some potential discoverer of a cure for cancer or AIDS is at this very moment deciding to give up on excellence or the pursuit of knowledge, in exchange for social satisfaction and acceptance?

Whether a far-reaching scientific discovery or ordinary achievement in your own life, you will experience neither happiness nor self-esteem if popularity and social status represent your primary motivations.

If you are presently unhappy with the state of your life, then ask yourself these questions:

Do I try to be popular, or do I try to be excellent?

Do I set goals based upon what is socially appropriate, or on what I, personally, judge to be desirable and achievable?

Am I trying to please others, or am I trying to please myself?

In short: Am I operating on a philosophy of mediocrity or a philosophy of excellence?

A philosophy of excellence does not mean sacrifice of others to yourself. It obviously does not mean robbing, lying, cheating, or acting in what *feels* like your interest in the short-term without reference to any sort of externalized, abstract principles.

A philosophy of excellence does not imply sacrifice of yourself to others. This is *your* life. It is up to you—not your family, not the government, not "society"—to decide what you want to do with it. Yes, you do have an obligation to leave others alone to pursue their own goals and values free of violence and coercion. But your duty to others stops there. Nobody has a right to tell you what career to choose, how many children to have, whether or not to have children, what shows you may watch on television, what books you may read, whom you should marry or have sex with, what you should do with your money or how much of it you may keep for yourself. The facts of reality—of existence—represent your only absolute; not the will of others.

Freedom demands profound respect for yourself, but it also requires responsibility. Not the sort of responsibility that you normally hear about, such as blind obedience to Church, country, government, society, or the poor. Rather, it requires a responsibility to yourself—to live rationally and by a set of moral principles which are possible to practice: to take what you want out of life, *provided you are willing to pay for it.* You have a right to happiness—provided you are willing to take responsibility for pursuing and achieving it. You have a right to life—provided you are willing to find a way to make a living for yourself without forcing others to make that living for you. You have a right to total control over everything you do and say on your own private property—provided you grant that same right to others, and provided you do not impose force or fraud on anyone.

People suffering from various forms of depression, anxiety and other psychological maladies usually overlook the "provided" part of the equation. Consciously or subconsciously they often believe that, "I have a right to happiness—so where is it?" When happiness does not simply appear to them, they displace their anger onto other sources. They may displace their anger on "God" for not bestowing happiness. Or they may displace their anger on "society," or the government, for not sufficiently legislating or mandating universal happiness into existence. Or they may displace their anger onto family members or children, for allegedly getting in the way or not sacrificing sufficiently for them.

Whatever or whomever the source, such displaced anger eventually festers and becomes psychological disorder. Very often, people with emotional problems believe that they can go to a psychological expert for purely passive "treatment" the same way a medically ill person goes for treatment and gets cured. In reality, quite the opposite is true. Sometimes, in fact, psychotherapy can become part of the problem rather than part of the solution because many therapists simply tell the patient, over and over, "Yes, you *do* have a right to happiness, and you should be angry. Get in touch with your anger, and you'll be better."

Well, the patient certainly "gets in touch" with the anger; but to "get in touch" is not necessarily to get better.

No real cure exists for such mental maladies, except the one that nobody ever wants to hear (but usually, upon honest reflection, everyone knows is true): Take responsibility for your life. Demand freedom, and then live up to that freedom.

Set goals. Choose them for yourself, and only for yourself. Yes, this means being self-ish. *Be selfish.* Being selfish, in the rational sense, also means being totally responsible for yourself. Responsibility is scary. There are many ways to make responsibility less scary. But there is no way to escape it. All attempts at escape lead to the volumes of psychological diseases, syndromes, and addictions so well documented today.

Adopt a philosophy of excellence. Discover knowledge and experience in whatever field is of interest to you: science, the arts, business, or raising children. Whatever you choose, be obsessive—yes, obsessive—in your pursuit of excellence. This is the only genuine path to self-esteem.

Above all, do not give a moment's thought to what anyone else thinks. Everyone else can be wrong, and sometimes they are. And if *you* turn out to be wrong, so long as you used your honest and most conscientious judgment, then at least it was your own mistake. Your only obligation to others is to leave them alone, to not impose violence or deceit upon them. You were not born to serve others. People who live exclusively to serve others will never achieve the kind of happiness most of us claim to want.

Your obligation to *yourself*—which is far more challenging than taking care of others—is to use your senses, trust your logical reasoning abilities, acquire knowledge in all fields relevant to your life, and to never put random emotions before your reasoned judgment. Think before you act, but do not be afraid to act once you have spent enough time thinking.

Do not worry too much about loneliness. Indeed, to *consistently* follow the ethics and psychology of self-interest, rationality and responsibility represents the road less traveled. But people who travel this road manage to eventually find genuine happiness—and each other—if they persevere and stay true to their approach.

JUSTICE, NOT FORGIVENESS

Adam Smith once wrote, "Mercy to the guilty is cruelty to the innocent."

This observation has a wide variety of applications.

Consider a concrete issue from everyday life. A mother sees her son hit his sister for no clear reason. When she confronts him, he defensively replies, "It's not my fault! She wouldn't share her toys with me!"

The mother does not accept this excuse. She points out that her son might have pursued several other options, including asking for her help. She also points out that nobody is obliged to share their toys unless they choose to do so. Nevertheless, her son shows no remorse until she informs him that he cannot watch his favorite television show that night because of the incident.

"You can't do that!" her son screams. "It's not fair!"

Most parents, if they experience any doubt at all in this situation, will worry about the *guilty* party. "Should I punish him or not?" will be the central question. "If I don't punish him, I might not teach him the proper lesson. But if I do punish him, then I might just alienate him and harm his self-esteem." Notice how both sides of this dilemma focus on the well-being of the guilty party.

What about the well-being of the innocent party—the child who was hit, without any legitimate provocation? What about *her* self-esteem, and what about the impact of the decision to punish (or not punish) the aggressor on her life?

To refuse to punish the boy in this case amounts to an injustice against his sister. It would influence his sister's precarious, developing view of the world as either a rational place where justice is possible, or an irrational place where nothing matters so you might as well get by with whatever you can.

The same principle applies on a wider social scale. Consider the growing prevalence of crime in recent decades. Most debates on the subject focus on the well-being and mental health of the violent criminal. Some claim that rehabilitation is best for the criminal. Others cite evidence that rehabilitation doesn't work, nevertheless conceding that it would be the preferred option if only it were feasible.

What about the victim? What about the loved ones of a murder victim? Even if a pill were discovered tomorrow to "cure" the murderer of his criminal intent, how fair would it be to the victim and his survivors to focus on rehabilitation instead of justice? Why talk of "rights" for the murderer once he has violated the most fundamental right of another—the right to life? To talk of "rights" for a convicted murderer represents cruelty to the victim. The murderer forfeited his rights when he chose to wipe out the life of someone else.

Most of us are taught to unthinkingly accept the idea that "forgiveness is virtue." Not surprisingly, we are taught to accept this edict on blind faith, rather than reason. The notion of forgiveness as always virtuous is fundamentally at odds with reason, and could never survive two minutes of rational analysis. How can you possibly "forgive" someone who assaults, robs or tries to murder you? Who benefits from a policy of forgiveness—you, or the aggressor? And why on earth is this considered moral?

Events of the past few decades have done great damage to the politically correct hypothesis that crime is caused by poverty or low self-esteem. As unprecedented measures have been taken to pour billions of dollars into programs to help "cure" criminals, or to "address" the alleged root causes of crime (such as poverty), violent crime continues unabated. The promised Great Society is turning into a nightmare. Clearly, other factors besides family and society (such as individual free will) must be contributing to the proliferation of crime.

Even if it could be proven, beyond any doubt, that poverty or low self-esteem causes crime, it would not matter. Justice is still justice, whether on the playground or in the Supreme Court. If "morality" refers to a set of practical, rational principles to help an individual—and a civilization——survive and achieve happiness, then it certainly cannot be moral to allow a guilty person to go free. If you want to live and be happy, you cannot and should not forgive those who try to destroy you. Nor will the larger society survive if criminals are allowed to go free.

Blind, unthinking forgiveness can only benefit the guilty at the expense of the innocent. In fact, if the guilty were smart enough to develop a philosophy to promote their own interests, they could not have devised a more suitable "ideal" than the notion of forgiveness as a virtue. Unearned forgiveness disarms the innocent and forces them to pay homage to the evil, the irrational, the guilty.

Instead of platitudes about forgiveness, parents should teach kids the principle of justice. How can justice be applied to everyday life? First, decide if the guilty party deserves a second chance. If he does, then make sure he provides objective evidence that he is remorseful. "Objective evidence" refers to consistent behaviors, over a lengthy period of time, which *prove* regret by the guilty person. Words without actions do not constitute proof; nor do inconsistent, half-hearted behaviors designed merely to "look good." In the case of minor theft, objective proof of remorse refers to returning the stolen object (or equivalent) with interest (financial or otherwise) as defined by the victim or a court of law. In the case of marital infidelity, if the victim decides a second chance is possible, then the guilty party must be willing to accept the burden of winning back the trust of his spouse over a reasonable period of time. A similar approach can be used with dishonesty, provided—once again—the victim of dishonesty has some very good reason to believe that a second chance is possible.

Providing a rational second chance is not the same as granting unearned forgiveness. Forgiveness in the sense of "turning the other cheek" implies pretending that the transgression never happened. This is not the same as earning back the trust of a person you may have victimized. Even when trust is earned back, neither party pretends the transgression never happened. They may see little need to discuss it, since what's done is done. Yet this does not mean they cannot make reference to the incident, since it remains a fact.

Beware of false alternatives. Advocates of the forgiveness "ideal" (most therapists and clergy) will try to tell you that you must either be blindly forgiving, on the one hand, or filled with unresolved anger and unhealthy rage, on the other. In the real world, no such choice is necessary. You can demand justice, in the objective sense, without becoming consumed by anger. If the person is objectively guilty and you cannot forgive him, then you prosecute him (either legally, if appropriate, or morally, by terminating your relationship with him). If a person has earned forgiveness, because the offense is moderate enough and objective proof of remorse exists, then you continue in your relationship, neither obsessing on the incident nor ignoring the fact that it happened.

Beware of the idea that unearned forgiveness is a virtue, or that you should "turn the other cheek" and invite the criminal to victimize you yet again. Such a viewpoint represents a ticking time-bomb in your life, a time-bomb that will sooner or later explode in the form of mistaken decisions. Judging others fairly and accurately constitutes virtue. Sacrificing your own well-being spells disaster.   ⊕

Chapter 24

The Psychology of
Honesty

THE PSYCHOLOGY OF HONESTY

There are two types of liars.

The first type does not feel comfortable with lying. He feels guilty for betraying other people with his lie. He also feels awkward because lying complicates his life and his mind. He has to remember who knows about the falsehood and who does not. He must keep two separate lists in his mind at all times: one for the actual facts, the other for the "facts" he has created.

The second type of liar is much more sophisticated—and dangerous. He believes his own lies. He convinces himself that the "alternate reality" he creates with his lies actually exists. He is the more persuasive, more "effective" type of liar. He can fool loved ones, business associates, juries—even millions.

The persuasive liar rationalizes his deceit by way of the subjectivist viewpoint. The subjectivist viewpoint holds that there are different realities for different people—that my reality and your reality may not be the same. It starts with the perfectly reasonable assertion that people have different perspectives and points-of-view. It then smuggles in the false and vicious conclusion that there is, therefore, no one *objective* reality.

What Does Objective Reality Have to Do With Dishonesty?

Take a simple example. You and I are standing in different parts of the room, looking at a lamp. To you, the lamp looks one way and to me it looks slightly different because we view the lamp from different angles. I can see the ornaments on the front of the lamp. You can't see the ornaments, but you can see the plug coming out of its side. I can only see the front of the lampshade, which looks clean and nice. You can primarily see the side of the lampshade, which has a spot on it.

Because of our different perspectives, I am more inclined to view the lamp as nice and pretty while you are more inclined to view the lamp as flawed. Do these different perspectives prove, therefore, that the lamp possesses no objective reality? Can we say: "In your reality the lamp is messed up, in my reality the lamp is pretty. Therefore, there is no one true reality"? No, of course not. The lamp *is what it is*, regardless of what you or I see or do not see. This is what common sense and reason tell us.

But the consistent subjectivist would have to say that yes, indeed, in your reality the lamp is one thing and in my reality the lamp is another. Normally, the subjectivist applies his thinking to moral dilemmas rather than to lamps; but this makes his reasoning no less illogical.

Once you dispense with the idea of objective reality, all hopes of morality (including honesty) disappear. Anything can be rationalized or justified or wished away, even by otherwise seemingly "reasonable" people.

The very notion of morality presupposes that there exists an objective reality upon which we base our moral choices. If your house and your car represent objective pieces of property, for example, then it is possible to claim them as your property rights. If they don't constitute objective items, then who's to say what belongs to whom? By what right do you demand that the police protect you from theft, murder, unlawful search, or seizure—if everything is relative?

If all reality is subjective, then all bets are off. Life becomes one big free-for-all with morality and ethics (including property rights and other ethical tenets most of us take for granted) thrown out the window. As a delinquent teenager once told me, "Who is anyone to tell me what's right and wrong? There is no true or untrue." So long as he holds the premise that reality is not objective, teaching him about the immorality of stealing or initiating violence remains pointless.

Do people who subscribe to the subjective viewpoint practice their philosophy consistently? Of course not. To do so would mean literal suicide. Only a psychopath would step in front of an oncoming truck, indifferent to its path because "there is no objective reality." Only a common criminal would assume that whatever he desires belongs to him.

The trick to making a subjectivist viewpoint "work" is to apply it only when it's convenient—propping it up with rationalizations that make the eyes of thinking people glaze over. For real-life examples, think of a con artist you know or have read about. Or turn on the television and watch some of our politicians or professional intellectuals in action.

Obscuring the existence of objective reality is much more common—yet difficult to detect—than either psychopathy or simple criminality. Careful, critical thinking is necessary to combat it.

How Can You Tell If Someone Is Lying?

Most research on the detection of lying focuses on external behaviors such as eye-blinking, stuttering, and evasive body language. While there may be some merit to these studies, in many cases other explanations for such behaviors are possible. On television, for instance, a person may blink excessively because of the bright lights. Sometimes people stutter because they're confused, but not because they're lying.

Strictly behavioral theories do not go deep enough. They do not address the mind and the personality *behind* the dishonest or evasive behaviors. They look at what the body does, but they totally disregard what the mind thinks and feels.

To predict whether a person might lie, you need to look at his underlying convictions as well as his behaviors. Examine critically what he says, thinks, and feels in order to find out his underlying beliefs. The underlying beliefs of a typical liar include such rationalizations as the following:

- It's OK to lie when it spares somebody else's feelings.
- It's OK to lie if I have a higher, more noble purpose in mind.
- It's OK to lie if the subject is nobody else's business.
- It's OK to lie if it works, if I fool everybody involved.

This is not an exhaustive list of rationalizations, of course. But they are the ones I most frequently encounter as a psychotherapist. If psychotherapists are experts on anything, it's hearing people's rationalizations—particularly about such behaviors as lying. Most of the rationalizations I hear from people boil down to one of the four premises above.

It's not enough to ask people, intellectually, if they subscribe to these rationalizations or not. They might say "no," they sincerely don't agree with these statements. Yet they could still feel something different on the emotional level, and practice something different on the behavioral level. If someone tells you that, no, she does not believe lying is right, then you can relax somewhat; but you still need to recognize that human beings have free will and in any given moment of their lives are free to reject something they consider a moral principle.

If someone tells you that "yes," intellectually he *does* agree with any of the above statements, then consider yourself forewarned. Such a person might lie to you at any time.

If you don't want a husband who cheats, or if you don't want a business partner who will steal from you, then spend some time getting to know how he thinks and what he believes, on the deepest level. To some, this may sound too judgmental. But the inescapable fact remains: You can't enjoy the expected security of a personal or business relationship with someone who believes that lying is OK.

Rationalization # 1:
"It's OK to lie when it spares somebody else's feelings."

This may be the most common rationalization for lying. Instead of holding others responsible for their emotional reactions—and respecting their right to know the truth, the same right we insist upon for ourselves—too many of us rationalize that we know what's best for others and therefore "shield" them from the truth. In effect, we end up treating grown, autonomous adults as if they were little children.

In order to resist this most common of rationalizations for lying, you must let go of the idea that you are personally responsible for other people's emotions. You must resist the idea that you are everyone's emotional keeper. Of course you should not go out of your way to be nasty, rude, or hurt others' feelings. At the same time, you should not spare valued friends and associates from the truth, even if it sometimes hurts.

Try to think of the nicest and most compassionate way to express the truth. Yet always remember that reality must come first—before *anyone's* feelings, yours or another's.

Does this mean you must express your opinion even when it's not solicited? Should you walk up to strangers on the street and tell them what you think of their taste in clothes or hairstyles, all in the name of honesty? Of course not. The principle of honesty between two parties presupposes a voluntary, mutual relationship between the two parties.

What about loved ones or close business associates? Should you give them your opinion even if it's not asked for? Generally it's not a good idea to give an opinion unless someone seeks it out. If you're not sure whether they're seeking it out, you can request their permission ahead of time. You can ask, for example, "Would you like to know what I honestly think?" Or: "Can I make a suggestion?" Usually people will reply "Yes, of course," but it's still considerate to prepare them. It's also in your own interest to prepare them, since they are more likely to listen to you and less likely to go on the defensive when you show them this courtesy.

If you already believe it's wrong to lie—even to spare other's feelings—then make sure people with whom you associate know of this fact early in the relationship. Make sure they know that you never want to have your feelings spared if this means sacrificing the truth. Show them you believe it's possible to communicate in a mature, sensitive way but still not to violate this very important principle. If this scares them off, so be it. You will know this was not a person with whom you ever needed to associate.

Rationalization # 2:
"It's OK to lie if I have a higher, more noble purpose in mind."

If you hold this belief, then ask yourself: What higher or more noble purpose is there than the truth? Is there anything more important than adherence to reality?

Again, the answer to this question presupposes a particular philosophical perspective. If you believe that truthfulness is important, your belief rests on the premises that: (a) there is an objective reality by which truth or falsehood can be assessed, and (b) that becoming competent and happy in the realm of objective reality is the central moral purpose of life.

To some people, adhering to the truth is indeed the most important aspect of morality. They practice this principle in their daily lives. Consequently, they are easier to trust. In any dilemma between the truth and something else, you have good reason to expect they will choose the truth.

Consistently truthful individuals are—contrary to popular opinion—among the most productive and successful, because consistent adherence to reality allows for more competent, effective work. If you doubt this assertion, then ask yourself which television set or computer products you prefer to purchase: ones which break down easily and don't honor their warranties; or ones with guarantees to stand by their products and that deliver on what they promise? What kind of surgeon do you want operating on you: one who lied his way through medical school, or one who makes adherence to objective reality his highest goal?

To many people, however, there are more important things than the truth. Charity, for instance, supersedes truth in the eyes of some. If somebody holds charity as the ideal, then he may feel justified in lying or even stealing in the name of that ideal. To such people, the end justifies the means.

People who lie and cheat in the name of "feeling your pain" or acting "compassionately" are merely cashing in on the very principle you hold so dear. Logically, they have every right to say to you, "So you hold compassion and service to others as the most important ideals? OK. Then that means I can lie and steal, if necessary, to achieve those ideals. The end justifies the means."

This is known as the Robin Hood approach to morality. The Robin Hood approach to ethics applies both materially and spiritually: materially, when self-appointed Robin Hoods take your money or property; and spiritually, when they steal a part of your mind or "soul" by lying to you.

So long as you keep on insisting that charity, sacrifice, and kindness to others represent the most important moral principles of life, then you have no business complaining when people lie to you. They're just practicing what you preach. They're simply giving you what you demanded.

Rationalization # 3:
"It's OK to lie if the subject is nobody else's business."

This rationalization implies that if someone is violating your privacy, you have no other choice but to lie to them. If, in fact, you have no other choice but to lie, then so be it. Such cases do exist, and your privacy should come first.

But in most cases you have other choices. You can simply say, "This is none of your business," or "I'm sorry, I don't want to discuss that." Or, depending upon the circumstances, you can call the police or an attorney. In the United States, you can (under certain conditions) even plead the Fifth Amendment and refuse to speak at all.

If you live under a repressive government, or under a negligent government that fails to consistently protect you from thugs or thieves, then you certainly have a right to lie if no other choice exists for saving yourself. The same applies if you are dealing with a terrorist, a kidnapper, or a known cheater whom you are trying to trap.

But in relationships where both you and the other party voluntarily enter in good faith, lying is not justified. Otherwise, a husband could lie to his wife that he's not having an affair when he *is* having an affair, rationalizing that "it's none of her business." Or a businessman could blatantly lie to his customer about the product he's selling him on the rationalization that "it's none of his business." The fact is that you have no business entering into any kind of association with anybody unless you intend to be truthful.

Rationalization # 4:
"It's OK to lie if it works, if I fool everybody involved."

This is the cynical, Machiavellian approach to truth. It is anti-reality and anti-truth on "principle." Perhaps it's the worst of all the rationalizations. It is not only a vicious idea; it's also foolish. Lying, over the long-run, does not work—*at least, not if others allow it or tolerate it.* Sooner or later the truth usually comes out and then the liar is exposed as a fraud.

Of course, lying is impractical only to the extent that a community or society is inhabited with alert, critical thinkers who are not afraid to make moral judgments. Today we live in a society where adherence to the truth and morality is, in general, on the decline. This is dangerous, because prospective liars see this situation and stand ready to take advantage. They recognize that people don't seem interested in making moral judgments any longer.

Ultimately, dishonesty is impractical even in a corrupt society where the majority of people tolerate it. If society is full of liars, it can't function. Nobody knows where anyone stands. Contracts are valid one moment and invalid the next. Nobody can be trusted to mean what they say; and nobody can be held responsible, legally or morally, for committing fraud or deceit. Trade and division of labor—two necessary components of a civilized, advanced society—become impossible. Government also becomes corrupt and unreliable. The advanced, productive, technological world we still enjoy today will flounder and eventually collapse if most of us give up on honesty.

Many say morality is on the decline because people do not believe in God or go to church enough. Actually, this is not the real cause of the problem. While many religions do teach the importance of telling the truth, most religions also emphasize that self-sacrifice and charity are more important than anything—including, presumably, the truth. Many religions also teach their members to "turn the other cheek" and resist judging others—ideas which liars are all too ready to cynically exploit. By advocating principles friendly to the cause of the liar, religion remains part of the problem rather than part of the solution.

Why Is Dishonesty Becoming More Acceptable Today?

The real cause of today's moral crisis is philosophical and psychological—not religious. Following the lead of our "talking heads" and professors in the intellectual-media establishment, fewer and fewer people believe there is such a thing as objective reality, at least in the realm of morality.

These "experts" don't think that the mind is capable of making objective judgments—particularly moral judgments. They claim it's unsophisticated and "simplistic" to assert that objective reality exists. Consider that today the greatest moral crime is not lying or cheating; the greatest ethical and social crime is to be "judgmental," which includes exercising the capacity to judge or think for oneself.

As the idea that there is no such thing as objective reality spreads, we will see less emphasis on truth as a virtue or an ideal. It may take many decades—but without objective truth as the central ideal in the minds of most people, you can be sure our culture is headed down the path of the Roman empire and other doomed civilizations.

Don't despair, however. There are still many virtuous people in American culture. Our economy and society could not continue to thrive and advance were this not the case. Spectacular breakthroughs continue to occur in the fields of science, business, and technology. Millions of decent, basically honest people continue to work and prosper every day. The ultimate fate of American civilization is still anybody's guess, because it has been very hard for irrational philosophies to take hold of the minds and hearts of most people.

The Real Meaning of Honesty

In the end, you can't have your honesty and eat it too. You can't claim to value honesty, on the one hand, while at the same time asserting or implying that something else (e.g. charity, turning the other cheek) is more important than honesty. To do so increases the risk not only that *you* will lie, but that you will inappropriately tolerate dishonesty in others. In so doing, you contribute to the spread of immorality in the world and turn yourself into your own victim.

Honesty means remaining truthful to reality, and refusing to fake reality for your own sake or the sake of others. Honesty, defined in this way, is either the cornerstone of morality or it is not. You can't have it both ways. You can't say that charity, love, kindness, and sensitivity are the most important things—and then wail when somebody you care about lies to you in the name of those things you hold most important.

If you expect others to be your emotional keepers, then you can't expect them to be truthful with you. If others truly are your keepers, and your caretakers, sometimes they need to decide what's in your best interest. This includes lying to you when they see fit.

To pursue charity as the ultimate end *and* to seek objective truth as the ultimate end represents a contradiction. Sooner or later, you have to decide which is more important.

If you want others to be honest with you, then start asserting honesty as the most fundamental of moral principles. Expect it in yourself, and in others. Once you grasp the true meaning of honesty as being rational and reality-oriented, then you will start to see that honesty is psychologically beneficial. Your life will become clean and free of the psychological distress from which so many suffer today.

Honesty is the best policy. Those who remember this principle will flourish because of it.   ⊕

Conclusion

GREATNESS UNREALIZED

A company hosts a press conference to show how caring and compassionate it is. The CEO of the company, dressed in a top-of-the-line suit, stands in front of the television cameras with his arms around a homeless man who has not bathed for several days. This, we are supposed to believe, makes the company's CEO a good person.

A head of state is impeached for moral and legal breaches while in office. The day after the impeachment, he and his wife volunteer in a soup kitchen. We're supposed to believe that he is still a good person, despite the wrongdoing he more or less acknowledged.

It is easy to become cynical and hopeless when faced with these kinds of examples, as we are almost every day. It just seems so easy to fake being ethical—and to get away with it. Pretending that you are altruistic and kind and giving seems to be all that is required anymore.

But there is another question. Why is the prevailing code of ethics so easy to exploit? *Might there be something wrong with the code itself?*

The prevailing code of ethics is sacrifice, selfless giving, and charity. In a word: selflessness. Because selflessness supposedly represents the supreme good, the CEO is supposed to be a good person when he selflessly sacrifices some pride and personal hygiene to stand with the homeless man. Because charity is supposedly the supreme good, we are to assume the political leader is a good man because he's still willing to do charity work despite his awesome power and well-publicized misdeeds.

What if the standard of supreme good were something different? What if the standard of supreme good were excellence, or competence? It's not easy to fake excellence or competence. In fact, it's not even possible.

Visualize a great work of art: a sculpture of a beautiful, godlike body such as Michelangelo's David. Or imagine a feat of engineering and design, such as a towering, state-of-the-art skyscraper or a Frank Lloyd Wright building.

Now try to conceive of pretending to be Michelangelo for a day; or throwing a press conference or photo-op for an architectural masterpiece you played no role in designing. It just wouldn't happen. True greatness cannot be faked. If something is capable of being faked even for a moment, it isn't greatness in the first place. Genuine greatness is objective, and real. It does not depend upon some "good" intention to cover up its failure to produce. It produces both good intentions *and* good results.

We all probably have some measure of greatness within us, at least potentially. But greatness is not what we are trained to think it is. Our greatness lies not in our capacity to write a check to a charity organization or to build houses for poor people. Our greatness lies in our individual willingness to create, to produce, and to use our minds. To selfishly—yes, *selfishly*—develop our interests and talents to their fullest potential represents the true measure of our worth.

An act of greatness consists of a businessman working long hours to make his company number one. An act of greatness consists of an engineer struggling to determine how to construct the Golden Gate Bridge or its equivalent. An act of greatness consists of a dancer or a musician or an artist working doggedly to bring absolute excellence, even perfection, to her craft. In selfishly developing our talents and pursuing our dreams and values, plenty of other people benefit—especially if we succeed.

In contemporary society we have lost sight of—or, more accurately, never truly grasped—the authentic meaning of greatness. Increasingly, we pay cynical lip service to the politically correct/religiously correct view that the essence of greatness lies in helping an old lady across the street. We don't even give a moment's thought to the science, ingenuity, and relentless effort which made the street possible in the first place. We simply take for granted that the traffic lights work, that cars are better and cheaper than ever before, and that the planes flying overhead somehow came out of nowhere.

We likewise ignore the advances in medical technology and the continuing work of doctors to enable older and older ladies to walk, increasingly, without any help at all. In fact, we hear it relentlessly lectured by people—who never would or could produce anything of objective value—that technology and progress represent an anti-environmental catastrophe rather than phenomena which make all of our lives infinitely easier and safer.

Like it or not: there's nothing so compassionate as the cold hand of science, reason, and objective knowledge. As Woody Allen said in the movie *Deconstructing Harry*: "If I had a choice between the Pope and air-conditioning...I'd choose air-conditioning." The same applies to business and capitalism, which makes the widespread, cheap distribution of the air-conditioning possible; and the much-maligned profit motive, which delivers the goods with masterful efficiency and the voluntary consent of everyone involved.

Science and business do more to help that old lady across the street than any self-anointed (or popularly elected) do-gooder ever could. Yet science and business continue to be despised by many of our cultural elites—and ignored or simply taken for granted by the masses.

The degree to which human beings have misplaced their priorities is shameful. In the midst of so much to admire, we instead focus on non-essentials (or anti-essentials). We stubbornly persist in the belief that greatness lies in *giving up* one's self rather than developing one's self with heroic and precise dedication. The core and essence of a self, after all, is the mind. And it is through the benefits of the human mind that all progress, great and small, occurs. It is through ideas that human beings master their environments and conquer the universe.

The dominant view today, tragically, is precisely the opposite.

Ted Turner, a truly courageous and accomplished entrepreneur, gives money to the United Nations—and he's instantly canonized as a saint by the cultural elites. Yet his true heroism is never acknowledged. Braving the new world of cable television, he dared to believe that a cable news network would survive. He was scorned by his peers and ignored by the masses. Yet he went ahead with what his judgment told him, and in the process revolutionized the media forever. *That* is heroism.

Bill Gates almost single-handedly triggered the entire Information Revolution. Instead of being given a hero's parade, he's put on trial for allegedly harming competition. Simply because millions of people choose to buy his superior product over second-rate competitors, he's somehow to blame. He's evil, in effect, because he's so competent that people voluntarily prefer to purchase his product over other products. So what does he do to defend himself? He holds a press conference to demonstrate how he's giving away a chunk of his money to charity.

The most tragic feature of today's ethical mess is that nobody, anywhere, seems to know what greatness really is. Not even the great individuals themselves.

In a sense, of course, the great innovators of the world do inhibit competition. Not by doing anything immoral or coercive or deceitful; simply by being who they are and, by their very natures and actions, towering above the crowd. For this, however, we should not be envious or resentful. For this we should all be eternally grateful—and inspired. The next time you log onto the Internet, or fly in a jet across the world in a matter of hours, or instantaneously obtain breaking news about an overseas war, take a moment to thank the best of the human spirit which made it all possible. ℗